USING A MAP
Compass and Direction

Compass

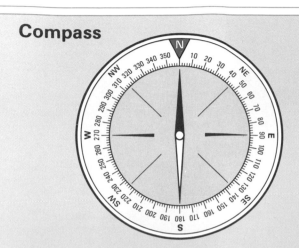

The Compass is an instrument for measuring Direction. The needle on a Compass always points North, and all directions are measured from North in a clockwise direction.
All the maps in this atlas have been drawn with North at the top of the page.

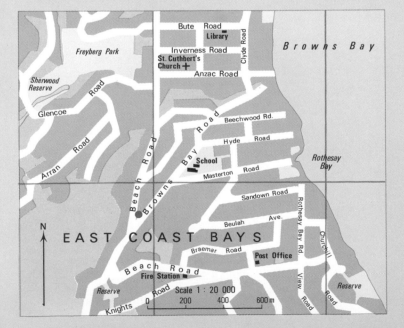

Direction

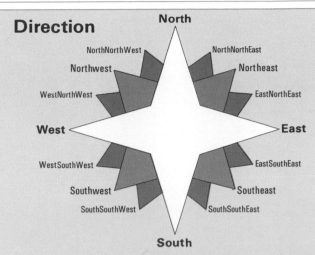

This diagram shows the four cardinal points, North, South, West, East, and twelve intermediate points. These can be used to describe the Direction of one place from another.

The children in the photograph on the left are using a map to find their way to Browns Bay. They have used a Compass to find North and have turned the map round so that the North point on the map is pointing in the same direction as the North point on the Compass. They can now tell which roads they should follow to reach Browns Bay.

The children are standing at the corner of Beach Road and Browns Bay Road, marked ● on the map on the left. In which direction is Browns Bay from where they are standing?

There are two routes to Browns Bay from where the children are standing. Using the Scale on the map, work out how far it is by each route. Which route is the shorter?

© Collins ◇ Longman Atlases

USING A MAP
Grid, Latitude and Longitude, Index

Grids

Many maps have Grids to help locate the names on the map. For example, the Grid References for some of the names on the map on the right are:

Auckland **B2**

Glenbrook **C2**

Hauraki Gulf **A3**

Whangamata **C6**

Work out the grid references for some of the other names on the map.

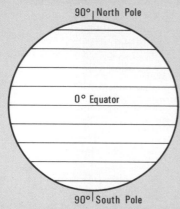

Latitude and Longitude

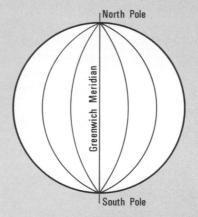

Lines of Latitude, or Parallels, range from 0 degrees, the Equator, to 90 degrees north, the North Pole, and from the Equator to 90 degrees south, the South Pole.

Lines of Longitude, or Meridians, range from 0 degrees, the Greenwich Meridian, west to 180 degrees and east to 180 degrees. There is a total of 360 degrees of longitude, so 180 degrees west and 180 east are the same line of longitude. This imaginary line runs north-south in the Pacific Ocean east of New Zealand. It is called the International Date Line.

Index

Latitude and Longitude can be used to locate places on a map more accurately than the grid reference letters and numbers described above.

Each degree of Latitude and Longitude is divided into 60 minutes.

All the important names on the maps in this atlas are listed in alphabetical order in the Index on pages 63 to 77. After the name of the place or feature and the name of the country, the page on which the map is found is given and then the Latitude and Longitude. The Latitude is the first figure, in degrees and minutes north or south of the Equator. The second figure is the Longitude in degrees and minutes west or east of the Greenwich Meridian.

On the map on the right each degree of Latitude and Longitude is shown. The extract from an Index below the map gives the Latitude and Longitude for several of the places on the map.

Waiouru New Zealand **9** 39.29S 175.40E
Waipukurau New Zealand **9** 40.00S 176.33E
Wairau r. New Zealand **9** 41.32S 174.08E
Wairoa New Zealand **9** 39.03S 177.26E
Waitaki r. New Zealand **9** 44.56S 171.09E
Waitara New Zealand **9** 39.00S 174.14E
Waiuku New Zealand **9** 37.15S 174.44E
Waiyevo Fiji **19** 16.50S 179.59W
Wakatipu, L. New Zealand **9** 45.04S 168.35E
Wakaya I. Fiji **18** 17.39S 179.01E
Wales U.K. **46** 53.00N 3.30W

WORLD ATLAS

Specially prepared for Ladybird Books Ltd by Collins—Longman Atlases

Ladybird

Ladybird Books   Loughborough

USING A MAP
Scale

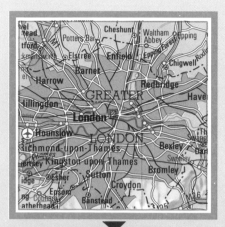

The scale of this map is 1:1 000 000 or one centimetre represents 10 kilometres.

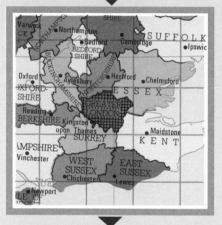

The scale of this map is 1:4 000 000 or one centimetre represents 40 kilometres.

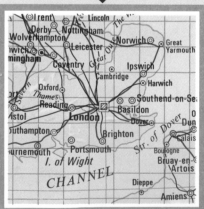

The scale of this map is 1:7 500 000 or one centimetre represents 75 kilometres.

The scale of this map is 1:30 000 000 or one centimetre represents 300 kilometres.

Maps tell us where places are and how far they are from each other. But maps are much smaller than the countries which they show. A kilometre on the ground may become less than a centimetre on the map. To measure how far one place is from another, we have to look at the *scale* of the map.

If the scale is 1:1 000 000 one centimetre of the map represents 1 000 000 centimetres on the ground, 10 kilometres.

If the scale is 1:30 000 000, one centimetre of the map represents 30 000 000 centimetres on the ground, 300 kilometres.

The scale becomes smaller as the number of centimetres becomes bigger.

In this atlas, the maps are drawn at different scales. For a map of a small part of our country, we use a large scale, so that many towns, roads and railways can be shown. But if there are many countries on one map, we have to use a small scale and we only have room to show the biggest towns.

Here are samples of 4 maps. In each one, **London** is at the centre. As we look down the page, we see that the scale becomes smaller as the area shown becomes bigger.

Look at the black squares on these maps. The sides of each square equal 50 km on the ground. As the scale becomes smaller, the squares become smaller too, and we can fit many more squares into the maps. But the sides of the squares always equal 50 km in all the maps.

Notice how the small square dot, or *symbol,* which shows us exactly where London is on each map, always stays the same size, even when the scale changes.

USING A MAP
Symbols

The different dots and lines on a map are known as Symbols. The different dots are used to show the size of towns and the different lines stand for rivers, roads, railways and boundaries. The Symbols used on the general maps in this atlas are explained below.

Highlands, Lowlands and Rivers

Relief

Relief is shown in two ways: by layer colouring to indicate elevation and by hill shading to indicate form.

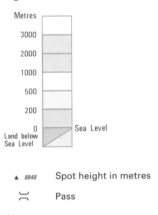

Metres	
3000	
2000	
1000	
500	
200	
0	Sea Level
Land below Sea Level	

▲ 8848   Spot height in metres

⌣   Pass

Water features

▢	Permanent ice cap
〰	Reef
〜	River
⋯	Intermittent river
─│─	Falls
─│─	Dam
⌇	Gorge
⋯⋯	Canal
◯	Lake/Reservoir
⋯	Intermittent lake
≈≈	Marsh/Swamp

Towns and Cities

Over 1 000 000	**Calcutta**	⊠
500 000–1 000 000	**Howrah**	◉
100 000–500 000	Ranchi	◎
Under 100 000	Jumla	⊙

Capital cities are shown in a square :-
Athens ⊠   **Dakar** ◉   **Katmandu** ◎   **Banjul** ⊡

Routes and Boundaries

———	International boundary
– – –	Undefined/disputed boundary
–·–·–	Internal boundary
———	Main road
– – –	Proposed road/desert track
———	Railway
– – –	Railway under construction

Lettering and Colours

Lettering :- Various styles and sizes of lettering are used for different features.

Physical features	*SAHARA*	*Pampas*	*Pemba*	*C. Cod* *Everest*
Water features	*INDIAN OCEAN*	*L. Erie*	*Bass Str.*	*Nile*
Country names	CHILE	KUWAIT		
Internal divisions	VICTORIA	INDIANA		
Territorial administrations	*(U.S.A.)* *(Port.)*			

Colours

The coloured parts of maps have special meanings. On the map on the right the different colours show the areas of the different countries. On other maps in this atlas the colours have special meanings. These are explained in the Key on each map.

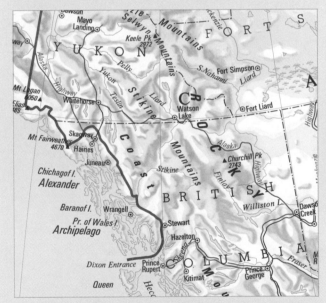

THE WORLD
Countries and Cities

A. : AUSTRIA
BELG. : BELGIUM
CZECH. : CZECHOSLOVAKIA
D. : DJIBOUTI
E. GER. : EAST GERMANY
H. : HUNGARY
L. : LUXEMBOURG
MAL : MALAŴI
NETH. : NETHERLANDS
ROM. : ROMANIA
SWITZ. : SWITZERLAND
YUGO. : YUGOSLAVIA

Largest continent   Asia (including Asiatic U.S.S.R.), 44 391 162 sq km
Largest country   U.S.S.R., Asia/Europe, 22 402 000 sq km
Smallest country   Monaco, 1.5 sq km
Most populous country   China, 1 031 883 000
Most populous city   New York, U.S.A., 16 121 297

OCEAN

Arkhangel'sk

UNION OF SOVIET SOCIALIST REPUBLICS

Aleutian Is.
(U.S.A.)

ningrad

Gorki   Sverdlovsk   Novosibirsk

sk   Moscow   Omsk

Kiev   Kharkov

Odessa

Ulan Bator
MONGOLIA

Shenyang   NORTH
KOREA
Pyongyang   JAPAN

charest   Aral
Black Sea   Sea   Tashkent   Beijing   Seoul   Tokyo
RIA   Caspian Sea   SOUTH   Osaka
stanbul   Baku   KOREA

Ankara   CHINA   Nanjing
TURKEY   Tehran   Kabul   JAMMU
CYPRUS   AFGHANI-   AND   Chongqing   Wuhan   Shanghai   PACIFIC
LEBANON   SYRIA   Baghdad   IRAN   STAN   KASHMIR
ISRAEL   IRAQ   Lahore   Islamabad
airo   JORDAN   KUWAIT   PAKISTAN   Delhi   NEPAL   BHUTAN   Taipei
GYPT   SAUDI   BAHRAIN   New Delhi   Katmandu   TAIWAN
    QATAR   Guangzhou   (FORMOSA)
Riyadh   UNITED ARAB   Karachi   Dhaka   Kowloon
ARABIA   EMIRATES   Muscat   Ahmadabad   INDIA   Calcutta   BANGLA-   Hanoi   HONG KONG
    Mecca   OMAN   DESH   BURMA   (U.K)   Mariana Is.
        Bombay   LAOS   (U.S.A.)
Sana   SOUTHERN   Vientiane   VIETNAM
YEMEN   YEMEN   Hyderabad   Rangoon   THAI-   Quezon City
hartoum   Aden   Madras   Andaman Is.   LAND   Manila
UDAN   D.   Lakshadweep Is.   (Ind.)   Bangkok   PHILIPPINES   OCEAN
        (Ind.)   KAMPUCHEA
Addis Ababa   SRI   Phnom Penh   Ho Chi
ETHIOPIA   LANKA   Minh City   Caroline Is.
        Colombo   Nicobar Is.   (U.S.A.)
UGANDA   SOMALI REPUBLIC   (Ind.)
KENYA   Mogadishu   MALDIVES   BRUNEI
Kampala   Kuala Lumpur   MALAYSIA
RWANDA   Nairobi   Singapore
BURUNDI   SEYCHELLES   SINGAPORE   INDONESIA   PAPUA
TANZANIA   NEW GUINEA
Dodoma   Dar es Salaam   Jakarta   Surabaya   SOLOMON
                IS
COMOROS   Christmas I.
AMBIA   Cocos Is.   (Austl.)
ka   Lilongwe   MOZAMBIQUE   (Austl.)   INDIAN   OCEAN
arare   MADAGASCAR
MBABWE   Antananarivo   MAURITIUS
aborone   SWAZILAND
Pretoria   Maputo   AUSTRALIA   New Caledonia
Johannesburg   LESOTHO   (Fr.)
Durban
ICA   Brisbane

Perth   Sydney
St. Paul   Amsterdam I.   Adelaide   Canberra   Auckland
(Fr.)   (Fr.)
        Melbourne   NEW
                ZEALAND
rince Edward Is.   Crozet Is.   Scale 1:72 500 000   Wellington
(S. Africa)   (Fr.)   0   500   1000   1500   2000   2500   3000 km

Kerguelen
(Fr.)

Heard I.
(Austl.)   © Collins ◇ Longman Atlases

THE WORLD
Highlands, Lowlands and Rivers

ARCTIC OCEAN

Queen Elizabeth Islands

Ellesmere Island

Greenland

Beaufort Sea

Banks I.

Victoria Island

Baffin Bay

Baffin Island

Norweg

Brooks Range

Yukon

Gt Bear Lake

Denmark Strait

Arctic Circle

Iceland

Sea

Mackenzie

Bering Strait

Alaska Range 6194
Mt. McKinley

Gt Slave Lake

Hudson Bay

Davis Strait

C. Farewell

British Isles

North Sea

Gulf of Alaska

Peace

NORTH

Saskatchewan

Nelson

Canadian Shield

Seine
Loire

Aleutian Is.

Vancouver I.

Cordillera

Missouri

AMERICA

L. Winnipeg

Great Lakes

St. Lawrence

Newfoundland

Mt. Blanc 481

Western Mts.

Rocky Mts.

Great Plains

Ohio

Appalachian Mts

C. Sable

Azores

Tagus

Atlas Mts.

Colorado

Arkansas

Mississippi

Bermuda

ATLANTIC

Canary Is.

Tropic of Cancer

Rio Grande

Altiplano Mexicano

Gulf of Mexico

Bahama Is.

Saha

S A F

Ahagga Mt.

Hawaiian Islands

C. San Lucas

Cuba

Puerto Rico Trench 8528

Cape Verde Is.

Senegal

Niger

PACIFIC

Caribbean Sea

Lesser Antilles

OCEAN

Futa Jalon S u d

Christmas I.

Equator

Galapagos Is.

Orinoco

Guiana Highlands

Gulf of Guinea

Negro

SOUTH

C. São Roque

Ascension I.

Marquesas Is.

Amazon

Selvas

Tapajós

Tocantins

São Francisco

OCEAN

AMERICA

Society Is.

Tuamotu Archipelago

Andes

Paraguay

Paraná

Brazilian Highlands

St. Helena

Cook Is.

Tropic of Capricorn

8066

Pampas

Tristan da Cunha

Gough I.

Patagonia

Easter I.

6960 Aconcagua

Falkland Is.

South Georgia

C. Horn

Tierra del Fuego

Peru - Chile Trench

South Shetland Is.

Antarctic Circle

Antarctic Peninsula

Amundsen Sea

Bellingshausen Sea

Weddell Sea

A N T A R

Relief

Metres	
3000	
2000	
1000	
500	
200	
0	Sea Level
Land Dep.	200
	4000
	7000
	Metres

Longest river Nile, Africa, 6 695 km
Largest lake/inland sea Caspian Sea, U.S.S.R./Iran, 371 795 sq km
Largest ocean Pacific, 165 384 000 sq km
Deepest ocean Mariana Trench, Pacific, 11 034 m
Highest mountain Mt. Everest, Nepal, 8 848 m
Largest island Greenland, 2 175 597 sq km

© Collins ◇ Longman Atlases

THE WORLD
Wet and Dry Lands, Hot and Cold Lands

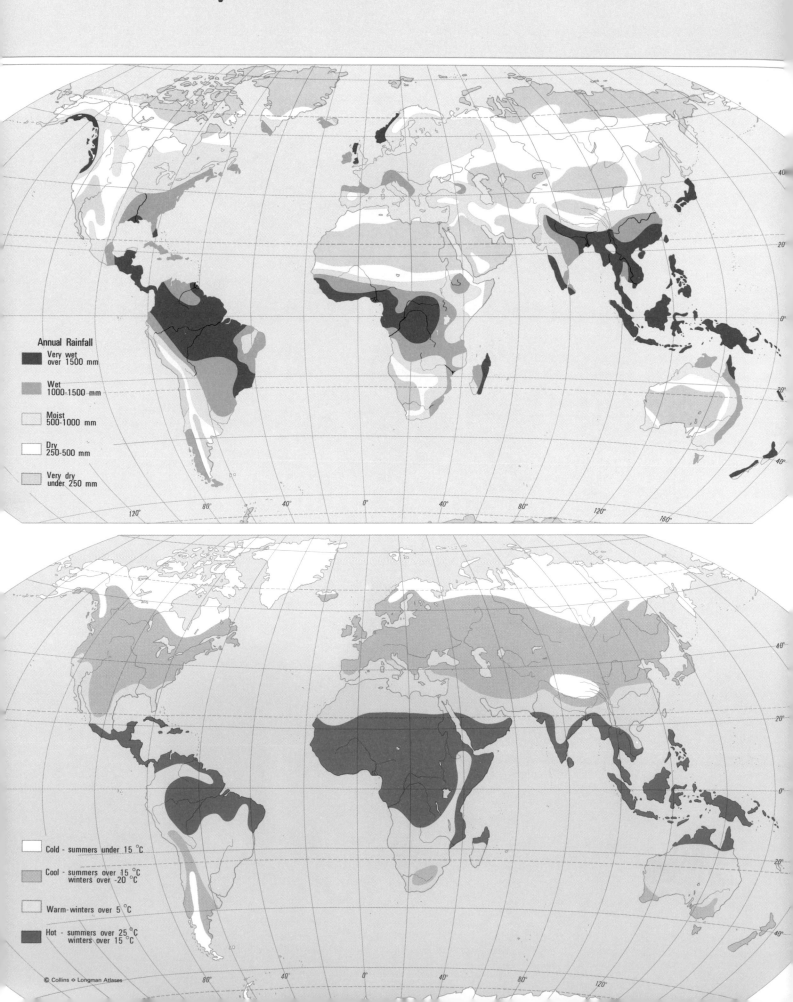

Annual Rainfall

Very wet
over 1500 mm

Wet
1000-1500 mm

Moist
500-1000 mm

Dry
250-500 mm

Very dry
under 250 mm

Cold - summers under 15 °C

Cool - summers over 15 °C
winters over -20 °C

Warm - winters over 5 °C

Hot - summers over 25 °C
winters over 15 °C

THE WORLD
Forests, Grasslands and Wastelands

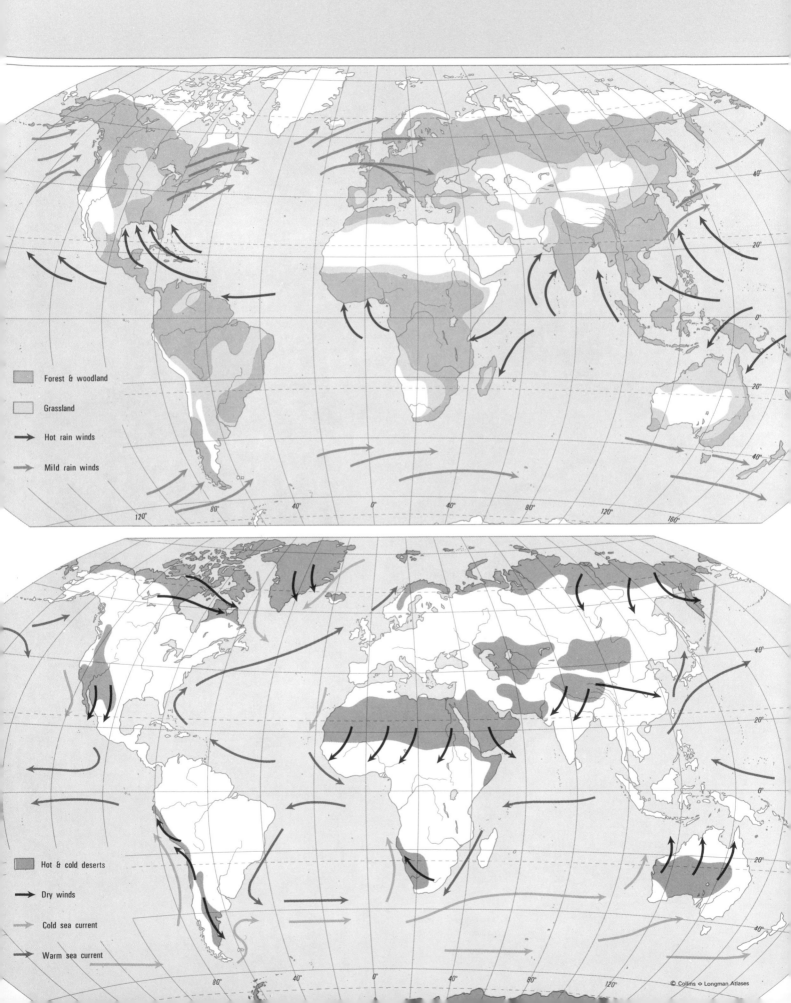

Forest & woodland

Grassland

→ Hot rain winds

→ Mild rain winds

Hot & cold deserts

→ Dry winds

→ Cold sea current

→ Warm sea current

© Collins ◇ Longman Atlases

THE WORLD
How we Use the Land

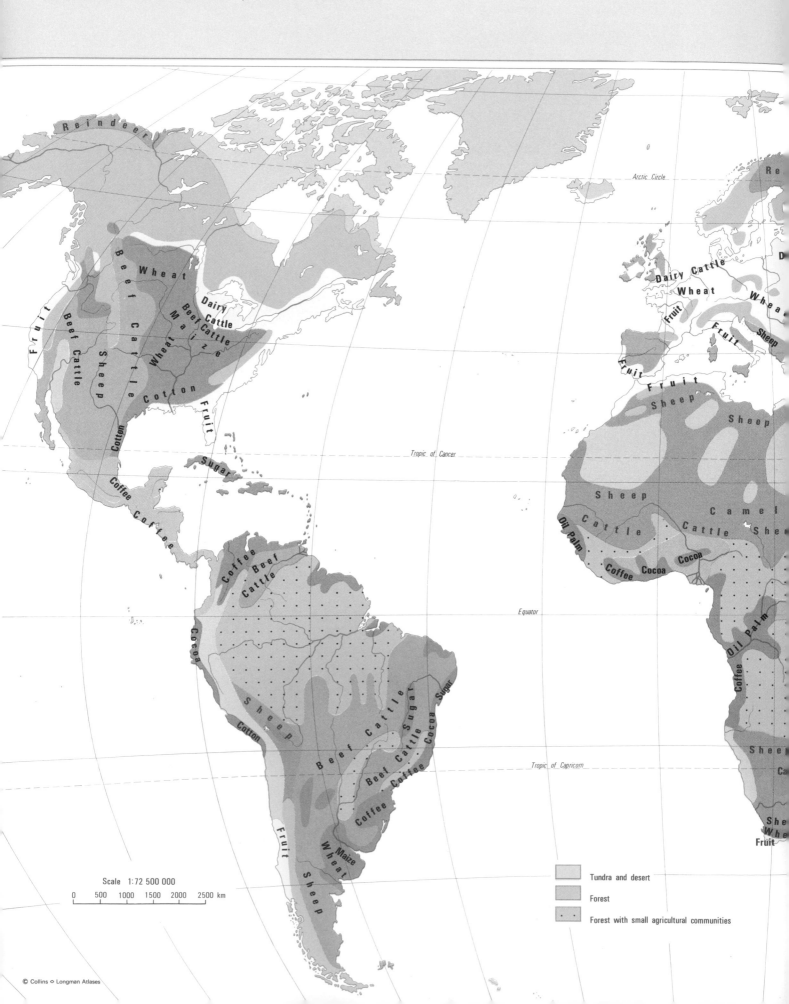

Reindeer

Beef Cattle
Wheat
Fruit
Beef Cattle
Sheep
Beef Cattle
Wheat
Cotton
Dairy Cattle
Beef Cattle
Maize
Cotton
Fruit
Sugar
Coffee
Coffee

Dairy Cattle
Wheat
Fruit
Fruit
Fruit
Sheep
Sheep

Sheep
Cattle
Oil Palm
Coffee
Cocoa
Cocoa
Camel
Cattle
Sheep

Coffee
Beef Cattle
Cocoa

Sheep
Cotton
Beef Cattle
Sugar
Cocoa
Sugar
Beef Cattle
Coffee
Coffee
Fruit
Maize
Wheat
Fruit
Sheep

Oil Palm
Coffee

Sheep
Ca
Sheep
Wheat
Fruit

Arctic Circle
Re

Tropic of Cancer

Equator

Tropic of Capricorn

Scale 1:72 500 000

0   500   1000   1500   2000   2500 km

Tundra and desert

Forest

Forest with small agricultural communities

Cattle

Wheat Wheat

Beef Cattle

Maize Sheep Cotton Fruit

Sheep Fruit

Fruit Wheat Sheep Wheat Yak Wheat Cotton Fruit Tea

Sheep Rice Fruit Tea

Cotton Rice Tea

Camels Cotton Sheep Tea Rice Rice Rice

Coffee Cotton Rice Rice

Rice Rice

Coffee Coffee Rubber Rice

Rubber Rice

Rubber Rice

Coffee Cattle Tea Rice Coffee

Cattle Tea

Cattle Maize

Reindeer

Sheep

Sugar Sheep Wheat Beef Cattle Fruit Sheep Fruit Wheat Fruit

Dairy Cattle

Sheep

	Commercial farming: crops dominant		Subsistence agriculture, crop based
	Commercial farming: animals dominant		Subsistence agriculture, animal based
	Commercial farming: mixed farming and horticulture		

Black names indicate main cash crops and stock, and
red names indicate main subsistence crops and stock.

THE WORLD
Where we Live and How we Travel

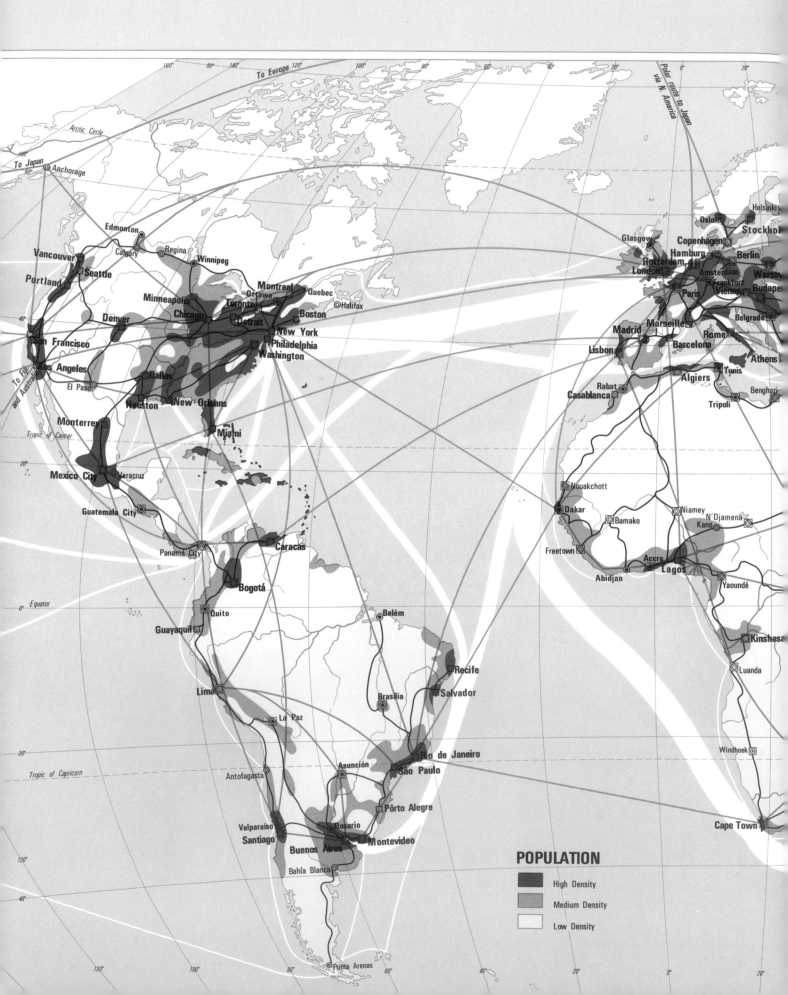

POPULATION

- High Density
- Medium Density
- Low Density

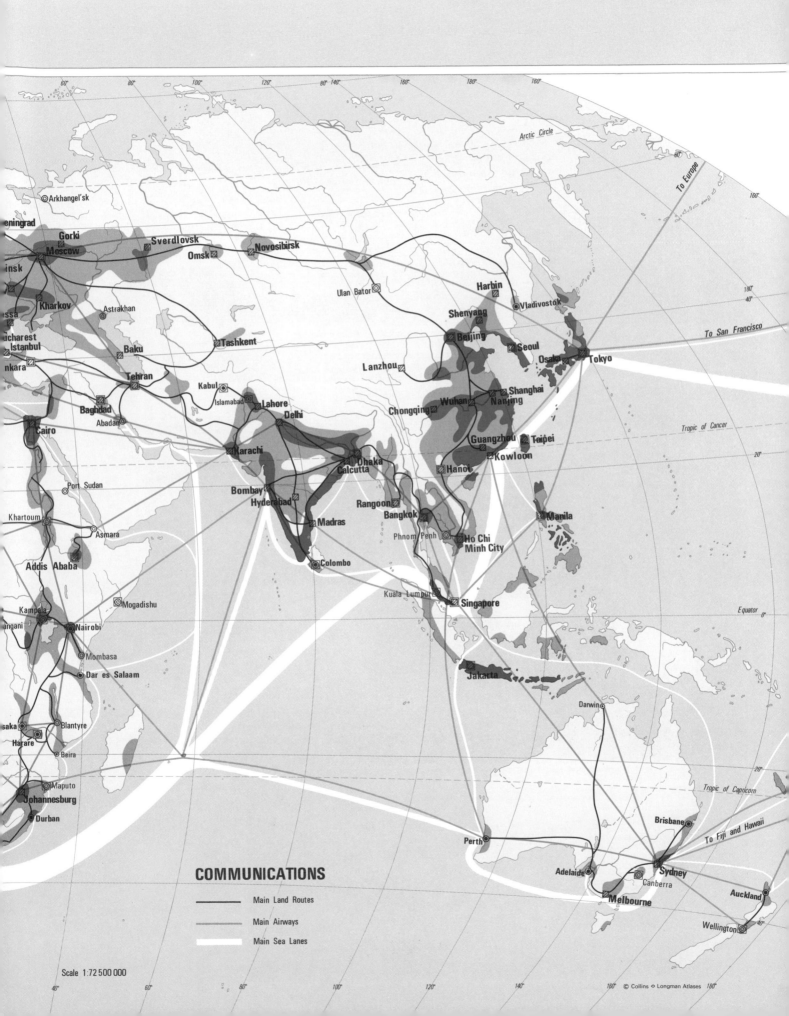

COMMUNICATIONS

	Main Land Routes
	Main Airways
	Main Sea Lanes

Scale 1:72 500 000

© Collins ◇ Longman Atlases

EUROPE

Area 10 354 636 sq km (including Europea
U.S.S.R.)
4 783 636 sq km (excluding Europea
U.S.S.R.)
Population 487 000 000 (excluding Europe
U.S.S.R.)
Number of countries 32
Largest country France, 547 026 sq km

Scale 1:20 000 000

allest country   Monaco, 1.5 sq km
st populous city   Paris, France, 8 612 531
hest mountain   Mt. Blanc, France,
807 m
west point   Netherlands coastal areas,
-5 m

Highest live volcano   Mt. Etna, Italy,
3 340 m
Longest river   Volga, U.S.S.R., 3 688 km
Largest lake/inland sea   Lake Ladoga,
U.S.S.R., 18 390 sq km
Highest waterfall   Gavarnie, France 422 m

1. The Pool of London, England

2. Buttermere, Lake District, England

3. St. Basil's Cathedral, Moscow, U.S.S.R.

4. Aqueduct, Pont du Gard, France

EL : BELGIUM
: LIECHTENSTEIN
UX : LUXEMBOURG
ETH : NETHERLANDS
M : SAN MARINO
WITZ : SWITZERLAND
: TURKEY (in Europe)

© Collins ○ Longman Atlases

BRITISH ISLES
Counties and Regions

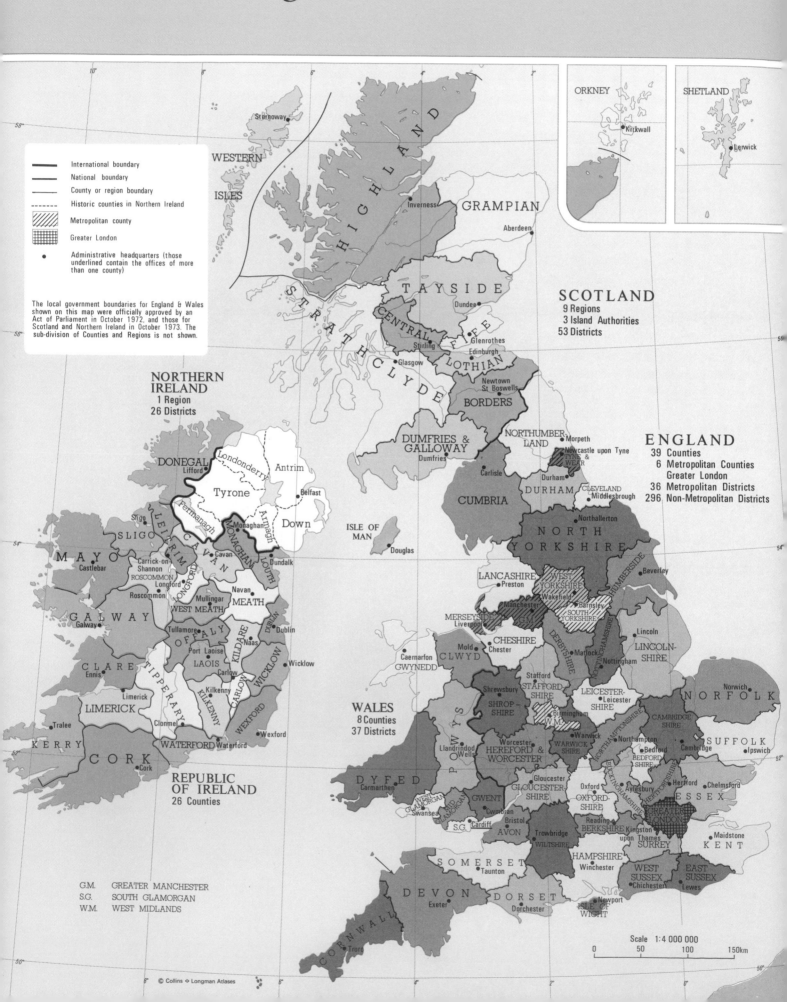

	International boundary
	National boundary
	County or region boundary
	Historic counties in Northern Ireland
	Metropolitan county
	Greater London
•	Administrative headquarters (those underlined contain the offices of more than one county)

The local government boundaries for England & Wales shown on this map were officially approved by an Act of Parliament in October 1972, and those for Scotland and Northern Ireland in October 1973. The sub-division of Counties and Regions is not shown.

SCOTLAND
9 Regions
3 Island Authorities
53 Districts

NORTHERN IRELAND
1 Region
26 Districts

ENGLAND
39 Counties
6 Metropolitan Counties
Greater London
36 Metropolitan Districts
296 Non-Metropolitan Districts

WALES
8 Counties
37 Districts

REPUBLIC OF IRELAND
26 Counties

G.M.   GREATER MANCHESTER
S.G.   SOUTH GLAMORGAN
W.M.   WEST MIDLANDS

Scale 1:4 000 000

0   50   100   150km

© Collins ◇ Longman Atlases

BRITISH ISLES

ORKNEY ISLANDS same scale
Westray
Sanday
Mainland
59° Kirkwall 59°
Hoy
Pentland Firth
Thurso
Wick

SHETLAND ISLANDS same scale
Unst
Yell
60° Mainland Lerwick 60°
Fair Isle

ATLANTIC OCEAN

NORTH SEA

Pentland Firth
Thurso
Wick
Cape Wrath
Butt of Lewis
Stornoway
Lewis
St. Kilda
Harris
Ullapool
North Uist
Portree
Skye
South Uist
Kyle of Lochalsh
Loch Ness
Inverness
Moray Firth
Dee
Aberdeen
Spey 1311
Highlands
Rhum
Mallaig
Coll
Fort William 1343
Ben Nevis
Grampian
Tobermory
Tiree
Mull
SCOTLAND
Oban
Firth of Lorn
Tay
Dundee
Jura
Perth
Firth of Tay
St. Andrews
Loch Fyne
Loch Lomond
Stirling
Kirkcaldy
Firth of Forth
Islay
Greenock
Forth
Falkirk
Paisley
Glasgow
Edinburgh
Berwick-upon-Tweed
Motherwell
Arran
Kilmarnock
Tweed
Firth of Clyde
Ayr
Southern Uplands
Hawick
Cheviot Hills
Campbeltown
Clyde
Malin Head
Lough Foyle
Nith
Dee
Dumfries
Newcastle upon Tyne
Tyne
Sunderland
Londonderry
Larne
Carlisle
Durham
NORTHERN IRELAND
Lough Neagh
Belfast
Solway Firth
Eden
893
Middlesbrough
Donegal
Bangor
Workington
Darlington
Donegal Bay
Lower Lough Erne
Armagh
Lurgan
Mourne Mts
Scafell Pike 978
Lake District
Pennines
Tees
Sligo
Dundalk
Isle of Man
Scarborough
Barrow-in-Furness
Douglas
Achill I.
Dundalk Bay
Morecambe Bay
York
Westport
IRISH SEA
Lancaster
Ouse
Lough Mask
Ribble
Leeds
Kingston upon Hull
Lough Corrib
Athlone
Boyne
Blackpool
Bradford
REPUBLIC
Galway
Preston
Blackburn
Huddersfield
Don
Doncaster
Grimsby
Galway Bay
Southport
Bolton
Oldham
Humber
Aran Is.
OF
Liverpool
St. Helens
Manchester
Dublin
Birkenhead
Stockport
Sheffield
Lincoln
Dun Laoghaire
Holyhead
Anglesey
Mersey
Lough Derg
Roscrea
Bangor
Colwyn Bay
Crewe
Stoke-on-Trent
Nottingham
Naas
KINGDOM
Limerick
IRELAND
Wicklow Mts
1085
Snowdon
Dee
Derby
Shannon
Barrow
Slaney
Mountains
Crewe
Shrewsbury
Trent
The Wash
King's Lynn
Clonmel
Wexford
Cardigan Bay
Walsall
Leicester
The Fens
Norwich
Great Yarmouth
Tralee
Blackwater
Aberystwyth
Cambrian
WALES
Wolverhampton
Birmingham
Coventry
Rugby
Northampton
Waveney
Carrauntoohil
1041
Waterford
Carnsore Point
Teifi
Mountains
West Bromwich
Dudley
Solihull
Nene
Bedford
Cambridge
Ipswich
Dingle Bay
Killarney
Tywi
Severn
Wye
Avon
Harwich
Cork
Fishguard
St. David's Head
Gloucester
Cotswold Hills
Oxford
Luton
Harlow
Milford Haven
Merthyr Tydfil
Rhondda
Newport
Thames
London
Basildon
Southend-on-Sea
Swansea
Port Talbot
Bristol
Reading
Grays
Gillingham
Cardiff
Avon
Bath
Canterbury
Bristol Channel
Swindon
Royal Tunbridge Wells
Dover
Exmoor
Exe
Taunton
Salisbury
Test
Southampton
Crawley
Brighton
Folkestone
Tamar
Dartmoor
Lyme Bay
Avon
Poole
Havant
Worthing
Dartmoor
Weymouth
Bournemouth
Portsmouth
Isle of Wight
Solent
Exeter
Torbay
Plymouth
Penzance
Land's End
Isles of Scilly

St. George's Channel
North Channel
The Minch
Outer Hebrides
Inner Hebrides
Mts of Antrim
Bann
Blackwater
Erne
Shannon
Suir
Nore
UNITED
ENGLAND

English Channel
FRANCE

Scale 1:4 000 000
0   50   100   150 km

© Collins ◇ Longman Atlases

WESTERN EUROPE

Scale 1:7 500 000

0   50   100   150   200km

EASTERN EUROPE

SCANDINAVIA and NORTHERN EUROPE

Straumnes
Ísafjördhur
Siglufjördhur
Húsavik
Langanes
Vopnafjördhur
Húna -flói
Breidhafjördhur
Seydhisfjördhur
ICELAND
Hofsjökull 1765
Odádhahraun
Hvíta
Grímsvötn 1725
Faxaflói
Thjórsá
Vatnajökull
2199
Reykjavik
Höfn
Keflavík
Mt. Hekla 1491
Vestmanna Is.
Surtsey
Same Scale

ATLANTIC OCEAN

Scale 1:7 500 000
0   100   200   300 km

Shetland Is.

NORTH CAPE
Hammerfest
Lopphavet
Tromsö
Vesterålen
Lofoten
Narvik
Torneträsk
Muonio
Kebnekaise 2123
LAPL...
Vest Fjord
Bodö
Sarek 2090
Gällivare
Vega
Mosjøen
Storavan
Haparanda
Vikna
Luleå
Törnio
Kemi
Frohavet
Ume
Oulu
Hitra
Skellefteå
Ouluärvi
Kristiansund
Ångerman
Vännäs
Umeå
Trondheim
Storsjön
Östersund
Sollefteå
Kokkola
FINLA...
Ålesund
Andalsnes
Dovrefjell 2286
Sundsvall
Kristinestad
Vaasa
Glittertind 2470
Jotunheimen
Ljusnan
Bergen
Sogne Fjord
Glåma
Lågen
Särna
Siljan
Näsijärvi
Lillehammer
Myösa
Klar
Tampere
Päijänne
Haugesund
Hardanger Fjord
Borlänge
Gävle
Dal
Åland Is.
Oslo
Drammen
Turku
Vantaa
Kotka
Stavanger
Karlstad
Västerås
Uppsala
Espoo
Helsinki
Frederikstad
Eskilstuna
Stockholm
GULF OF FIN...
C. Lindesnes
Arendal
Vänern
Örebro
Mälaren
Tallinn
Kristiansand
Motala
Norrköping
Hiiumaa
ESTONIA S.S.R.
NORTH SEA
SKAGERRAK
Trollhättan
Göta Canal
Vättern
Linköping
Pärnu
Tartu
Göteborg
Borås
Saaremaa
Frederikshavn
Jönköping
Gulf of Riga
Lim Fjord
Ålborg
Halmstad
Växjö
Gotland
Ventspils
Fårösund
Holstebro
Randers
Kalmar
Öland
BALTIC SEA
DENMARK
Zealand
Hälsingborg
Lund
Karlskrona
Riga
Esbjerg
Århus
Odense
Funen
Store Bælt
Copenhagen
Malmö
Liepāja
LATVIA S.S.R.
North Frisian Islands
Flensburg
Lolland
Bornholm (Den.)
Siauliai
Daugavpils
Frisian Islands
Kiel Canal
Kiel
Rügen
Rostock
Gulf of Danzig
Klaipeda
LITHUANIA S.S.R.
Den Helder
Gröningen
Bremerhaven
Wilhelmshaven
Lübeck
Gdynia
Gdańsk
Kaliningrad
Kaunas
NETHERLANDS
Oldenburg
WEST GERMANY
Hamburg
EAST GERMANY
POLAND
Vilnius
R.S.F.S.R.

NORWAY
SWEDEN
GULF OF BOTHNIA
Oslo Fjord
Kattegat

BARENTS

SEA

Varangeren Fjord

Kirknes

Pechenga

Murmansk

C. Kanin

Kanin
Peninsula

Naryan Mar

Pechora

Ust'Tsilma

Lake
Imandra

Kirovsk

Kola

Peninsula

Mezen

Mezen

Ukhta

Troitsko-
Pechersk

Kandalaksha

Kandalakskaya Gulf

WHITE
SEA

Kelloselkä

L. Pya

L. Top

Severodvinsk

Arkangel'sk

UNION OF SOVIET

N. Dvina

Syktyvkar

Taivalkoski

Kajaani

Belomorsk

Onega

Vychegda

Kotlas

SOCIALIST REPUBLICS

Pielinen

Medvezhyegorsk

Kuopio

Kallavesi

Petrozavodsk

Lake
Onega

Konosha

Sukhona

Vytegra

RUSSIAN SOVIET

Kirov

ikkeli

Lake
Ladoga

FEDERAL

Vetluga

Vyatka

aimaa

Vyborg

SOCIALIST

Volkhov

Vologda

AND

Leningrad

Cherepovets

REPUBLIC

Yoshkar Ola

Rybinsk
Reservoir

Luga

Novgorod

Andropov

Kostroma

Dzerzhinsk

Gorki

Cheboksary

Kazan

Lake
Peipus

Bologoye

Yaroslavl

Vyshniy-Volochek

Volga

Ivanovo

Volga

Pskov

Dno

Valdai

Volga

Kovrov

Chistopol

Hills

Kalinin

Vladimir

Kuybyshev
Reservoir

Velikiye - Luki

EAST

Rzhev

Orekhovo-
Zuyevo

Murom

Oka

Ul'yanovsk

Dvina

EUROPEAN

PLAIN

Mytishchi

Sura

Dvina

Moscow

Elektrostal

Polotsk

Lyubertsy

Kolomna

Saransk

Tol'yatti

WHITE

Vitebsk

Podolsk

Vyazma

Serpukhov

Ryazan

Volga Uplands

RUSSIA

Orsha

Smolensk

Dnieper

Kaluga

Tula

© Collins ◇ Longman Atlases

Syzran

ASIA

Area	44 391 162 sq km (including Asiatic U.S.S.R.)
	27 560 162 sq km (excluding Asiatic U.S.S.R.)
Population	2 672 000 000 (excluding Asiatic U.S.S.R.), U.S.S.R. 271 000 000
Number of countries	41
Largest country	China, 9 596 961 sq km

1. Oil drilling rig in the desert, Iran

2. Drying grapes to make raisins, Turkey

3. Building supertankers, Japan

4. Houseboats crowding the harbour, Hong Kong

5. Planting rice, Madras, India

allest country Maldives, 298 sq km
st populous city Tokyo, Japan,
1 634 428
hest mountain Mt. Everest, Nepal,
848 m
west point Dead Sea, Jordan, —393 m

Highest live volcano Klyuchevskaya,
U.S.S.R., 4 750 m
Longest river Chang Jiang, China, 5471 km
Largest lake/inland sea Caspian Sea,
U.S.S.R./Iran, 371 795 sq km
Highest waterfall Gersoppa, India, 253 m

Scale 1:40 000 000

© Collins ◇ Longman Atlases

UNION OF SOVIET SOCIALIST REPUBLICS

Scale 1:20 000 000

0   200   400   600   800 km

© Collins · Longman Atlases

Severnaya
Zemlya
I N D I A
C
Komsomolets
October Revolution
Bolshevik
C. Chelyuskin

Taymyr Peninsula
Byrranga Mts.
Taymyr
Upper
L.Taymyr
Pyasina
Khatangskiy G.
Nordvik
Olenekskiy Gulf
L A P T E V
S E A
New Siberian Is
Novaya Siberia
Bolshoi
Lyakhovskiy
Kotelnyy
E A S T   S I B E R I A N
S E A
Wrangel I.
De Long Str.
Bering Str.
Arctic Circle
Chuckchee Pen

Khatanga
Anabar
Ust Olenek
Tiksi
G. of Tona
Kazachye
Yana
Indigirka
Ambarchik
Anadyr
Gulf of Anadyr

Dudinka
Norilsk
Kamen
2037
Putoran Mts
Kotuy
Olenek
Olenek
Central
Bulun
Lena
Verkhoyansk
V e r k h o y a n s k
Verkhoyansk
Cherskogo
Srebne
Kolymskaya
Kolyma
Omolon
Kamenskoye
Koryak
Range
Gizhiga
G. of Penzhina
Uka
Palana

Siberian
Markha
Plateau
Vilyuy
Vilyuysk
Mt Chen
2682
Mt Pobeda
3147
Oymyakon
Magadan
Okhotsk
Kamchatka
Klyuchevskaya
Ust Kamchatsk
1750

S O C I A L I S T   R E P U B L I C S   R a n g e
Aldan
Amga
Ust Maya
Dzhugdhur Range
Mt Topko
1906
B E R I N G
S E A

Lower
Tunguska
Tura
C E N T R A L
P l a t e a u
S O C I A L I S T   R E P U B L I C
Yakutsk
Amga
Aldan
Lena
Ayan
Shantar Is
S E A   O F
O K H O T S K
Petropavlovsk-
Kamchatskiy
Kamchatka
Peninsula

Yartsevo
Yeniseysk
Stony Tunguska
Angara
Chuna
Olekminsk
Lena
Aldan
Olekma
Skalintyy
2482
Okha
Aleksandrovsk
Sakhalinskiy
Sakhalin

Krasnoyarsk
Kansk
Tayshet
Tulun
Nizhneudinsk
Eastern
Sayan
Kirensk
Ust Kut
Bratsk
Resr
Vitim
Stanovoy Range
Skovorodino
Zeya
Komsomolsk-
na-Amur
Nikolayevsk-na-
Amur
Uglegorsk
Poronaysk

abakan
Sayan
Cheremkhovo
Angarsk
Irkutsk
Bratsk
Tulun
Y a b l o n o v y   R a n g e
Shilka
Svobodnyy
Amur
Sovetskaya
Gavan
Yuzhno-
Sakhalinsk
Gulf of Tartary
La Perouse Str.

Kyzyl
annu Ola Ra
Munku
Sardyk 3492
Khöbsögöl
Dalai
Ulan-Ude
Petrovsk
Zabaykal'skiy
L. Baikal
Chita
Zeya
Blagoveshchensk
Birobidzhan
Khabarovsk
Wakkanai
Asahi daki
2290
Hokkaido

Ubsa
Nur
t
a
i
M O N G O L I A
Ulan Bator
Undur Khan
Da Hinggan Ling
Shilka
C H I N A
Amur
Shuhua Jiang
L.Khanka
Ussuriysk
Nakhodka
Vladivostok
Ust' Olga
Khote-Alin Range
Sapporo
Hakodate
Z

Inner Mongolia
Harbin
Mudanjiang
Yilin
Songhua Jiang
S E A   O F
J A P A N
Honshu
Kuril Islands
Niigata
Tokyo
Yokohama
Fujiyama
3776
Nagoya

G
b
i
Changchun
Shenyang
Fushun
Anshan
NORTH
KOREA
Pyongyang
SOUTH
KOREA
Seoul
J A P A N
Kyoto
Kobe
Osaka

Zhangjiakou
Baotou
Hohhot
Beijing
Liaodong
Bay
Lüda
Korea
Bay
Hachinohe

MIDDLE EAST and SOUTH ASIA

Scale 1:20 000 000

0   200   400   600   800 km

FAR EAST
and SOUTHEAST ASIA

© Collins • Longman Atlases

O C E A N

BELAU

New Guinea

Maoke Range ▲5030 Puntjak Jaya

Schouten Is.

Javapura

Mappi

Kolapoun

c. Vals

Manokwari

Vogelkop

Aru Is.

Tanimbar Is.

Misoöl

Buru

Ceram

Sula Is.

Halmahera

A R A F U R A   S E A

c. Arnhem

Gulf of Carpentaria

Arnhem Land

Darwin

Melville I.

Katherine

Ropet

Birdum

A U S T R A L I A

c. Londonderry

Wyndham

Old

c. Lévêque

PHILIPPINES

Butuan

Davao

Samar

Cebu

Cebu

Mindanao

Talaud Is.

Sangihe Is.

Menado

M O L U C C A S

Dili

Wetar

Timor

Aparri

Luzon

Quezon City

Manila

Iloilo

Panay

Negros

Dipolog

Zamboanga

Menado

C E L E B E S   S E A

Poso

Celebes

Kendari

Butung

Kolaka

Kabia

Roti

Kupang

TIMOR SEA

Lingayen

Batangas

Mindoro

Palawan

Donggala

Mamuju

Ujung Pandang

Makassar

Strait

FLORES SEA

Flores

Sumba

Roti

S O U T H

C H I N A

S E A

Tawau

Kudat

Kinabalu ▲4101

Kota Kinabalu

SABAH

Samarinda

B o r n e o

Barito

Banjarmasin

Bali

Sumbawa

Surabaya

SARAWAK

Kuching

Pontianak

Schwaner Mts

Kapuas

Sintang

Semarang

Surakarta

Kediri

Yogyakarta

I N D O N E S I A

Bandar Seri Begawan

BRUNEI

J a v a

Jakarta

Bandung

Bogor

V I E T N A M

Qui Nhon

Nha Trang

Da Nang

Hué

Ho Chi Minh City

Can Tho

Gulf of Tonking

Vietnam Highlands

Mekong

Pakse

KAMPUCHEA

Tonle Sap

Phnom Penh

Battambang

Kampot

Palembang

Telukbetung

Christmas I. (Aus.)

M A L A Y S I A

Johor Bahru

SINGAPORE

Singapore

Jambi

THAILAND

Bangkok

Ubon Ratchathani

Gulf of Thailand

Kota Bharu

Kuala Lumpur

Kuantan

Lahat

Vientiane

Uttaradit

Songkhla

Ipoh

Straits of Malacca

G. Kerinci 3806

Barisan Range

Pakanbaru

Pematangsiantar

Medan

George Town

L. Toba

Padang

S u m a t e r a

Pegu

Moulmein

Rangoon

Phuket

Mergui Archipelago

Mentawai Islands

Banda Aceh

I N D I A N   O C E A N

Scale 1:20 000 000

0   200   400   600   800 km

MALAYSIAN PENINSULA
and SINGAPORE

THAILAND

SOUTH CHINA

SEA

Songkhla
Ban Hat Yai
Pattani
Padang Besar
Yala
Kangar
PERLIS
LANGKAWI
(Kedah)
Jitra
Tumpat
Alor Setar
Kota Bharu
Pasir Mas
Betong
Pasir Puteh
P. Redang
Keroh
Tanah Merah
K E D A H
Sai Buri
Pattani
Sungai Petani
Kuala Krai
G. Lawit
1517
P. Pinang
George Town
Butterworth
G. Bintang
1880
Kuala Trengganu
Bukit Mertajam
Kulim
G. Inas
1818
Kg.
Merchang
PULAU
PINANG
SEBER
PERAI
Belum (Perak)
G. Chamah
2170
Nenggiri
K E L A N T A N
T R E N G G A N U
Kuala
Brang
Bagan Serai
Tasik
Chenderoh
Dungun
Port Weld
Taiping
S. Siput
Merapoh
T A M A N   N E G A R A
Dungun
Kuala Kangsar
Lebir
Trengganu
Gt. Korbu
2204
G. Tahan
2190
Ipoh
G. Swettenham
1980
Batu Gajah
Cameron
Highlands
Jelai
G. Irong
1202
Chukai
Kampar
G. Batu Puteh
2130
Kuala Lipis
P E R A K
Lumut
Perak
G. Tapis
1511
Jerantut
Kuantan
Teluk Intan
M A L A Y S I A
Kuantan
Bernam
Bukit
Fraser
Raub
G. Benom
2108
Sabak
P A H A N G
Pekan
Kuala Kuba
Baharu
Bentong
Mentakab
Maran
Pahang
SELANGOR
Karak
Kuala Selangor
Tasik
Bera
Shah
Alam
Kuala Lumpur
Petaling Jaya
Serdang
Tasik
Dampar
P. Tioman
Pelabuhan Kelang
Kelang
Kajang
Ayer Hitam
Rompin
N E G E R I
Kuala
Pilah
Port Dickson
Seremban
S E M B I L A N
Gemas
Segamat
G. Besar
1037
Mersing
INDONESIA
SUMATERA
UTARA
Tampin
G. Ledang
1288
Labis
P. Tinggi
Melaka
Tangkak
J O H O R
Muar
G. Belumut
1009
SUMATRA
Pulau Rupat
Rokan
Keluang
Batu Pahat
R I A U
Kulai
Kota Tinggi
Pontian Kechil
Johor Bahru
S. Siak
P. Padang
P. Rangsang
SINGAPORE
Singapore
P. Bengkalis
Straits of Singapore
P. Batam
P. Bintan

Straits of Malacca

Scale 1:2 850 000
0   20   40   60   80   100 km

© Collins © Longman Atlases

JAPAN

CHINA

Mutankiang

U.S.S.R.

Lake Khanka

Ussuriysk

Sikhote Alin Range

▲1448

Sea of Okhotsk

Kunashir (U.S.S.R.)

Nemuro kaikyo

Wakkanai

Vladivostok

Yenki

Asahikawa

Asahi daki ▲2290

Sapporo

Otaru

Obihiro

Kushiro

Nemuro

HOKKAIDO

NORTH KOREA

SEA OF

Muroran

Hakodate

Tsugaru kaikyo

Shiriya saki

SOUTH KOREA

JAPAN

Aomori

Iwaki

Hirosaki

Hachinohe

Akita

Morioka

Chokai san ▲2230

Omono

Sakata

Yamagata

Sendai

Sado

Niigata

Iide yama ▲2105

Fukushima

Suzu misaki

Nagaoka

Agano

Kōriyama

Shinano

Iwaki

Takaoka

Toyama

Nagano

Utsunomiya

Hitachi

Kanazawa

Matsumoto

▲3180

Maebashi

Ashikaga

Fukui

Ontaki san ▲3063

Kumagaya

Kawagoe

Oki gunto

Shirane san ▲3192

Kofu

Tokyo

Chiba

Boso Hanto

Wakasa wan

Tsuruga

Ogaki

Gifu

Kawasaki

Yokohama

Matsue

Tottori

Maizuru

Biwa ko

Fujiyama ▲3776

Odawara

Pusan

Chugoku sanchi

Nagoya

Shimizu

Korea Strait

Kyoto

Amagasaki

Okazaki

Oshima

Tsushima

Okayama

Kobe

Osaka

Ise

Hamamatsu

Hiroshima

Takamatsu

Sakai

Miyake jima

Iwakuni

Wakayama

Kitakyushu

Ube

Suo nada

Matsuyama

Yoshino

Tokushima

Shikoku sanchi

Kii suido

Fukuoka

Beppu

Shiono misaki

Sasebo

Kuju san ▲1788

Kochi

SHIKOKU

Nagasaki

Omuta

Ashizuri saki

Hachijo jima

Kumamoto

Nobeoka

Shimo jima

Kyushu sanchi

KYUSHU

Miyazaki

Kagoshima

Osumi kaikyo

Osumi gunto

Tanega shima

Yakujima kaikyo

PACIFIC OCEAN

Scale 1:7 500 000

0 50 100 150 200km

AFRICA

Area 30 244 049 sq km
Population 499 000 000
Number of countries 53
Largest country Sudan, 2 505 813 sq km

1. Kariba Dam, Zambia/Zimbabwe

2. A Kenyan village

3. A town made of mud bricks, Nigeria

4. The Pyramids, Egypt

5. An oil refinery, Algeria

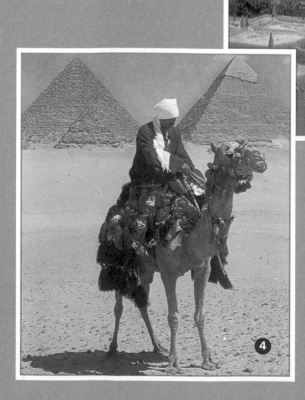

allest country Seychelles, 280 sq km
st populous city Cairo, Egypt, 5 074 000
ghest mountain Kilimanjaro, Tanzania, 895 m
west point Qattara Depression, Egypt, −134 m

Highest live volcano Mt. Cameroon, Cameroon, 4 070 m
Longest river Nile, 6 695 km
Largest lake/inland sea Lake Victoria, 69 485 sq km
Highest waterfall Kalambo Falls, Tanzania, 215 m

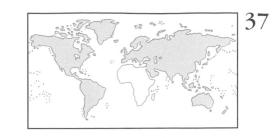

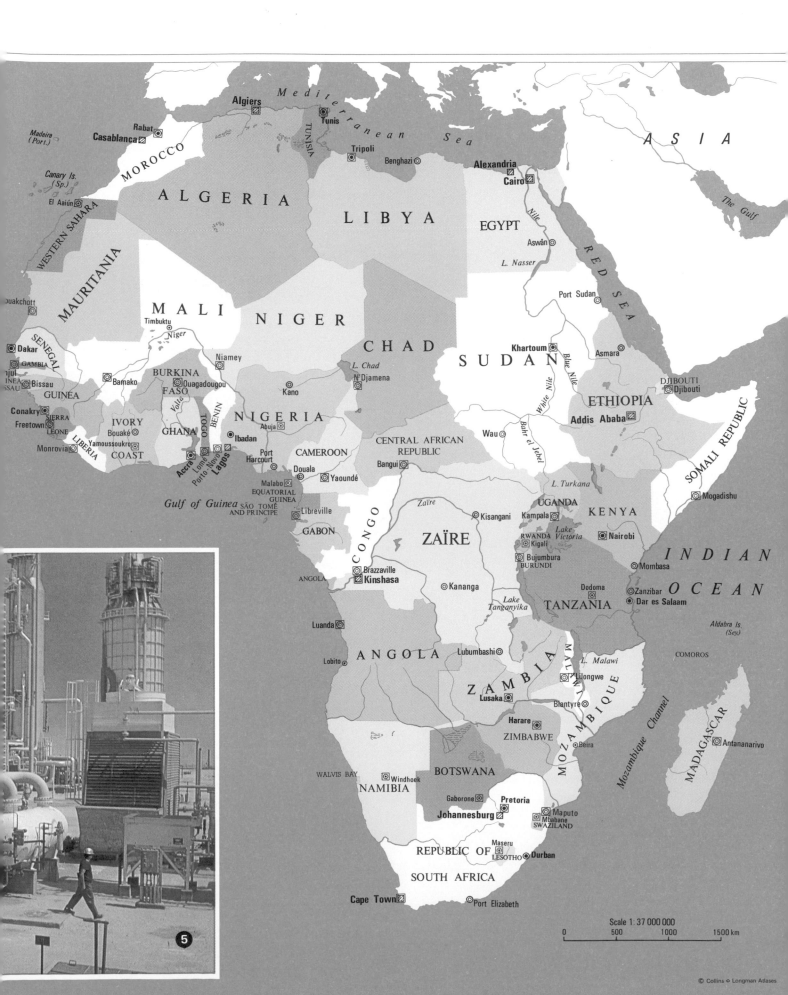

Mediterranean Sea

Madeira (Port.)

Algiers
Rabat
Casablanca
Tunis
TUNISIA
Tripoli
Benghazi
Alexandria
Cairo

MOROCCO
Canary Is. (Sp.)
El Aaiún
WESTERN SAHARA

A L G E R I A

L I B Y A

E G Y P T

Nile
Aswân
L. Nasser

ASIA

The Gulf

RED SEA

MAURITANIA
uakchott

M A L I
Timbuktu
Niger

N I G E R
Niamey
Kano

C H A D
L. Chad
N'Djamena

S U D A N
Khartoum

Port Sudan

Asmara
DJIBOUTI
Djibouti

Dakar
SENEGAL
GAMBIA
njul
INEA
ssau
Bissau
GUINEA
Conakry
Freetown
SIERRA
LEONE
LIBERIA
Monrovia

BURKINA FASO
Bamako
Ouagadougou
Volta

NIGERIA
Abuja
Ibadan

TOGO
BENIN
GHANA
Accra
Lomé
Porto-Novo
Lagos

IVORY COAST
Bouaké
Yamoussoukro

Port Harcourt
CAMEROON
Douala
Yaoundé
Malabo
EQUATORIAL GUINEA
SÃO TOMÉ AND PRINCIPE

Gulf of Guinea

CENTRAL AFRICAN REPUBLIC
Bangui

Wau
White Nile
Blue Nile
Bahr el Jebel

ETHIOPIA
Addis Ababa

SOMALI REPUBLIC
Mogadishu

Libreville
GABON
Zaïre
CONGO
Z A Ï R E
Kisangani

UGANDA
Kampala
Lake Victoria
RWANDA
Kigali
BURUNDI
Bujumbura

KENYA
Nairobi
L. Turkana

Mombasa

INDIAN OCEAN

ANGOLA
Brazzaville
Kinshasa
Kananga

Luanda

A N G O L A
Lobito

Dodoma
Zanzibar
Dar es Salaam

TANZANIA
Lake Tanganyika

Aldabra Is. (Sey.)
COMOROS

Lubumbashi

Z A M B I A
Lusaka

L. Malawi
MALAWI
Lilongwe
Blantyre

Mozambique Channel

MADAGASCAR
Antananarivo

WALVIS BAY
NAMIBIA
Windhoek

BOTSWANA
Gaborone

Harare
ZIMBABWE
Beira

MOZAMBIQUE

Pretoria
Johannesburg
Maputo
Mbabane
SWAZILAND

Maseru
LESOTHO
Durban

REPUBLIC OF SOUTH AFRICA

Cape Town
Port Elizabeth

Scale 1: 37 000 000
0   500   1000   1500 km

⑤

© Collins ○ Longman Atlases

NORTHERN AFRICA

Scale 1:20 000 000

0   200   400   600   800 km

CENTRAL and SOUTHERN AFRICA

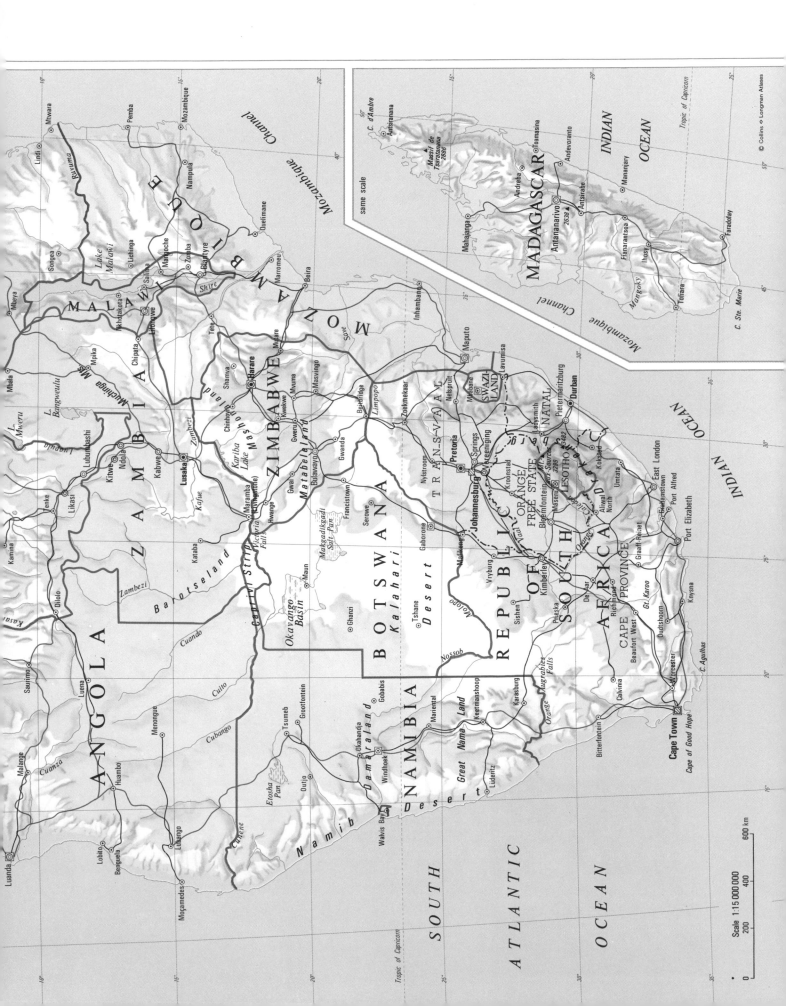

OCEANIA

Area   8 547 000 sq km
Population   23 500 000
Number of countries   11
Largest country   Australia, 7 686 848 sq k

Bonin Is.   (Japan)

Marcus I.

Wake I.
(U.S.A.)

Mariana
Islands

Trust Territory of the
Pacific Islands (U.S.A.)

Guam
(U.S.A.)

M I C R O N E S I

Marshall
Islands

Caroline Islands

M E L

NAURU   Ocean I.   KIRIBAT

New
Ireland

PAPUA
NEW
GUINEA

New
Britain

SOLOMON
ISLANDS

Honiara

TUVALU

Port
Moresby

Santa Cruz
Is.

Darwin

Coral
Sea

VANUATU

Vila

Suva
FIJI

New
Caledonia
(France)

Noumea

Loyalty Is.

A U S T R A L I A

Brisbane

Norfolk I.
(Aus.)

INDIAN

Lord Howe I.
(Aus.)

Perth

OCEAN

Darling

Sydney

Adelaide

Murray

Canberra

Melbourne

North
Island

Auckland

Tasman

NEW
ZEALAND

Tasmania

Sea

Hobart

South
Island

Wellington

Christchurch

Dunedin

Boun
Is
(N.

1. A Koala bear, Australia

2. Sheep shearing, New Zealand

3. Fishing in a lagoon, Western Samoa

4. Coastal village, Viti Levu, Fiji

5. Haymaking, South Island, New Zealand

Auckland Is.
(N.Z.)

allest country   Nauru, 21 sq km
st populous city   Sydney, Australia,
 280 900
hest mountain   Mt. Wilhelm, Papua
Jew Guinea, 4 694 m
west point   Lake Eyre, Australia, —12 m

Highest live volcano   Mauna Loa, Hawaii,
4 169 m
Longest river   Murray-Darling, Australia,
3 717 km
Largest lake/inland sea   Lake Eyre,
Australia, 9 583 sq km
Highest waterfall   Wollomombie, Australia,
335 m

way
s.

Hawaiian Islands
(U.S.A.)

◉ **Honolulu**
Hawaii

P A C I F I C

O C E A N

Howland I. (U.S.A.)
Baker I. (U.S.A.)

Christmas I.

Line Islands

Phoenix Is.

P O L Y N E S I A

Tokelau Is.

Apia ◙
**WESTERN
SAMOA**
e)   *(U.S.A.)*

(N.Z.)

Cook Is.

Society Is.

Papeete ◙
Tahiti   *(France)*

TONGA

Avarua ◙

◙
Nuku'alofa

*Marquesas
Islands*

Tuamotu Archipelago

(U.K.)
Pitcairn I.

Easter I.
(Chile)

Scale 1:40 000 000

0   400   800   1200   1600 km

Kermadec Is.
(N.Z.)

ham
)

AUSTRALIA

INDONESIA

Makassar Strait
Celebes
Sula Is.
Misool
Ceram
3055
Buru
Kendari
Butung
Ujung Pandang
Kabia
FLORES SEA
Wetar
Flores
Dili
Timor
Sumbawa
Sumba
Kupang
Roti

Aru Is.
Tanimbar Is.
Kolepom
C. Vals
Mappi

Maoke Range
Puntjak Jaya 5030
Sepik
PAPUA NEW
GUINEA
NEW GUINEA
Mt. Hagen
Mt Wilhelm 4694
Madang
Lae
Wewak

Jayapura

Admiralty Is.
New Hanover
Bismarck Sea
New Ireland
New Brita
Solomon Sea
Mt. Victoria 3987
Owen Stanley Range
Port Moresby

Gulf of Papua
Torres Strait

ARAFURA SEA

TIMOR SEA

Melville I.
Bathurst I.
Darwin
Arnhem Land
C. Wessel
C. Arnhem
Groote Eylandt
Gulf of Carpentaria

CORAL SEA

C. Londonderry
Joseph Bonaparte Gulf
Katherine
Roper
Birdum

C. Melville
C. York
Cape York Peninsula

C. Lévêque
Wyndham
King Leopold Ranges
Kimberley Plateau
Derby
Broome
Fitzroy Crossing
Hall's Creek

Cooktown
Mitchell
Cairns 1611
Ingham
Great Barrier Reef

NORTHERN
Barkly Tableland
Flinders
Normanton
Townsville
Bowen

Eighty Mile Beach
Great Sandy Desert
Port Hedland
Tennant Creek
TERRITORY
Barrow Creek
Mount Isa
Hughenden
Mackay

Barrow I.
Dampier
Marble Bar
L. Mackay
QUEENSLAND
Winton

Hamersley Range
Tom Price 1227
Ashburton
Mount Newman
L. Disappointment
Macdonnell Ranges 1510
Alice Springs
Simpson Desert
Barcaldine
Great

Tropic of Capricorn
Barlee Range
Gascoyne
WESTERN
Gibson Desert
L. Amadeus
Artesian
Grey Range
Rockhampton
Gladstone
Bundab

Murchison
AUSTRALIA
L. Carnegie
Musgrave Ranges
L. Eyre
Basin
Cunnamulla
Maryborough
Charleville
Dividing

Meekatharra
SOUTH AUSTRALIA
Great Victoria Desert
Toowoomba
Brisba

Mount Magnet
Leonora
Laverton
L. Torrens
Flinders Range
L. Frome
Bourke
Goondiwindi
Warwick
Lismore 1510

Geraldton
L. Barlee
Rawlinna
Forrest
Woomera
Broken Hill
Darling
Cobar
Nyngan
Narrabri
Armidale
Range
1615
Grafton

Moora
Kalgoorlie
Boulder
Eucla
Nullarbor Plain
L. Gairdner
Whyalla
Port Augusta
NEW SOUTH WALES
Dubbo
Tamworth
Taree

Perth
Coolgardie
L. Cowan
Ceduna
Port Pirie
Cobar
Orange
Bathurst
Maitland

Fremantle
York
Southern Cross
Norseman
Great Australian Bight
Port Lincoln
Murray
Lachlan
Cessnock
Newcastle
Sydney
Wollongong

Narrogin
Esperance
Spencer Gulf
Adelaide
Murrumbidgee
Wagga Wagga
Goulburn

Bunbury
Kojonup
Mount Barker
Kangaroo I.
Murray
Albury
Mt Kosciusko 2230
AUST. CAP. TER.
Canberra

Busselton
Augusta
Albany
Denmark
Mount Gambier
Ballarat
Bendigo
VICTORIA
Great
Snowy Mts
C. Howe
TASMAN SEA

C. Leeuwin
Warrnambool
Geelong
Yallourn
Melbourne
Morwell

INDIAN OCEAN
King I.
Bass Strait
Flinders I.

Burnie
Devonport
Launceston
TASMANIA
Mt. Ossa 1617
South East C.
Hobart

Scale 1:20 000 000
0   200   400   600   800 km

© Collins ◇ Longman Atlases

SOUTHEAST AUSTRALIA

Scale 1:7 500 000

0   100   200   300 km

© Collins ○ Longman Atlases

NEW ZEALAND

Scale 1:6 000 000

0 50 100 150 200 250 km

© Collins ◇ Longman Atlases

PACIFIC OCEAN

Equatorial Scale 1:80 000 000

3000km
2000
1000
0

© Collins © Longman Atlases

NORTH AMERICA

Area   24 247 038 sq km
Population   383 000 000
Number of countries   23
Largest country   Canada, 9 976 139 sq km

1. Lumbering (floating logs down river), Maine, U.S.A.

2. Cutting sugar cane, Antigua

3. Monument Valley, Arizona/Utah, U.S.A.

4. Brooklyn Bridge, New York, U.S.A.

allest country   St. Kitts — Nevis,
66 sq km
st populous city   New York, U.S.A.,
6 121 297
ghest mountain   Mt. McKinley, U.S.A.,
194 m
west point   Death Valley, U.S.A., —84 m

Highest live volcano   Mt. Wrangell, Alaska,
4 317 m
Longest river   Mississippi-Missouri, U.S.A.,
6 020 km
Largest lake/inland sea   Lake Superior,
U.S.A./Canada, 82 413 sq km
Highest waterfall   Ribbon Fall, U.S.A.,
491 m

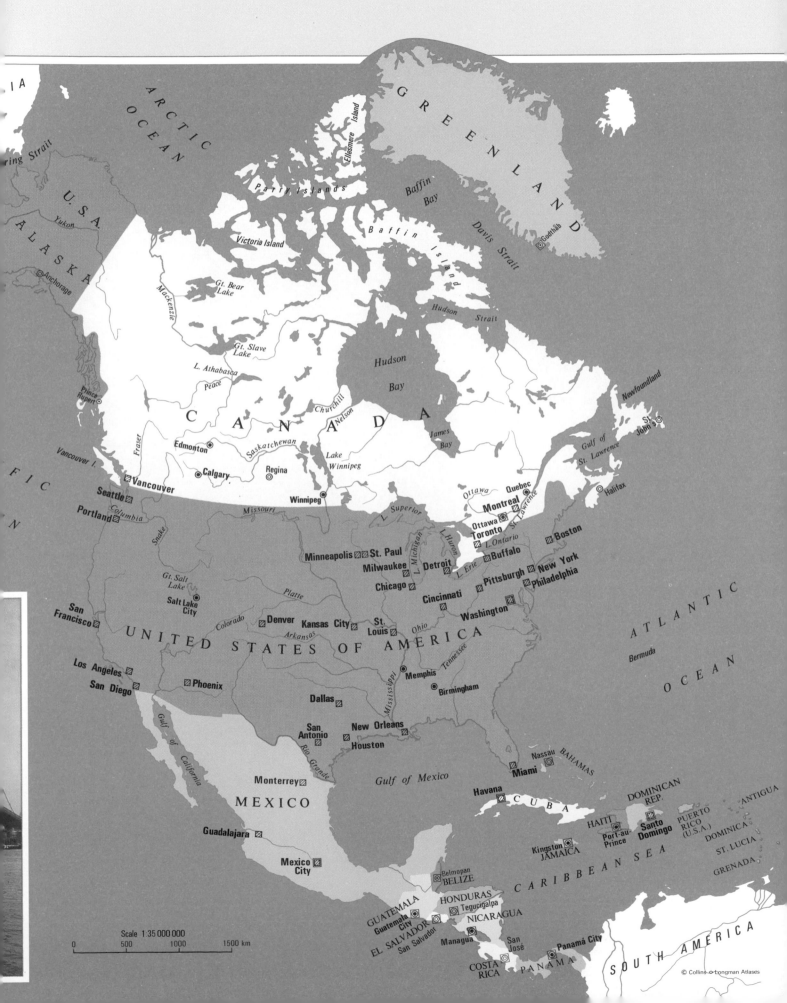

I A

ARCTIC OCEAN

G R E E N L A N D

Ellesmere Island

ring Strait

Parry Islands

Baffin Bay

Victoria Island

Baffin Island

Davis Strait

Godthåb

U.S.A.

Yukon

ALASKA

Anchorage

Gt. Bear Lake

Mackenzie

Hudson Strait

Gt. Slave Lake

L. Athabasca

Peace

Hudson Bay

James Bay

C A N A D A

Churchill

Nelson

Newfoundland

St. John's

Prince Rupert

Edmonton

Fraser

Saskatchewan

Calgary

Regina

Lake Winnipeg

Gulf of St. Lawrence

Halifax

Vancouver I.

Vancouver

Seattle

Winnipeg

Missouri

Ottawa

Quebec

Montreal

Portland

Columbia

L. Superior

Ottawa

St. Lawrence

Toronto

L. Ontario

Boston

Snake

Minneapolis

St. Paul

L. Michigan

L. Huron

Detroit

Buffalo

PACIFIC

Milwaukee

L. Erie

Pittsburgh

New York

Gt. Salt Lake

Platte

Chicago

Cincinnati

Philadelphia

OCEAN

San Francisco

Salt Lake City

Denver

Kansas City

St. Louis

Ohio

Washington

ATLANTIC

U N I T E D   S T A T E S   O F   A M E R I C A

Colorado

Arkansas

Tennessee

Bermuda

Los Angeles

San Diego

Phoenix

Mississippi

Memphis

Birmingham

OCEAN

Dallas

Gulf of California

San Antonio

New Orleans

Houston

Rio Grande

Miami

Nassau

BAHAMAS

Monterrey

Gulf of Mexico

MEXICO

Havana

C U B A

DOMINICAN REP.

ANTIGUA

Guadalajara

HAITI

Santo Domingo

PUERTO RICO (U.S.A.)

DOMINICA

Kingston

JAMAICA

Port-au-Prince

ST. LUCIA

Mexico City

Belmopan

BELIZE

C A R I B B E A N   S E A

GRENADA

GUATEMALA

HONDURAS

Tegucigalpa

Guatemala City

NICARAGUA

EL SALVADOR

San Salvador

Managua

San José

Panamá City

S O U T H   A M E R I C A

COSTA RICA

PANAMA

© Collins · Longman Atlases

Scale 1:35 000 000

0   500   1000   1500 km

CANADA

B E R I N G   S E A

P A C I F I C   O C E A N

B E A U F O R T   S E A

Scale 1:17 000 000

0   200   400   600   800 km

GREENLAND

King Christian IX Land

Mt Forel ▲ 3360

King Frederik VI Coast

Arctic Circle

Ammassalik (Tasiilaq)

Queen Axel Heiberg I.
zabeth Heiberg I.
Islands

Bathurst I.
Islands
Cornwallis I.
Resolute
Devon Island

Thule (Qaanaaq)

C. Parry

Nares Strait

Ellesmere Island

Lancaster Sound

Iville
Prince of Wales Island
Somerset Island

Bylot I.
Pond Inlet

Baffin Bay

Upernavik

Disko

Godthåb (Nuuk)

B a f f i n

Gulf of Boothia
Melville Peninsula
Prince Charles I.
Foxe Basin

Home Bay

Penny Highland 2591

C. Dyer

Pangnirtung

Cumberland Sound

Frederikshåb (Paamiut)

Julianehåb (Qaqortoq)

C. Farewell

Davis Strait

ATLANTIC OCEAN

ueen Maud Gulf

N O R T H W E S T

I s l a n d

Frobisher Bay

Frobisher Bay

Spence Bay

Foxe Channel

T E R R I T O R I E S

Southampton Island

Fisher Strait
Coats I.

Hudson

Saglouc

Strait
Akpatok I.
C. Chidley

Mansel I.

Ungava Bay

C. Harrison
Indian Harbour

KEEWATIN

Dubawnt Lake

Garry L.

Amaud

Leaf

Kokoak

Nain

Whale

George

NEWFOUNDLAND

C A N A D A

Eskimo Point

Ottawa Is.

Larch

Clearwater Lake

Schefferville

Labrador

Churchill

Battle Harbour

C. Bauld

Seal
Churchill
C. Churchill

Nelson

Hudson Bay

Belcher Is.

Gt. Whale

Romaine

Grand Falls

Gander

St. John's

Lynn Lake

Hayes

C. Tatnam

York Factory

C. Henrietta Maria

Fort George
La Grande

Gagnon

Moisie
Sept Iles
Port Cartier

Anticosti I.

Newfoundland

Channel Port aux Basques

MANITOBA

Winisk

Seven

James
Akimiski I.
Bay

Eastmain

Peribonca

Manicouagan

Gulf of St. Lawrence

Cape Breton I. St. Pierre and
Str. Miquelon (Fr.)

The Pas

Fort Rupert

Lake Mistassini

Q U E B E C

Gaspé

Belle Isle Str.

L. Winnipeg

O N T A R I O

Albany

Abitibi

St. Maurice

Chicoutimi-Jonquière

St. Lawrence

NEW BRUNSWICK

PR. EDWARD I.
Charlottetown

Sydney

Bathurst

Moncton

NOVA SCOTIA

Sable I.

legostis

L. Manitoba

Winnipeg
St Boniface
Kenora

Sioux Lookout

Nipigon

L. Nipigon

Longlac

Hearst

Timmins

Quebec
Lévis

Edmundston

Fredericton
Saint John

Bay of Fundy

Halifax

Liverpool

Portage la Prairie
Brandon
Morden

Thunder Bay

Trans Canada Highway

Michipicoten Harbour

North Bay

Trois Rivières

Montreal

Sherbrooke

MAINE

Bangor

Yarmouth

C. Sable

Minot
Red

Grand Forks

MINNESOTA
Duluth

L. Superior

Sault Ste Marie

Sudbury

Ottawa
Hull

Lake Champlain

Portland

Bismarck
TH DAKOTA

Fargo

WISC.

Manistique

Georgian Bay

Owen Sound

Kingston

NEW YORK

VERMONT N.H.
Manchester

Boston
C. Cod

Aberdeen
St Cloud

St Paul

Green Bay

Kitchener

Oshawa

Toronto

Rochester
Syracuse
Utica

Albany

Worcester
Hartford
CONN.

Providence

Minneapolis

MICH.

Cadillac

Bay City

London

Hamilton

Niagara Falls

Buffalo

Scranton

Newhaven

Long Island

DAKOTA
Pierre

Milwaukee

L. Michigan

Grand Rapids

St Catharines

Erie

Newark

New York

Sioux Falls
IOWA

Madison

Detroit

Windsor

PENNSYLVANIA

Philadelphia

Sioux City

Waterloo
Cedar Rapids

Chicago

Toledo

Cleveland

Pittsburgh

Baltimore

ILL.

IND.

OHIO

© Collins ○ Longman Atlases

UNITED STATES

Hawaiian Islands
(U.S.A.)

PACIFIC
OCEAN

Honolulu

Scale 1:20 000 000

© Collins ○ Longman Atlases

Scale 1:12 000 000

0   200   400   600km

NORTHEAST UNITED STATES and SOUTH CENTRAL CANADA

Fort Frances
Rainy L.
International Falls
Atikokan
L. Nipigon
Lac des Mille Lacs
Dog L.
Long L.
Nipigon
Pic
Hearst
Cochrane

C A N A D A

Heron Bay
Timmins
Kirkla Lake

MINNESOTA
Grand Rapids
Virginia
Ely
Grand Marais
Thunder Bay
Isle Royale
Michipicoten Harbour
Michipicoten I.
Chapleau
Biskotasi L.
Timagami L.

Duluth
Two Harbors
Apostle Is.
Lake Superior
Keweenaw Pt.
Keweenaw Bay

Cloquet
Superior
Ashland
Hancock
Ontonagon

Mille Lacs L.
St. Croix
Ironwood
Marquette
Whitefish Pt.
Sault Ste. Marie
Sault Ste. Marie
Blind River
Sudbury
Sturgeon Falls
L. Nipissing
Ludgate

Park Falls
Newberry
North Channel
Manitoulin I.

Minneapolis
St Paul
Rhinelander
Iron Mountain
Escanaba
Manistique
Mackinaw City
Cheboygan
Lake Huron
Georgian Bay
Parry Sound

WISCONSIN
Chippewa Falls
Chippewa
Wausau
Wisconsin
Marinette
Green Bay
Beaver I.
Manitou Is.
C. Hurd
Owen Sound

Hastings
Eau Claire
Marshfield
Shawano
Green Bay
Alpena
North Pt.

MICHIGAN
Lake Michigan
Manitou Is.
Traverse City
Au Sable
Grayling

Wisconsin Rapids
Appleton
Manitowoc
Manistee
Cadillac
Au Sable Pt.
Saginaw Bay
Port Austin

Winona
Sparta
L. Winnebago
Fond du Lac
Ludington
Clare
Goderich

Austin
La Crosse
Portage
Sheboygan
Muskegon
Alma
Bay City
Saginaw

Black
Wisconsin
Watertown
Muskegon
Grand Rapids
Flint
Port Huron
Waterloo
Kitchener
Guelph

Cedar Falls
Waterloo
Madison
Milwaukee
Waukesha
Lansing
Pontiac
London
Brantford

IOWA
Dubuque
Janesville
Racine
Kenosha
Battle Creek
Kalamazoo
Detroit
Windsor
L. St. Clair
Chatham
Port Burwell

Cedar Rapids
Rockford
Waukegan
Jackson
Ann Arbor
Pt. Pelee
Lake Erie

Iowa City
Elgin
Evanston
Benton Harbour
Adrian
Monroe

Davenport
Chicago
Joliet
Hammond
Gary
Michigan City
South Bend
Toledo
Sandusky
Lorain
Lakewood
Cleveland
Ashtabula
Painesville

La Salle
Aurora
Kankakee
Fort Wayne
Defiance
Maumee
Findlay
Fostoria
Akron
Wooster
Youngstown
Aliquippa

Galesburg
Fort Madison
Peoria
Logansport
Peru
Decatur
Lima
Marion
Mansfield
Canton
Pittsburgh
Weirton

ILLINOIS
Bloomington
Lafayette
Kokomo
Portland
Piqua
Springfield
Coshocton
Wheeling

Quincy
Champaign
Danville
Anderson
INDIANA
Springfield
Columbus
Zanesville
Cambridge

Hannibal
Decatur
Tuscola
Richmond
Dayton
Hamilton
Chillicothe
Athens
Parkersburg

Mexico
Jacksonville
Springfield
Indianapolis
Franklin
OHIO
Miami
Scioto
Fairmont
Clarksburg

Missouri
Effingham
Terre Haute
Bloomington
Cincinnati
Covington
A M E R
Elkins

Jefferson City
St. Louis
East St. Louis
Lawrenceville
Vincennes
Seymour
Bedford
Ohio
Portsmouth
WEST VIRGINIA

MISSOURI
Salem
Centralia
Princeton
KENTUCKY

Scale 1:5 000 000

| 0 | 50 | 100 | 150 | 200 | 250 | 300 km |

CENTRAL AMERICA and the CARIBBEAN

Mexican States numbered on map
1. AGUASCALIENTES
2. DISTRITO FEDERAL
3. TLAXCALA

Scale 1:12 500 000

0   100   200   300   400   500   600 km

© Collins ○ Longman Atlases

Inset map (upper right):

on the same scale

Virgin Is.(U.K.) Anguilla(U.K.)
Bayamon San Juan Virgin Sint Maarten(Neth.) St. Martin(Fr.)
Carolina Is. (U.S.A.) St. Barthélemy(Fr.) Barbuda
Ponce Caguas Saba(Neth.) St. KITTS ANTIGUA
PUERTO Sint Eustatius(Neth.) NEVIS St. John's
RICO (U.K.) Montserrat Leeward Islands
(U.S.A.) Guadeloupe Pointe-à-Pitre
(Fr.) Basse-Terre Marie Galante
Lesser Roseau DOMINICA

Fort-de-France Martinique
Castries (Fr.)
ST. LUCIA
St. Kingstown BARBADOS
VINCENT Bridgetown
AND THE Windward Islands
GRENADINES
St. George's GRENADA

Lesser Antilles

La Blanquilla TOBAGO
Dragon's Mouth Port of Spain
Bonaire San Fernando
Los Orchila G. of TRINIDAD
Roques Tortuga Margarita I. Paria Serpent's
Cumaná Mouth

Barcelona Maturín

Main map:

TENNESSEE NORTH
Pickwick L. Asheville Charlotte Fayetteville C. Lookout
Chattanooga SOUTH CAROLINA
Guntersville Greenville Wilmington
Tennessee Columbia CAROLINA C. Fear
SSIPPI Atlanta Augusta
ALABAMA GEORGIA Savannah
Birmingham Macon Ogeechee C. Romain
Meridian Montgomery Columbus Charleston
Mobile Albany ATLANTIC
Tuscaloosa Flint
Alabama Suwannee
New Okeefenokee OCEAN
Orleans Biloxi Pensacola Swamp
Tallahassee Jacksonville 30°
Mississippi Apalachee
Delta C. San Blas Bay Gainesville Daytona Beach
Orlando Cape Canaveral
Tampa Lakeland
St. Petersburg
Tampa B. Lake West
OF Okeechobee Palm
Fort Myers Beach Freeport Great
The Fort Grand Abaco I.
Everglades Lauderdale Bahama I.
C. Romano Miami Eleuthera I.
C. Sable New BAHAMAS
Key West Providence Nassau
Florida Keys Cat I. San
RICO Straits Andros I. Exuma Is. Salvador
of Florida Gt. Long I.
Havana Matanzas Exuma
(La Habana) Crooked I. Mayaguana I.
Pinar del Rio Guines Santa Clara Caibarién Acklin's I. Turks and Caicos Is.
Gulf of Sancti Morón Little Caicos Is. (U.K.)
Guane Batabanó Cienfuegos Spíritus Inagua Turks Is.
Nueva Trinidad Ciego de Avila Nuevitas Great
Gerona CUBA Camagüey Holguín Inagua I.
Yucatán Isle of Pines Victoria Baracoa Tortue
C. San de las Tunas Cap Haitien Puerto Plata
Progreso Antonio Jardines de la Bayamo Sa. Maestra San Francisco
Tizimín Reina Manzanillo Guantánamo de Macorís Samaná
Mérida Santiago G. of Gonaïves Santiago San Juan
YUCATAN C. Catoche de Cuba Gonâve St. Marc La Vega DOMINICAN REP. Bayamon
Puerto Little Windward Jérémie HAITI Azua S. Pedro Ponce Caguas
Juárez Cayman Cayman Brac Passage Port-au- S. Cristóbal Santo La Romana PUERTO
Cozumel I. Prince Domingo Saona RICO
QUINTANA Cayman Is. Les Barahona Hispaniola (U.S.A.)
Chetumal ROO Grand Cayman (U.K.) Cayes
Chetumal Georgetown Montego Bay St. Ann's Bay Antilles
Bay Black River Port
BELIZE Antonio
Belize JAMAICA Kingston
Belmopan Turneffe Is.
Mts. Gulf of Honduras CARIBBEAN SEA
Maya Bay Is.
Pto. Netherlands
Pto. Cortés Caratasca Antilles
La Ceiba Lagoon Aruba Curaçao Bonaire
Barrios Willemstad
S. Pedro Sula Patuca Mosquitia
Zacapa Sta. HONDURAS Juticalpa Plain C. Gracias á Dios Guajira Gulf
Sta. Rosa Comayagua Peninsula of
Chiquimula Tegucigalpa Coco Pto. Cabezas Paraguaná Venezuela
ALA Ana Danlí Pen. Punto Fijo
San Salvador 2400 Isabella Ríohacha Coro Puerto
S. Vicente Mosquito Sta. Marta Cabello
DOR S. Miguel Chontales Cord. Coast Ciénaga Cristóbal San Felipe
G. of Fonseca NICARAGUA Rio Grande Barranquilla Colón Maracaibo Cabimas Barquisimeto Valencia Maracay
Chinandega Escondido Valledupar Lagunillas
Corinto León Managua Cartagena Lake VENEZUELA
Managua Rama Bluefields Maracaibo Valera Mérida
Jinotepe Granada Lake Arjona Trujillo Barinas
Rivas Nicaragua Magangue Montería Bolívar
Liberia San Juan Magdalena Cúcuta Apure
Nicoya COSTA Turbo San Cristóbal
Peninsula Límon Gulf of Barrancabermeja
Puntarenas San Colón Darién Bucaramanga
C. Blanco José Cartago Gatun Gulf COLOMBIA Meta
G. of Nicoya Quepos Chiriquí Lake of Uraba
Pto. David Balboa Panama City
RICA Santiago Golfito PANAMA Gulf
Pta. Armuelles Penonomé of
Burica Azuero Archp. de
Peninsula las Perlas

SOUTH AMERICA

Area	17 821 028 sq km
Population	252 000 000
Number of countries	13
Largest country	Brazil, 8 511 965 sq km

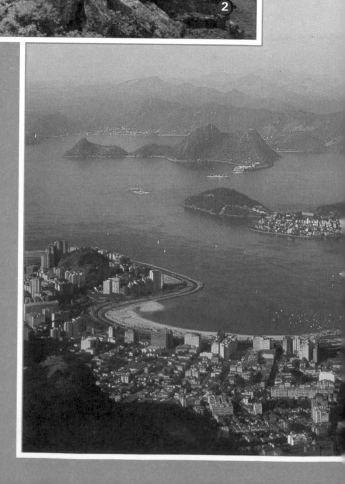

1. A Llama, Peru

2. The ruined city of Machu Picchu, Peru

3. Ignazu Falls, Brazil

4. Sugar-Loaf Mountain, Rio de Janeiro, Brazil

...allest country Trinidad and Tobago,
128 sq km
...st populous city Buenos Aires,
...rgentina, 9 927 404
...ghest mountain Aconcagua, Argentina,
...960 m
...west point Salinas Grande, Argentina,
...40 m

Highest live volcano Cotopaxi, Ecuador,
5 897 m
Longest river Amazon, Brazil, 6 570 km
Largest lake/inland sea Lake Maracaibo,
Venezuela, 16 300 sq km
Highest waterfall Angel Falls, Venezuela,
979 m

NORTH AMERICA

Caribbean Sea

ATLANTIC OCEAN

L. Nicaragua

Barranquilla
Cartagena
Curaçao (Neth.)
Maracaibo
L. Maracaibo
Caracas
Ciudad Bolívar
TRINIDAD
Port of Spain

VENEZUELA

Medellín
Manizales
Bogotá
COLOMBIA
Cali

Georgetown
Paramaribo
Cayenne
Orinoco
GUYANA
SURINAM
GUIANA (Fr.)
Essequibo

PACIFIC OCEAN

Quito
ECUADOR
Guayaquil
Iquitos
Galapagos Is. (Ec.)

Negro
Manaus
Amazon
Amazon
Belém
Madeira
Tapajós
Xingu

P E R U

Trujillo

B R A Z I L

Araguaia
Tocantins
Fortaleza
Natal
Recife

Callao
Lima
Cuzco

São Francisco
Salvador

L. Titicaca
Arequipa
La Paz
Cochabamba
Santa Cruz
Arica
Sucre

Goiânia
Brasília

BOLIVIA

Iquique

PARAGUAY
Paraguay

Paraná

Belo Horizonte

Rio de Janeiro
Niterói
São Paulo

Antofagasta

Asunción

Curitiba

San Miguel de Tucumán
Salado
Paraná

C H I L E

Valparaíso
Santiago
Mendoza
Córdoba
Rosario
Uruguay
URUGUAY
Montevideo
Buenos Aires

Juan Fernandez Is. (Chile)

Pôrto Alegre

SOUTH

Concepción
Bahía Blanca
Mar del Plata

A R G E N T I N A

San Antonio Oeste

ATLANTIC OCEAN

Puerto Montt

Comodoro Rivadavia

Falkland Is. (U.K.)

Punta Arenas
Tierra del Fuego

OCEAN

Scale 1:35 000 000
0   500   1000   1500 km

© Collins ○ Longman Atlases

SOUTH AMERICA

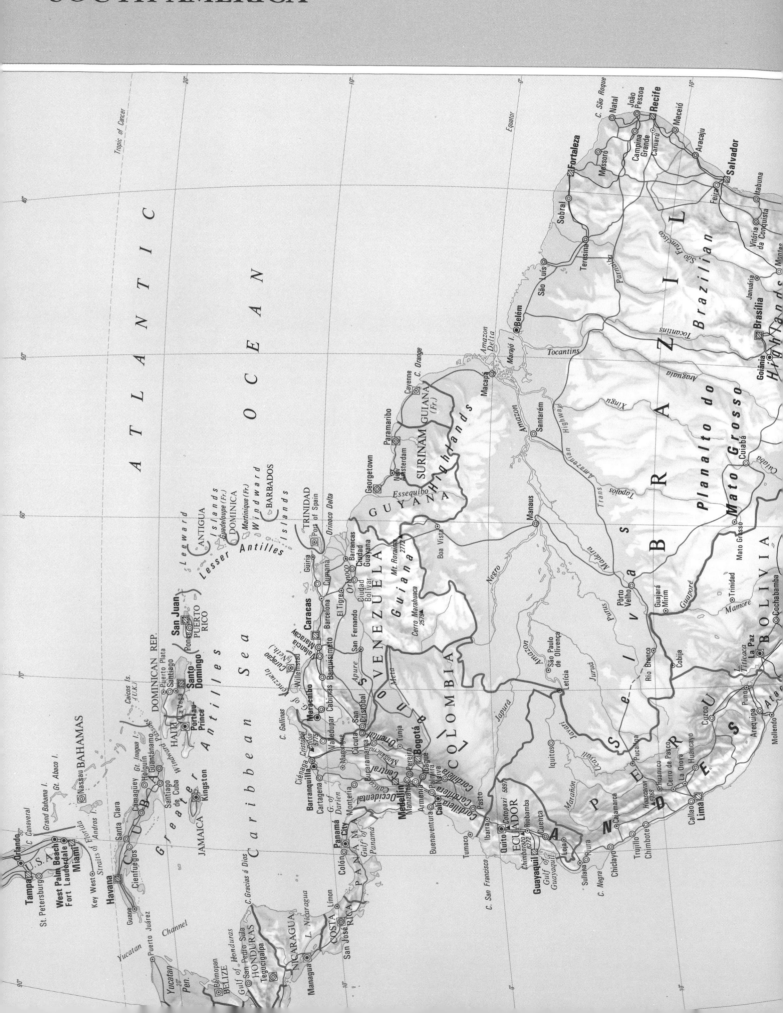

Scale 1:25 000 000

1500 km

1000

500

0

POLAR REGIONS

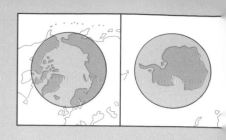

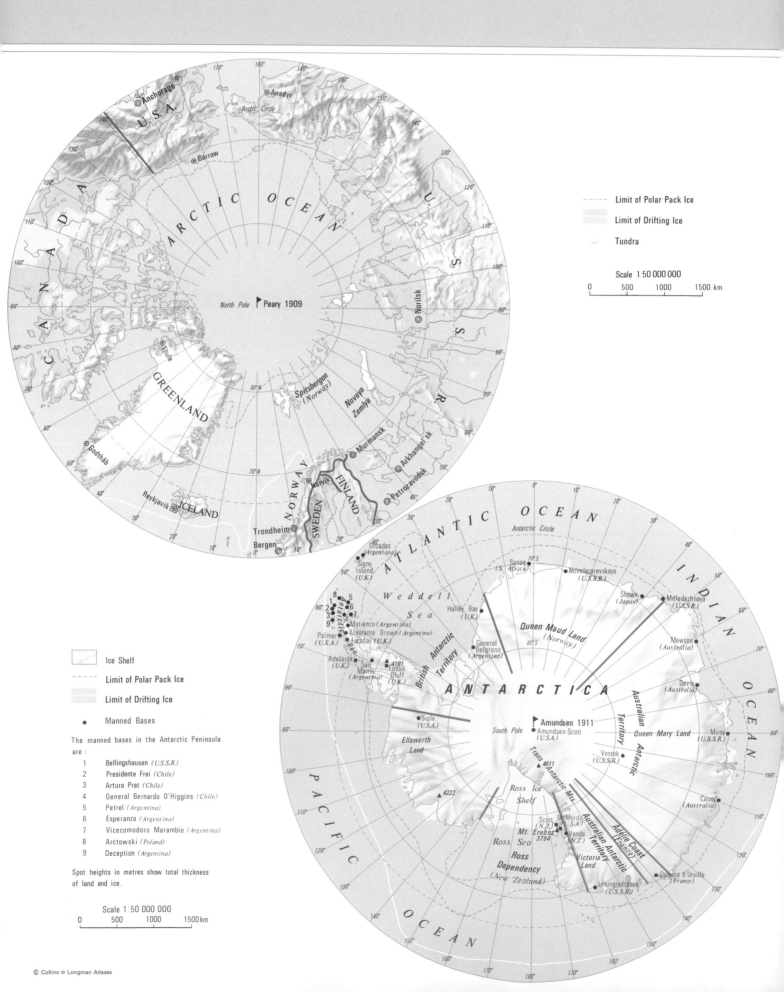

Legend (top right):

----- Limit of Polar Pack Ice

Limit of Drifting Ice

Tundra

Scale 1:50 000 000

0   500   1000   1500 km

Legend (left, lower):

Ice Shelf

----- Limit of Polar Pack Ice

Limit of Drifting Ice

• Manned Bases

The manned bases in the Antarctic Peninsula are :

1 Bellingshausen (U.S.S.R.)
2 Presidente Frei (Chile)
3 Artura Prat (Chile)
4 General Bernardo O'Higgins (Chile)
5 Petrel (Argentina)
6 Esperanza (Argentina)
7 Vicecomodoro Marambio (Argentina)
8 Arctowski (Poland)
9 Deception (Argentina)

Spot heights in metres show total thickness of land and ice.

Scale 1:50 000 000

0   500   1000   1500km

© Collins ◇ Longman Atlases

ll the important names on the physical-political maps in the atlas will be found in this index. Each entry indicates he country or region of the world in which the name is located, followed by the number of the most appropriate page n which the name appears — generally the largest scale map. Lastly the latitude and longitude in degrees and ninutes is given. Where a name applies to a very large area of the map these coordinates are sometimes omitted. For ames that do apply to an area the reference is to the centre of the feature, which will usually also be the centre of he name on the map. In the case of rivers the mouth or confluence is always taken as the point of reference. 'herefore it is necessary to follow the river upstream from this point to find its name on the map. The abbreviations ısed in the index are explained below.

INDEX

fghan.	Afghanistan
la.	Alabama
las.	Alaska
rctic Oc.	Arctic Ocean
riz.	Arizona
rk.	Arkansas
tlantic Oc.	Atlantic Ocean
, **B.**	bay, Bay
aja Calif. Sur	Baja California Sur
angla.	Bangladesh
.C.	British Columbia
., **C.**	cape, Cape
alif.	California
.A.R.	Central African Republic
. America	Central America
onn.	Connecticut
zech.	Czechoslovakia
.	internal division, e.g. county, region, state
. and G.	Dumfries and Galloway
el.	Delaware
erbys.	Derbyshire
es.	desert
om. Rep.	Dominican Republic
. Germany	East Germany
quat. Guinea	Equatorial Guinea
st.	estuary
	physical feature e.g. valley, plain, geographic district or region
la.	Florida
g., **G.**	gulf, Gulf
Ga.	Georgia
Glos.	Gloucestershire
Humber.	Humberside
i., **I.**, *is.*, **Is.**	island, Island, islands, Islands
Ill.	Illinois
Ind.	Indiana
Indian Oc.	Indian Ocean
Kans.	Kansas
Ky.	Kentucky
l., **L.**	lake, Lake
La.	Louisiana
Liech.	Liechtenstein
Lux.	Luxembourg
Man.	Manitoba
Mass.	Massachusetts
Md.	Maryland
Med. Sea	Mediterranean Sea
Mich.	Michigan
Minn.	Minnesota
Miss.	Mississippi
Mo.	Missouri
Mont.	Montana
Mt.	Mount
mtn., **Mtn.**	mountain, Mountain
mts., **Mts.**	mountains, Mountains
N. America	North America
N.B.	New Brunswick
N.C.	North Carolina
N. Dak.	North Dakota
Nebr.	Nebraska
Neth.	Netherlands
Nev.	Nevada
Nfld.	Newfoundland
N.H.	New Hampshire
N. Ireland	Northern Ireland
N.J.	New Jersey
N. Korea	North Korea
N. Mex.	New Mexico
N.S.W.	New South Wales
N.W.T.	Northwest Territories
N.Y.	New York State
N. Yorks.	North Yorkshire
Ont.	Ontario
Oreg.	Oregon
Pacific Oc.	Pacific Ocean
pen., **Pen.**	peninsula, Peninsula
Penn.	Pennsylvania
Phil.	Philippines
P.N.G.	Papua New Guinea
Pt.	Point
Qld.	Queensland
Que.	Quebec
r., **R.**	river, River
Rep. of Ire.	Republic of Ireland
Resr.	Reservoir
R.I.	Rhode Island
R.S.A.	Republic of South Africa
R.S.F.S.R.	Russian Soviet Federal Socialist Republic
S.A.	South Australia
S. America	South America
S.C.	South Carolina
S. Dak.	South Dakota
S. Korea	South Korea
Somali Rep.	Somali Republic
Sd.	Sound
str., **Str.**	strait, Strait
Switz.	Switzerland
S. Yemen	Southern Yemen
Tas.	Tasmania
Tenn.	Tennessee
Tex.	Texas
U.A.E.	United Arab Emirates
U.K.	United Kingdom
U.S.A.	United States of America
U.S.S.R	Union of Soviet Socialist Republics
Va.	Virginia
Vic.	Victoria
Vt.	Vermont
W.A.	Western Australia
W. Germany	West Germany
Wisc.	Wisconsin
W. Sahara	Western Sahara
W. Samoa	Western Samoa
W. Va.	West Virginia
Wyo.	Wyoming
Yugo.	Yugoslavia

A

Aachen W. Germany **20** 50.46N 6.06E
Abadan Iran **30** 30.21N 48.15E
Abadla Algeria **38** 31.01N 2.45W
Abakan U.S.S.R. **29** 53.43N 91.25E
Abaya, L. Ethiopia **41** 6.20N 38.00E
Abéché Chad **39** 13.49N 20.49E
Aberdeen U.K. **19** 57.08N 2.07W
Aberdeen S. Dak. U.S.A. **52** 45.28N 98.30W
Aberystwyth U.K. **19** 52.25N 4.06W
Abidjan Ivory Coast **38** 5.19N 4.01W
Abilene Tex. U.S.A. **52** 32.27N 99.45W
Abitibi *r.* Canada **53** 51.15N 81.30W
Abitibi, L. Canada **55** 48.40N 79.35W
Abrantes Portugal **21** 39.28N 8.12W
Abu Dhabi U.A.E. **30** 24.27N 54.23E
Abu Hamed Sudan **41** 19.32N 33.20E
Abuja Nigeria **38** 9.12N 7.11E
Acámbaro Mexico **56** 20.01N101.42W
Acapulco Mexico **56** 16.51N 99.56W
Accra Ghana **38** 5.33N 0.15W
Achill I. Rep. of Ire. **19** 53.57N 10.00W
Achinsk U.S.S.R. **28** 56.10N 90.10E
Acklin's I. Bahamas **57** 22.30N 74.10W
Aconcagua *mtn.* Argentina **61** 32.37S 70.00W
Adamawa Highlands Nigeria **38** 7.05N 12.00E
Adams, Mt. U.S.A. **52** 46.13N121.29W
Adana Turkey **23** 37.00N 35.19E
Adapazari Turkey **23** 40.45N 30.23E
Adda *r.* Italy **21** 45.08N 9.55E
Addis Ababa Ethiopia **41** 9.03N 38.42E
Adelaide Australia **45** 34.56S138.36E
Adélie Coast Antarctica **62** 73.00S140.00E
Aden S. Yemen **30** 12.50N 45.00E
Aden, G. of Indian Oc. **30** 13.00N 50.00E
Adige *r.* Italy **21** 45.10N 12.20E
Adirondack Mts. U.S.A. **55** 44.00N 74.15W
Admiralty Is. P.N.G. **44** 2.30S147.30E
Adour *r.* France **21** 43.28N 1.35W
Adrian Mich. U.S.A. **54** 41.55N 84.01W
Adriatic Sea Med.Sea **22** 42.30N 16.00E
Aduwa Ethiopia **41** 14.12N 38.56E
Aegean Sea Med. Sea **23** 39.00N 25.00E
Afghanistan Asia **31** 33.00N 66.00E
Africa 8
Afyon Turkey **23** 38.46N 30.32E
Agades Niger **38** 17.00N 7.56E
Agano *r.* Japan **35** 37.58N139.02E
Agedabia Libya **38** 30.48N 20.15E
Agen France **21** 44.12N 0.38E
Agordat Ethiopia **41** 15.35N 37.55E
Agra India **31** 27.09N 78.00E
Aguascalientes Mexico **56** 21.51N102.18W
Aguascalientes *d.* Mexico **56** 22.00N102.00W
Agulhas, C. R.S.A. **41** 34.55S 20.00E
Agulhas Negras *mtn.* Brazil **61** 22.20S 44.43W
Ahaggar Mts. Algeria **38** 24.00N 5.50E
Ahmadabad India **31** 23.03N 72.40E
Ahwaz Iran **30** 31.17N 48.44E
Ain Salah Algeria **38** 27.12N 2.29E
Aïn Sefra Algeria **38** 32.45N 0.35W
Aïr *mts.* Niger **38** 18.30N 8.30E
Ajaccio France **21** 41.55N 8.43E
Ajmer India **31** 26.29N 74.70E
Aketi Zaïre **40** 2.46N 23.51E
Akhdar, Jebel *mts.* Libya **39** 32.10N 22.00E
Akimiski I. Canada **51** 53.00N 81.20W
Akita Japan **35** 39.44N140.05E
Akobo *r.* Sudan/Ethiopia **40** 8.30N 33.15E
Akola India **31** 20.44N 77.00E
Akpatok I. Canada **51** 60.30N 68.30W
Akron Ohio U.S.A. **54** 41.04N 81.31W
Aktyubinsk U.S.S.R. **28** 50.16N 57.13E
Alabama *d.* U.S.A. **53** 33.00N 87.00W
Alabama *r.* U.S.A. **53** 31.05N 87.55W
Åland Is. Finland **24** 60.20N 20.00E
Alaska *d.* U.S.A. **50** 65.00N153.00W
Alaska, G. of U.S.A. **50** 58.45N145.00W
Alaska Pen. U.S.A. **50** 56.00N160.00W
Alaska Range *mts.* U.S.A. **50** 62.10N152.00W
Albacete Spain **21** 39.00N 1.52W
Alba-Iulia Romania **22** 46.04N 23.33E
Albania Europe **23** 41.00N 20.00E
Albany Australia **44** 34.57S117.54E
Albany *r.* Canada **53** 52.10N 82.00W
Albany Ga. U.S.A. **53** 31.37N 84.10W
Albany N.Y. U.S.A. **55** 42.40N 73.49W
Albemarle Sd. U.S.A. **53** 36.10N 76.00W
Albert, L. Africa **41** 1.45N 31.00E
Alberta *d.* Canada **50** 55.00N115.00W
Albert Nile *r.* Uganda **41** 3.30N 32.00E
Ålborg Denmark **24** 57.03N 9.56E
Albuquerque U.S.A. **52** 35.05N106.38W
Albury Australia **45** 36.03S146.53E
Alcazar Spain **21** 39.24N 3.12W
Alcira Spain **21** 39.10N 0.27W
Aldan U.S.S.R. **29** 58.44N125.22E
Aldan *r.* U.S.S.R. **29** 63.30N130.00E
Aleksandrovsk Sakhalinskiy U.S.S.R. **29** 50.55N142.12E
Aleppo Syria **30** 36.14N 37.10E
Ålesund Norway **24** 62.28N 6.11E
Aleutian Is. U.S.A. **7** 57.00N180.00
Aleutian Range *mts.* U.S.A. **50** 58.00N156.00W
Aleutian Trench Pacific Oc. **9** 50.00N178.00E
Alexander Archipelago *is.* U.S.A. **50** 56.30N134.30W
Alexandra New Zealand **46** 45.14S169.26E
Alexandria Egypt **39** 31.13N 29.55E
Alexandria La. U.S.A. **53** 31.19N 92.29W
Alexandroúpolis Greece **23** 40.50N 25.53E
Algeria Africa **38** 28.00N 2.00E
Algiers Algeria **38** 36.50N 3.00E
Aliákmon *r.* Greece **23** 40.30N 22.38E
Alicante Spain **21** 38.21N 0.29W
Alice Springs *town* Australia **44** 23.42S133.52E
Aliquippa U.S.A. **54** 40.38N 80.16W
Aliwal North R.S.A. **41** 30.41S 26.41E
Al Jauf Saudi Arabia **30** 29.49N 39.52E
Allagash *r.* U.S.A. **55** 47.08N 69.10W
Allahabad India **31** 25.57N 81.50E
Allegheny *r.* U.S.A. **55** 40.26N 80.00W
Allegheny Mts. U.S.A. **55** 40.00N 79.00W
Allentown U.S.A. **55** 40.37N 75.30W
Allier *r.* France **21** 46.58N 3.04E
Alma Mich. U.S.A. **54** 43.23N 84.40W
Alma-Ata U.S.S.R. **28** 43.19N 76.55E
Almeria Spain **21** 36.50N 2.26W
Alor Setar Malaysia **34** 6.06N100.23E
Alpena U.S.A. **54** 45.04N 83.27W
Alps *mts.* Europe **21** 46.00N 9.00E
Altai *mts.* Mongolia **32** 46.30N 93.30E
Altamaha *r.* U.S.A. **53** 31.15N 81.23W
Altiplano Mexicano *mts.* N. America **8** 24.00N105.00W
Altoona U.S.A. **55** 40.32N 78.23W
Alvarado Mexico **56** 18.49N 95.46W
Amadeus, L. Australia **44** 24.50S131.00E
Amagasaki Japan **35** 34.43N135.20E
Amarillo U.S.A. **52** 35.14N101.50W
Amazon *r.* Brazil **60** 2.00S 50.00W
Amazon Delta *f.* Brazil **60** 0.00 50.00W
Ambala India **31** 30.19N 76.49E
Ambarchik U.S.S.R. **29** 69.39N162.27E
Ambre, C. d' Madagascar **41** 11.57S 49.17E
Amga U.S.S.R. **29** 60.51N131.59E
Amga *r.* U.S.S.R. **29** 62.40N135.20E
Amgun *r.* U.S.S.R. **29** 53.10N139.47E
Amiens France **20** 49.54N 2.18E
Amman Jordan **30** 31.57N 35.56E
Ammassalik Greenland **51** 65.40N 38.00W
Amraoti India **31** 20.58N 77.50E
Amritsar India **31** 31.35N 74.56E
Amsterdam Neth. **20** 52.21N 4.54E
Amsterdam I. Indian Oc. **7** 37.00S 79.00E
Amu Darya *r.* U.S.S.R. **28** 43.50N 59.00E
Amundsen G. Canada **50** 70.30N122.00W
Amur *r.* U.S.S.R. **29** 53.17N140.00E
Anabar *r.* U.S.S.R. **29** 72.40N113.30E
Anadyr U.S.S.R. **29** 64.40N177.32E
Anadyr *r.* U.S.S.R. **29** 65.00N176.00E
Anadyr, G. of U.S.S.R. **29** 64.30N177.50W
Anaiza Saudi Arabia **30** 26.05N 43.57E
Anatolia *f.* Turkey **30** 38.00N 35.00E
Anchorage U.S.A. **50** 61.10N150.00W
Ancona Italy **22** 43.38N 13.30E
Andalsnes Norway **24** 62.33N 7.43E
Andaman Is. India **31** 12.00N 93.00E
Andaman Sea Indian Oc. **31** 11.15N 95.30E
Anderson *r.* Canada **50** 69.45N129.00W
Anderson Ind. U.S.A. **54** 40.05N 85.41W
Andes *mts.* S. America **60** 15.00S 72.00W
Andevoranto Madagascar **41** 18.57S 48.56E
Andizhan U.S.S.R. **28** 40.48N 72.23E
Andorra Europe **21** 42.30N 1.32E
Andreba Madagascar **41** 17.40S 48.30E
Andropov U.S.S.R. **25** 58.01N 38.52E
Andros *i.* Greece **23** 37.50N 24.50E
Andros I. Bahamas **57** 24.30N 78.00W
Aneto, Pico de *mtn.* Spain **21** 42.40N 0.19E
Angara *r.* U.S.S.R. **29** 58.00N 93.00E
Angarsk U.S.S.R. **29** 52.31N103.55E
Angel de la Guarda *i.* Mexico **56** 29.10N113.20W
Ångerman *r.* Sweden **24** 62.52N 17.45E
Angers France **21** 47.29N 0.32W
Anglesey *i.* U.K. **19** 53.16N 4.25W
Angola Africa **41** 12.00S 17.00E
Angoulême France **21** 45.40N 0.10E
Anguilla *i.* Leeward Is. **57** 18.14N 63.05W
Ankara Turkey **23** 39.55N 32.50E
Ankober Ethiopia **41** 9.32N 39.43E
Annaba Algeria **38** 36.55N 7.47E
An Nafud *des.* Saudi Arabia **30** 28.40N 41.30E
Annam Highlands *mts.* Asia **33** 17.40N105.50E
Annan *r.* U.K. **19** 54.59N 3.16W
Annapolis U.S.A. **55** 38.59N 76.30W
Annapurna *mtn.* Nepal **31** 28.34N 83.50E
Ann Arbor U.S.A. **54** 42.18N 83.43W
Anqing China **32** 30.40N117.03E
Anshan China **32** 41.06N122.58E
Antalya Turkey **23** 36.53N 30.42E
Antalya, G. of Turkey **23** 36.38N 31.00E
Antananarivo Madagascar **41** 18.55S 47.31E
Antarctica 62
Antarctic Pen. Antarctica **61** 65.00S 64.00W
Anticosti I. Canada **51** 49.20N 63.00W
Antigua Guatemala **56** 14.33N 90.42W
Antigua *i.* Leeward Is. **57** 17.09N 61.49W
Antipodes Is. Pacific Oc. **47** 49.42S178.50E
Antofagasta Chile **61** 23.40S 70.23W
Antrim *d.* U.K. **18** 54.58N 6.20W
Antrim, Mts. of U.K. **19** 55.00N 6.10W
Antsirabe Madagascar **41** 19.51S 47.02E
Antsiranana Madagascar **41** 12.16S 49.17E
Antwerp Belgium **20** 51.13N 4.25E
Anyang China **32** 36.05N114.20E
Anzhero-Sudzhensk U.S.S.R. **28** 56.10N 86.10E
Aomori Japan **35** 40.50N140.43E
Apalachee B. U.S.A. **53** 29.30N 84.00W
Aparri Philippines **33** 18.22N121.40E
Apennines *mts.* Italy **22** 42.00N 13.30E
Apia W. Samoa **47** 13.48S171.45W
Apostle Is. U.S.A. **54** 47.00N 90.30W
Appalachian Mts. U.S.A. **53** 39.30N 78.00W
Appleton U.S.A. **54** 44.17N 88.24W
Apure *r.* Venezuela **60** 7.44N 66.38W
Aqaba Jordan **30** 29.32N 35.00E
Arabia Asia **9** 25.00N 45.00E
Arabian Sea Asia **30** 16.00N 65.00E
Aracaju Brazil **60** 10.54S 37.07W
Arad Romania **22** 46.12N 21.19E
Arafura Sea Austa. **44** 9.00S133.00E
Araguaia *r.* Brazil **60** 5.30S 48.05W
Araguari Brazil **61** 18.38S 48.13W
Arakan Yoma *mts.* Burma **31** 20.00N 94.00E
Aral Sea U.S.S.R. **28** 45.00N 60.00E
Aralsk U.S.S.R. **28** 46.56N 61.43E
Aran Is. Rep. of Ire. **19** 53.07N 9.38W
Ararat Australia **45** 37.20S143.00E
Ararat, Mt. Turkey **30** 39.45N 44.15E
Araxes *r.* U.S.S.R. **28** 40.00N 48.48E
Arctic Ocean 62
Arctic Red *r.* Canada **50** 67.26N133.48W
Ardennes *mts.* Belgium **20** 50.10N 5.30E
Arena, Pt. U.S.A. **52** 38.58N123.44W
Arendal Norway **24** 58.27N 8.56E
Arequipa Peru **60** 16.25S 71.32W
Argentina S. America **61** 35.00S 65.00W
Argos Greece **23** 37.37N 22.45E
Århus Denmark **24** 56.10N 10.13E
Arica Chile **61** 18.30S 70.20W
Arizona *d.* U.S.A. **52** 34.00N112.00W
Arkansas *d.* U.S.A. **53** 35.00N 92.00W
Arkansas *r.* U.S.A. **53** 33.50N 91.00W
Arkhangel'sk U.S.S.R. **28** 64.32N 41.10E
Armagh U.K. **19** 54.21N 6.41W
Armagh *d.* U.K. **18** 54.21N 6.41W
Armavir U.S.S.R. **28** 44.59N 41.10E
Armenia Colombia **60** 4.32N 75.40W
Armenia S.S.R. *d.* U.S.S.R. **28** 40.00N 45.00E
Armidale Australia **45** 30.32S151.40E
Arnaud *r.* Canada **51** 60.00N 69.45W
Arnhem Neth. **20** 52.00N 5.53E
Arnhem, C. Australia **44** 12.10S137.00E
Arnhem Land *f.* Australia **44** 13.00S132.30E
Arran *i.* U.K. **19** 55.35N 5.14W
Arthur's Pass New Zealand **46** 42.50S171.45E
Arua Uganda **40** 3.02N 30.56E
Aruba *i.* Neth. Ant. **57** 12.30N 70.00W
Aru Is. Indonesia **33** 6.00S134.30E

INDEX

Arusha Tanzania 40 3.21S 36.40E
Asahi daki *mtn.* Japan 35 43.42N142.54E
Asahikawa Japan 35 43.46N142.23E
Asansol India 31 23.40N 87.00E
Ascension I. Atlantic Oc. 6 8.00S 14.00W
Ashburton *r.* Australia 44 21.15S115.00E
Ashburton New Zealand 46 43.54S171.46E
Ashikaga Japan 35 36.21N139.26E
Ashizuri saki *c.* Japan 35 32.45N133.05E
Ashkhabad U.S.S.R. 28 37.58N 58.24E
Ashland Wisc. U.S.A. 54 46.34N 90.45W
Ashtabula U.S.A. 54 41.53N 80.47W
Asir *f.* Saudi Arabia 30 19.00N 42.00E
Asmara Ethiopia 41 15.20N 38.58E
Aspiring, Mt. New Zealand 46 44.20S168.45E
Assab Ethiopia 39 13.01N 42.47E
Assiniboine, Mt. Canada 52 50.51N115.39W
Astoria U.S.A. 52 46.12N123.50W
Astrakhan U.S.S.R. 28 46.22N 48.00E
Asunción Paraguay 61 25.15S 57.40W
Aswân Egypt 39 24.05N 32.56E
Aswân High Dam Egypt 39 23.59N 32.54E
Asyût Egypt 39 27.14N 31.07E
Atacama Desert S. America 61 20.00S 69.00W
Atar Mauritania 38 20.32N 13.08W
Atbara Sudan 41 17.42N 34.00E
Atbara *r.* Sudan 41 17.47N 34.00E
Atchafalaya B. U.S.A. 53 29.30N 92.00W
Athabasca *r.* Canada 50 58.30N111.00W
Athabasca, L. Canada 50 59.30N109.00W
Athens Greece 23 37.59N 23.42E
Athens Ohio U.S.A. 54 39.20N 82.06W
Athlone Rep. of Ire. 19 53.26N 7.57W
Áthos, Mt. Greece 23 40.09N 24.19E
Atikokan Canada 54 48.45N 91.38W
Atlanta Ga. U.S.A. 53 33.45N 84.23W
Atlantic City U.S.A. 55 39.23N 74.27W
Atlantic Ocean 8
Atlas Mts. Africa 8 33.00N 4.00W
Atrek *r.* Asia 30 37.23N 54.00E
At Tã'if Saudi Arabia 30 21.15N 40.21E
Auckland New Zealand 46 36.55S174.45E
Auckland Is. Pacific Oc. 47 50.35S166.00E
Augrabies Falls *f.* R.S.A. 41 28.33S 20.27E
Augsburg W. Germany 21 48.21N 10.54E
Augusta Australia 44 34.19S115.09E
Augusta Ga. U.S.A. 53 33.29N 82.00W
Augusta Maine U.S.A. 55 44.17N 69.50W
Aurora Ill. U.S.A. 54 41.45N 88.20W
Au Sable *r.* U.S.A. 54 44.25N 83.20W
Au Sable Pt. U.S.A. 54 44.21N 83.20W
Austin Minn. U.S.A. 54 43.40N 92.58W
Austin Tex. U.S.A. 52 30.18N 97.47W
Australia Austa. 44
Australian Alps *mts.* Australia 45 36.30S148.45E
Australian Antarctic Territory Antarctica 62 73.00S 90.00E
Australian Capital Territory *d.* Australia 45 35.30S149.00E
Austria Europe 21 47.00N 11.30E
Austria Europe 22 47.30N 14.35E
Avarua Cook Is. 47 21.12S159.46W
Avignon France 21 43.56N 4.48E
Avon *d.* U.K. 18 51.25N 2.40W
Avon *r.* Avon U.K. 19 51.30N 2.43W
Avon *r.* Dorset U.K. 19 50.43N 1.45W
Avon *r.* Glos. U.K. 19 52.00N 2.10W
Axel Heiberg I. Canada 51 79.30N 90.00W
Ayaguz U.S.S.R. 28 47.59N 80.27E
Ayan U.S.S.R. 29 56.29N138.00E
Aydin Turkey 23 37.52N 27.50E
Ayer Hitam Malaysia 34 2.56N102.25E
Aylesbury U.K. 18 51.48N 0.49W
Ayr U.K. 19 55.28N 4.37W
Ayr *r.* U.K. 19 55.28N 4.38W
Azbine *mts.* see Aïr *mts.* Niger 38
Azerbaijan S.S.R. *d.* U.S.S.R. 28 40.10N 47.50E
Azores *is.* Atlantic Oc. 6 39.00N 30.00W
Azoum *r.* Chad 40 9.20N 18.00E
Azov, Sea of U.S.S.R. 28 46.00N 36.30E
Azua Dom. Rep. 57 18.29N 70.44W
Azuero Pen. Panama 57 7.30N 80.30W
Azul Argentina 61 36.46S 59.50W

B

Bab el Mandeb *str.* Asia 30 13.00N 43.10E
Baboua C.A.R. 40 5.49N 14.51E
Bacãu Romania 22 46.32N 26.59E
Back *r.* Canada 51 66.37N 96.00W
Badajoz Spain 21 38.53N 6.58W
Baffin *d.* Canada 51 68.00N 80.00W
Baffin B. Canada 51 74.00N 70.00W
Baffin I. Canada 51 68.50N 70.00W
Bagan Serai Malaysia 34 5.01N100.32E
Baghdad Iraq 30 33.20N 44.26E
Baghlan Afghan. 31 36.11N 68.44E
Bahamas C. America 57 23.30N 75.00W
Bahía Blanca Argentina 61 38.45S 62.15W
Bahrain Asia 30 26.00N 50.00E
Bahr Aouk *r.* C.A.R./Chad 40 8.50N 18.50E
Bahr el Ghazal *r.* Sudan 41 9.30N 31.30E

Bahr el Jebel *r.* Sudan 41 9.30N 30.20E
Baikal, L. U.S.S.R. 29 53.30N108.00E
Bairnsdale Australia 45 37.51S147.38E
Baja California Norte *d.* Mexico 56 30.00N115.00W
Baja California Sur *d.* Mexico 56 26.00N112.00W
Baker Oreg. U.S.A. 52 44.46N117.50W
Baker, Mt. U.S.A. 52 48.48N121.10W
Baker I. Pacific Oc. 47 0.14N176.28W
Bakersfield U.S.A. 52 35.25N119.00W
Baku U.S.S.R. 28 40.22N 49.53E
Balakovo U.S.S.R. 28 52.04N 47.46E
Balaton, L. Hungary 22 46.55N 17.50E
Balboa Panama 57 8.37N 79.33W
Balclutha New Zealand 46 46.16S169.46E
Balearic Is. Spain 21 39.30N 3.00E
Balearic Sea Med. Sea 21 40.30N 2.00E
Bali *i.* Indonesia 33 8.30S115.05E
Balikesir Turkey 23 39.38N 27.51E
Balkan Mts. Bulgaria 22 42.50N 24.30E
Balkhash U.S.S.R. 28 46.51N 75.00E
Balkhash, L. U.S.S.R. 28 46.40N 75.00E
Ballarat Australia 45 37.36S143.58E
Ballenas B. Mexico 56 26.40N113.30W
Balranald Australia 45 34.37S143.37E
Balsas *r.* Mexico 56 18.10N102.05W
Baltic Sea Europe 24 57.00N 19.00E
Baltimore U.S.A. 55 39.18N 76.38W
Baluchistan *f.* Pakistan 31 28.00N 66.00E
Bamako Mali 38 12.40N 7.59W
Banda Aceh Indonesia 33 5.35N 95.20E
Bandar India 31 16.13N 81.12E
Bandar Abbas Iran 30 27.10N 56.15E
Bandar Seri Begawan Brunei 33 4.56N114.58E
Bandeira *mtn.* Brazil 61 20.25S 41.45W
Bandirma Turkey 23 40.22N 28.00E
Bandung Indonesia 33 6.57S107.34E
Banff Canada 52 51.10N115.54W
Bangalore India 31 12.58N 77.35E
Bangkok Thailand 33 13.45N100.35E
Bangladesh Asia 31 24.00N 90.00E
Bangor N. Ireland U.K. 19 54.40N 5.41W
Bangor Wales U.K. 19 53.13N 4.09W
Bangor Maine U.S.A. 55 44.49N 68.47W
Bangui C.A.R. 40 4.23N 18.37E
Bangweulu, L. Zambia 41 11.15S 29.50E
Ban Hat Yai Thailand 34 7.00N100.28E
Banja Luka Yugo. 22 44.47N 17.10E
Banjarmasin Indonesia 33 3.22S114.36E
Banjul Gambia 38 13.28N 16.39W
Banks I. N.W.T. Canada 50 73.00N122.00W
Banks Pen. New Zealand 46 43.45S173.10E
Banks Str. Australia 45 40.37S148.07E
Bann *r.* U.K. 19 55.10N 6.46W
Baoji China 32 34.20N107.17E
Baoshan China 32 25.07N 99.08E
Baotou China 32 40.35N109.59E
Baracoa Cuba 57 20.23N 74.31W
Barahona Dom. Rep. 57 18.13N 71.07W
Baranof I. U.S.A. 50 57.05N135.00W
Baranovichi U.S.S.R. 22 53.09N 26.00E
Barbados Lesser Antilles 57 13.20N 59.40W
Barbuda *i.* Leeward Is. 57 17.41N 61.48W
Barcaldine Australia 44 23.31S145.15E
Barcelona Spain 21 41.25N 2.10E
Barcelona Venezuela 60 10.08N 64.43W
Bardera Somali Rep. 39 2.18N 42.18E
Bareilly India 31 28.20N 79.24E
Barents Sea Arctic Oc. 28 73.00N 40.00E
Bari Italy 23 41.08N 16.52E
Barisan Range *mts.* Indonesia 33 3.30S102.30E
Barito *r.* Indonesia 33 3.35S114.35E
Barkly Tableland *f.* Australia 44 19.00S136.40E
Barlee, L. Australia 44 29.30S119.30E
Barlee Range *mts.* Australia 44 23.40S116.00E
Barnaul U.S.S.R. 28 53.21N 83.15E
Barnsley U.K. 18 53.33N 1.29W
Barotseland *f.* Zambia 41 16.00S 23.00E
Barquisimeto Venezuela 60 10.03N 69.18W
Barrancas Venezuela 60 8.55N 62.05W
Barranquilla Colombia 60 11.00N 74.50W
Barren Desert see Dasht-e-Lut Iran 30
Barrie Canada 55 44.22N 79.42W
Barrington Tops Australia 45 32.03S151.55E
Barrow *r.* Rep. of Ire. 19 52.17N 7.00W
Barrow U.S.A. 50 71.16N156.50W
Barrow Creek *town* Australia 44 21.32S133.53E
Barrow I. Australia 44 21.40S115.27E
Barrow-in-Furness U.K. 19 54.08N 3.15W
Barstow U.S.A. 52 34.55N117.01W
Barwon *r.* Australia 45 30.00S148.03E
Basel Switz. 21 47.33N 7.36E
Basildon U.K. 19 51.34N 0.25E
Baskatong L. Canada 55 46.50N 75.46W
Basra Iraq 30 30.33N 47.50E
Bassein Burma 31 16.45N 94.30E
Basse-Terre Guadeloupe 57 16.00N 61.43W
Bass Str. Australia 45 39.45S146.00E
Bastia France 21 42.41N 9.26E
Bata Equat. Guinea 40 1.51N 9.49E
Batabanó, G. of Cuba 57 23.15N 82.30W

Batam, Pulau *i.* Indonesia 34 1.05N104.00E
Batangas Philippines 33 13.46N121.01E
Bath U.K. 19 51.22N 2.22W
Bath Maine U.S.A. 55 43.56N 69.50W
Bathurst Australia 45 33.27S149.35E
Bathurst Canada 51 47.37N 65.40W
Bathurst I. Australia 44 11.45S130.15E
Bathurst I. Canada 51 76.00N100.00W
Bathurst Inlet *town* Canada 50 66.48N108.00W
Baton Rouge U.S.A. 53 30.30N 91.10W
Battambang Kampuchea 33 13.06N103.13E
Battle Creek *town* U.S.A. 54 42.20N 85.10W
Battle Harbour Canada 51 52.16N 55.36W
Batu Gajah Malaysia 34 4.27N101.02E
Batumi U.S.S.R. 28 41.57N 41.56E
Batu Pahat Malaysia 34 1.50N102.57E
Batu Puteh, Gunung *mtn.* Malaysia 34 4.14N101.26E
Bauchi Nigeria 38 10.16N 9.50E
Bauld, C. Canada 51 51.30N 55.45W
Bauru Brazil 61 22.19S 49.07W
Bayamo Cuba 57 20.23N 76.39W
Bayamon Puerto Rico 57 18.24N 66.10W
Bay City Mich. U.S.A. 54 43.35N 83.52W
Baydaratskaya B. U.S.S.R. 28 70.00N 66.00E
Bay Is. Honduras 57 16.10N 86.30W
Bayonne France 21 43.30N 1.28W
Bayreuth W. Germany 20 49.56N 11.35E
Beaufort Sea N. America 50 72.00N141.00W
Beaufort West R.S.A. 41 32.20S 22.34E
Beaumont Tex. U.S.A. 53 30.04N 94.06W
Beaver I. U.S.A. 54 45.40N 85.35W
Béchar Algeria 38 31.35N 2.17W
Bedford U.K. 19 52.08N 0.29W
Bedford U.S.A. 54 38.51N 86.30W
Bedfordshire *d.* U.K. 18 52.04N 0.28W
Bega Australia 45 36.41S149.50E
Beida Libya 39 32.50N 21.50E
Beijing China 32 39.52N116.20E
Beira Mozambique 41 19.49S 35.00E
Beirut Lebanon 23 33.52N 35.30E
Beitbridge Zimbabwe 41 22.10S 30.00E
Bejaïa Algeria 38 36.45N 5.05E
Belau Pacific Oc. 33 7.00N134.25E
Belaya *r.* U.S.S.R. 28 55.40N 52.30E
Belaya Tserkov U.S.S.R. 22 49.49N 30.10E
Belcher Is. Canada 51 56.00N 79.00W
Belém Brazil 60 1.27S 48.29W
Belfast U.K. 19 54.36N 5.57W
Belgaum India 31 15.54N 74.36E
Belgium Europe 20 51.00N 5.00E
Belgorod U.S.S.R. 22 50.38N 36.36E
Belgrade Yugo. 22 44.49N 20.28E
Belize Belize 57 17.29N 88.20W
Belize C. America 57 17.00N 88.30W
Belle Isle Str. Canada 51 50.45N 58.00W
Belleville Canada 55 44.10N 77.22W
Belmopan Belize 57 17.25N 88.46W
Belo Horizonte Brazil 61 19.45S 43.53W
Belomorsk U.S.S.R. 25 64.34N 34.45E
Beltsy U.S.S.R. 22 47.45N 27.59E
Belukha, Mt. U.S.S.R. 28 49.56N 86.40E
Belum *r.* Malaysia 34 4.56N101.00E
Belumut, Gunung *mtn.* Malaysia 34 2.02N103.34E
Benalla Australia 45 36.35S145.58E
Bend U.S.A. 52 44.04N121.20W
Bendery U.S.S.R. 22 46.50N 29.29E
Bendigo Australia 45 36.48S144.21E
Bengal, B. of Indian Oc. 31 17.00N 89.00E
Benghazi Libya 38 32.07N 20.05E
Bengkalis, Pulau *i.* Indonesia 34 1.30N102.20E
Benguela Angola 41 12.34S 13.24E
Beni *r.* Bolivia 60 10.30S 66.00W
Benin Africa 38 9.30N 2.15E
Benin City Nigeria 38 6.19N 5.41E
Ben Nevis *mtn.* U.K. 19 56.48N 5.00W
Benom, Gunung *mtn.* Malaysia 34 3.49N102.05E
Bentong Malaysia 34 3.32N101.55E
Benton Harbor U.S.A. 54 42.07N 86.27W
Benue *r.* Nigeria 38 7.52N 6.45E
Benxi China 32 41.21N123.47E
Beppu Japan 35 33.18N131.30E
Berber Sudan 40 18.01N 33.59E
Berbera Somali Rep. 39 10.28N 45.02E
Berens *r.* Canada 53 52.25N 97.00W
Berezniki U.S.S.R. 28 59.26N 56.49E
Bergamo Italy 21 45.42N 9.40E
Bergen Norway 24 60.23N 5.20E
Bering Sea N. America/Asia 50 65.00N170.00W
Bering Str. U.S.S.R./U.S.A. 50 65.00N170.00W
Berkshire *d.* U.K. 18 51.25N 1.03W
Berlin E. Germany 22 52.32N 13.35E
Berlin N.H. U.S.A. 55 44.27N 71.13W
Bermejo *r.* Tucumán Argentina 61 26.47S 58.30W
Bermuda Atlantic Oc. 6 32.18N 65.00W
Bernam *r.* Malaysia 34 3.51N100.52E
Berne Switz. 21 46.57N 7.26E
Berri Australia 45 34.17S140.36E
Berwick-upon-Tweed U.K. 19 55.46N 2.00W
Besançon France 21 47.14N 6.02E

Besar, Gunung *mtn.* Malaysia 34 2.30N103.09E
Bessarabia *f.* U.S.S.R. 22 46.30N 28.40E
Bethlehem U.S.A. 55 40.36N 75.22W
Betong Thailand 34 5.47N101.06E
Beverley U.K. 18 53.52N 0.26W
Beyla Guinea 38 8.42N 8.39W
Béziers France 21 43.21N 3.13E
Bhagalpur India 31 25.14N 86.59E
Bhopal India 31 23.17N 77.28E
Bhutan Asia 31 28.00N 90.00E
Białystok Poland 22 53.09N 23.10E
Biarritz France 21 43.29N 1.33W
Biddeford U.S.A. 55 43.29N 70.27W
Biel Switz. 21 47.09N 7.16E
Bielefeld W. Germany 20 52.02N 8.32E
Bielsko-Biała Poland 22 49.49N 19.02E
Bighorn *r.* U.S.A. 52 46.05N107.20W
Bighorn Mts. U.S.A. 52 44.30N107.30W
Big Snowy Mtn. U.S.A. 52 46.46N109.31W
Big Spring *town* U.S.A. 52 32.15N101.30W
Bijagos Archipelago *is.* Guinea Bissau 38 11.30N 16.00W
Bikaner India 31 28.01N 73.22E
Bilbao Spain 21 43.15N 2.56W
Billings U.S.A. 52 45.47N108.30W
Biloxi U.S.A. 53 30.30N 88.53W
Bingara Australia 45 29.51S150.38E
Binghamton U.S.A. 55 42.06N 75.55W
Bintan, Pulau *i.* Indonesia 34 1.00N104.30E
Bintang, Gunung *mtn.* Malaysia 34 5.26N100.52E
Birdum Australia 44 15.38S133.12E
Birhan *mtn.* Ethiopia 41 11.00N 37.50E
Birkenhead U.K. 19 53.24N 3.01W
Birmingham U.K. 19 52.30N 1.55W
Birmingham Ala. U.S.A. 53 33.30N 86.55W
Birni N'Konni Niger 38 13.49N 5.19E
Birobidzhan U.S.S.R. 29 48.49N132.54E
Biscay, B. of France 21 45.30N 4.00W
Biskotasi L. Canada 54 47.15N 82.15W
Biskra Algeria 38 34.48N 5.40E
Bismarck U.S.A. 52 46.50N100.48W
Bismarck Sea Pacific Oc. 44 4.00S147.30E
Bissau Guinea Bissau 38 11.52N 15.39W
Bitola Yugo. 23 41.02N 21.21E
Bitterfontein R.S.A. 41 31.02S 18.14E
Bitterroot Range *mts.* U.S.A. 52 46.00N113.50W
Biwa ko *l.* Japan 35 35.20N136.10E
Biysk U.S.S.R. 28 52.35N 85.16E
Bizerta Tunisia 38 37.17N 9.51E
Black *r.* Ark. U.S.A. 53 35.30N 91.20W
Black *r.* Wisc. U.S.A. 54 43.55N 91.20W
Blackburn U.K. 19 53.44N 2.30W
Black Forest *f.* W. Germany 21 48.00N 7.45E
Blackpool U.K. 19 53.48N 3.03W
Black River *town* Jamaica 57 18.02N 77.52W
Black Rock Desert U.S.A. 52 41.10N118.45W
Black Sea Europe 30 43.00N 35.00E
Black Sea Europe 30 43.00N 36.00E
Black Volta *r.* Ghana 38 8.14N 2.11W
Blackwater *r.* Waterford Rep. of Ire. 19 51.58N 7.52W
Blackwater *r.* U.K. 19 54.31N 6.36W
Blagoveshchensk U.S.S.R. 29 50.19N127.30E
Blanc, Cap *c.* Mauritania 38 20.44N 17.05W
Blanc, Mont *mtn.* Europe 21 45.50N 6.52E
Blanca, Bahía *b.* Argentina 61 39.15S 61.00W
Blanche, L. Australia 45 29.15S139.40E
Blanco, C. Costa Rica 57 9.36N 85.06W
Blanco, C. U.S.A. 52 42.50N124.29W
Blantyre Malaŵi 41 15.46S 35.05E
Blenheim New Zealand 46 41.32S173.58E
Blida Algeria 38 36.30N 2.50E
Blind River *town* Canada 54 46.12N 82.59W
Bloemfontein R.S.A. 41 29.00S 26.14E
Bloomington Ill. U.S.A. 54 40.29N 89.00W
Bloomington Ind. U.S.A. 54 39.10N 86.31W
Bloomsburg U.S.A. 55 41.01N 76.27W
Bluefield U.S.A. 53 37.14N 81.17W
Bluefields Nicaragua 57 12.00N 83.49W
Blue Mts. U.S.A. 52 45.00N118.00W
Blue Nile *r.* Sudan 41 15.45N 32.25E
Bluff New Zealand 46 46.38S168.21E
Bo Sierra Leone 38 7.58N 11.45W
Boa Vista Brazil 60 2.51N 60.43W
Bobo-Dioulasso Burkina Faso 38 11.11N 4.18W
Bobruysk U.S.S.R. 22 53.08N 29.10E
Bodö Norway 24 67.18N 14.26E
Bogong, Mt. Australia 45 36.45S147.21E
Bogor Indonesia 33 6.34S106.45E
Bogotá Colombia 60 4.38N 74.05W
Bohemian Forest *mts.* Czech. 22 49.20N 13.10E
Boise U.S.A. 52 43.38N116.12W
Boké Guinea 38 10.57N 14.13W
Bolivia S. America 60 17.00S 65.00W
Bologna Italy 21 44.30N 11.20E
Bologoye U.S.S.R. 25 57.58N 34.00E
Bolshevik *i.* U.S.S.R. 29 78.30N102.00E
Bolshoi Lyakhovskiy *i.* U.S.S.R. 29 73.30N142.00E
Bolton U.K. 19 53.35N 2.26W
Bolzano Italy 21 46.30N 11.20E
Bombay India 31 18.56N 72.51E
Bomu *r.* C.A.R. 41 4.05N 22.27E

on, C. Tunisia 38 37.05N 11.02E
onaire i. Neth. Antilles 57 12.15N 68.27W
onifacio, Str. of Med. Sea 21 41.18N 9.10E
onin Is. Pacific Oc. 47 27.00N142.00E
onn W. Germany 20 50.44N 7.06E
oothia, G. of Canada 51 70.00N 90.00W
orah Peak mtn. U.S.A. 52 44.09N113.47W
ordeaux France 21 44.55N 0.34W
orden I. Canada 50 78.30N111.00W
orders d. U.K. 18 55.30N 3.00W
ordertown Australia 45 36.18S140.49E
orisov U.S.S.R. 22 54.09N 28.30E
orlänge Sweden 24 60.29N 15.25E
orneo i. Asia 33 1.00N114.00E
ornholm i. Denmark 24 55.02N 15.00E
oso Hanto pen. Japan 35 35.08N140.00E
osporus str. Turkey 23 41.07N 29.04E
oston U.S.A. 55 42.20N 71.05W
otany B. Australia 45 34.04S151.08E
othnia, G. of Europe 24 63.30N 20.30E
otswana Africa 41 22.00S 24.00E
ouaké Ivory Coast 38 7.42N 5.00W
oulder Australia 44 30.55S121.32E
oulder U.S.A. 52 40.02N105.16W
oundary Peak mtn. U.S.A. 52 37.51N118.23W
ounty Is. Pacific Oc. 47 46.00S180.00
ourke Australia 45 30.09S145.59E
ournemouth U.K. 19 50.43N 1.53W
owen Australia 44 20.00S148.15E
oyne r. Rep. of Ire. 18 53.43N 6.17W
oyoma Falls f. Zaïre 41 0.18N 25.30E
radford U.K. 19 53.47N 1.45W
rahmaputra r. Asia 31 23.50N 89.45E
räila Romania 22 45.18N 27.58E
ranco r. Brazil 60 1.30S 62.00W
randon Canada 52 49.50N 99.57W
rantford Canada 54 43.09N 80.17W
rasília Brazil 60 15.54S 47.50W
ragov Romania 22 45.40N 25.35E
ratislava Czech. 22 48.10N 17.10E
ratsk U.S.S.R. 29 56.20N101.15E
ratsk Resr. U.S.S.R. 29 54.40N103.00E
raunschweig W. Germany 20 52.15N 10.30E
razil S. America 60 10.00S 52.00W
razilian Highlands Brazil 60 14.00S 45.00W
razos r. U.S.A. 52 28.55N 95.20W
razzaville Congo 40 4.14S 15.10E
ream B. New Zealand 46 36.00S174.30E
reidhafjördhur est. Iceland 24 65.15N 23.00W
remen W. Germany 20 53.05N 8.48E
remerhaven W. Germany 20 53.33N 8.35E
rescia Italy 21 45.33N 10.12E
rest France 21 48.23N 4.30W
rest U.S.S.R. 22 52.08N 23.40E
rett, C. New Zealand 46 35.15S174.20E
rewarrina Australia 45 29.57S147.54E
ridgeport Conn. U.S.A. 55 41.12N 73.12W
ridgetown Barbados 57 13.06N 59.37W
righton U.K. 19 50.50N 0.09W
rindisi Italy 23 40.38N 17.57E
risbane Australia 45 27.30S153.00E
ristol U.K. 19 51.26N 2.35W
ristol B. U.S.A. 50 58.00N158.50W
ristol Channel U.K. 19 51.20N 3.30W
ritish Antarctic Territory Antarctica 62 70.00S 50.00W
ritish Columbia d. Canada 50 55.00N125.00W
ritish Isles Europe 8 54.00N 5.00W
rittany f. France 21 48.00N 3.00W
rno Czech. 22 49.11N 16.39E
roadback r. Canada 53 51.15N 78.55W
rockton U.S.A. 55 42.06N 71.01W
rockville Canada 54 44.35N 75.44W
rod Hrvatska Yugo. 22 45.09N 18.02E
roken Hill town Australia 45 31.57S141.30E
rooks Range mts. U.S.A. 50 68.50N152.00W
roome Australia 44 17.58S122.15E
ruay-en-Artois France 20 50.49N 2.33E
runei Asia 33 5.00N114.00E
runy I. Australia 45 43.15S147.16E
russels Belgium 20 50.50N 4.21E
ryansk U.S.S.R. 22 53.15N 34.09E
ucaramanga Colombia 60 7.08N 73.10W
ucharest Romania 22 44.25N 26.06E
uckinghamshire d. U.K. 18 51.50N 0.50W
udapest Hungary 22 47.30N 19.03E
uenaventura Colombia 60 3.54N 77.02W
uenos Aires Argentina 61 34.40S 58.30W
uffalo N.Y. U.S.A. 55 42.52N 78.55W
ug r. U.S.S.R. 22 46.55N 31.59E
uggs Island l. U.S.A. 53 36.35N 78.20W
ugulma U.S.S.R. 28 54.32N 52.46E
ujumbura Burundi 40 3.22S 29.21E
ukavu Zaïre 40 2.30S 28.49E
ukhara U.S.S.R. 28 39.47N 64.26E
Bukit Mertajam town Malaysia 34 5.21N100.27E
ulawayo Zimbabwe 41 20.10S 28.43E
ulgaria Europe 23 42.30N 25.00E
uller r. New Zealand 46 41.45S171.35E

Bulloo r. Australia 45 28.43S142.27E
Bulun U.S.S.R. 29 70.50N127.20E
Bunbury Australia 44 33.20S115.34E
Bundaberg Australia 44 24.50S152.21E
Bungo suido str. Japan 35 32.52N132.30E
Burgas Bulgaria 23 42.30N 27.29E
Burgos Spain 21 42.21N 3.41W
Burica, Punta c. Panama 57 8.05N 82.50W
Burkina Faso Africa 38 12.15N 1.30W
Burlington Vt. U.S.A. 55 44.28N 73.14W
Burma Asia 33 22.00N 95.00E
Burnie Australia 45 41.03S145.55E
Burra Australia 45 33.40S138.57E
Burrinjuck Resr. Australia 45 35.00S148.40E
Bursa Turkey 23 40.11N 29.04E
Buru i. Indonesia 33 3.30S126.30E
Burundi Africa 40 3.00S 30.00E
Büshehr Iran 30 28.57N 50.52E
Busselton Australia 44 33.43S115.15E
Buta Zaïre 41 2.49N 24.50E
Butte Mont. U.S.A. 52 46.00N112.31W
Butterworth Malaysia 34 5.25N100.23E
Butt of Lewis c. U.K. 19 58.31N 6.15W
Butuan Philippines 33 8.56N125.31E
Butung i. Indonesia 33 5.00S122.50E
Bydgoszcz Poland 22 53.16N 17.33E
Bylot I. Canada 51 73.00N 78.30W
Byrock Australia 45 30.40S146.25E
Byrranga Mts. U.S.S.R. 29 74.50N101.00E
Bytom Poland 22 50.22N 18.54E

C

Cabimas Venezuela 60 10.26N 71.27W
Cabonga Resr. Canada 55 47.35N 76.40W
Cabot Str. Canada 51 47.00N 59.00W
Cadillac U.S.A. 54 44.15N 85.23W
Cádiz Spain 21 36.32N 6.18W
Cádiz, G. of Spain 21 37.00N 7.10W
Caen France 20 49.11N 0.22W
Caernarfon U.K. 18 53.08N 4.17W
Cagliari Italy 21 39.14N 9.07E
Caguas Puerto Rico 57 18.08N 66.00W
Caibarien Cuba 57 22.31N 79.28W
Caicos Is. Turks & Caicos Is. 57 21.30N 72.00W
Cairns Australia 44 16.51S145.43E
Cairo Egypt 39 30.03N 31.15E
Cairo Ill. U.S.A. 53 37.02N 89.02W
Cajamarca Peru 60 7.09S 78.32W
Calabar Nigeria 38 4.56N 8.22E
Calais France 20 50.57N 1.52E
Calcutta India 31 22.35N 88.21E
Caledon r. R.S.A. 41 30.27S 26.12E
Calgary Canada 52 51.05N114.05W
Cali Colombia 60 3.24N 76.30W
Caliente U.S.A. 52 37.36N114.31W
California d. U.S.A. 52 37.00N120.00W
California, G. of Mexico 56 28.30N112.30W
Callabonna r. Australia 45 29.37S140.08E
Callabonna, L. Australia 45 29.47S140.07E
Callao Peru 60 12.05S 77.08W
Calvinia R.S.A. 41 31.29S 19.44E
Camagüey Cuba 57 21.25N 77.55W
Cambay, G. of India 31 20.30N 72.00E
Cambrian Mts. U.K. 19 52.30N 3.35W
Cambridge New Zealand 46 37.53S175.29E
Cambridge U.K. 19 52.13N 0.08E
Cambridge Mass. U.S.A. 55 42.22N 71.06W
Cambridge Ohio U.S.A. 54 40.02N 81.36W
Cambridge Bay town Canada 50 69.09N105.00W
Cambridgeshire d. U.K. 18 52.30N 0.05E
Camden Australia 45 34.04S150.40E
Camden N.J. U.S.A. 55 39.52N 75.07W
Cameron Highlands mts. Malaysia 34 4.24N101.26E
Cameron Mts. New Zealand 46 45.50S167.00E
Cameroon Africa 40 5.30N 12.15E
Cameroon, Mt. Cameroon 40 4.20N 9.05E
Campbell, C. New Zealand 46 41.45S174.15E
Campbellton Canada 55 48.00N 66.41W
Campbelltown Australia 45 34.04S150.49E
Campbeltown U.K. 19 55.25N 5.36W
Campeche Mexico 56 19.50N 90.30W
Campeche d. Mexico 56 19.00N 90.00W
Campeche B. Mexico 56 19.30N 94.00W
Campina Grande Brazil 60 7.15S 35.53W
Campinas Brazil 61 22.54S 47.06W
Campo Grande Brazil 60 20.24S 54.35W
Campos Brazil 61 21.46S 41.21W
Camrose Canada 50 53.01N112.48W
Canada N. America 50 60.00N105.00W
Canadian r. U.S.A. 53 35.20N 95.40W
Canary Is. Atlantic Oc. 38 29.00N 15.00W
Canaveral, C. U.S.A. 53 28.28N 80.28W
Canberra Australia 45 35.18S149.08E
Canea Greece 23 35.30N 24.02E
Cannes France 21 43.33N 7.00E
Cañoas Brazil 61 29.55S 51.10W
Cantabrian Mts. Spain 21 42.55N 5.10W
Canterbury U.K. 19 51.17N 1.05E
Canterbury Bight New Zealand 46 44.15S172.00E
Can Tho Vietnam 33 10.03N105.46E

Canton Ohio U.S.A. 54 40.48N 81.23W
Cape Barren I. Australia 45 40.22S148.15E
Cape Breton I. Canada 51 46.00N 61.00W
Cape Province d. R.S.A. 41 32.00S 23.00E
Cape Town R.S.A. 41 33.55S 18.27E
Cape Verde Is. Atlantic Oc. 6 17.00N 25.00W
Cape York Pen. Australia 44 12.40S142.20E
Cap-Haïtien town Haiti 57 19.47N 72.17W
Capri i. Italy 23 40.33N 14.13E
Caprivi Strip f. Namibia 41 17.50S 23.00E
Caracas Venezuela 60 10.35N 66.56W
Caratasca Lagoon Honduras 57 15.10N 84.00W
Carbondale Penn. U.S.A. 55 41.35N 75.31W
Carcassonne France 21 43.13N 2.21E
Cardiff U.K. 19 51.28N 3.11W
Cardigan B. U.K. 19 52.30N 4.20W
Caribbean Sea C. America 57 15.00N 75.00W
Caribou Mts. Canada 50 58.30N115.00W
Carlisle U.K. 19 54.54N 2.55W
Carlow Rep. of Ire. 18 52.50N 6.50W
Carlow d. Rep. of Ire. 18 52.43N 6.50W
Carmarthen U.K. 18 51.52N 4.20W
Carmen Mexico 56 18.38N 91.50W
Carmen I. Baja Calif.Sur Mexico 56 25.55N111.10W
Carmen I. Campeche Mexico 56 18.35N 91.40W
Carnegie, L. Australia 44 26.15S123.00E
Carnot C.A.R. 40 4.59N 15.56E
Carnsore Pt. Rep. of Ire. 19 52.10N 6.21W
Carolina Puerto Rico 57 18.23N 65.57W
Caroline Is. Pacific Oc. 47 5.00N150.00E
Carpathian Mts. Europe 22 48.45N 23.45E
Carpentaria, G. of Australia 44 14.00S140.00E
Carrauntoohil mtn. Rep. of Ire. 19 52.00N 9.45W
Carrick-on-Shannon Rep. of Ire. 18 53.57N 8.06W
Carson City U.S.A. 52 39.10N119.46W
Cartagena Colombia 60 10.24N 75.33W
Cartagena Spain 21 37.36N 0.59W
Cartago Costa Rica 57 9.50N 83.52W
Carterton New Zealand 46 41.01S175.31E
Caruaru Brazil 60 8.15S 35.55W
Casablanca Morocco 38 33.39N 7.35W
Cascade Pt. New Zealand 46 44.01S168.22E
Cascade Range mts. U.S.A. 52 44.00N122.00W
Casino Australia 45 28.50S153.02E
Casper U.S.A. 52 42.50N106.20W
Caspian Depression f. U.S.S.R. 28 47.00N 48.00E
Caspian Sea U.S.S.R. 28 42.00N 51.00E
Castaños Mexico 56 26.48N101.26W
Castellón Spain 21 39.59N 0.03W
Castlebar Rep. of Ire. 18 53.52N 9.19W
Castlemaine Australia 45 37.05S144.19E
Castries St. Lucia 57 14.01N 60.59W
Catamarca Argentina 61 28.28S 65.46W
Catania Italy 23 37.31N 15.05E
Cat I. Bahamas 57 24.30N 75.30W
Catoche, C. Mexico 57 21.38N 87.08W
Catskill Mts. U.S.A. 55 42.15N 74.15W
Cauca r. Colombia 60 8.57N 74.30W
Caucasus Mts. U.S.S.R. 28 43.00N 44.00E
Cavan Rep. of Ire. 18 54.00N 7.22W
Cavan d. Rep. of Ire. 18 54.00N 7.10W
Caxias do Sul Brazil 61 29.14S 51.10W
Cayenne Guiana 60 4.55N 52.18W
Cayman Brac i. Cayman Is. 57 19.44N 79.48W
Cayman Is. C. America 57 19.00N 81.00W
Cayuga L. U.S.A. 55 42.40N 76.40W
Cebu Philippines 33 10.17N123.56E
Cebu i. Philippines 33 10.15N123.45E
Cedar r. U.S.A. 54 41.10N 91.25W
Cedar Falls town U.S.A. 54 42.34N 92.26W
Cedar Rapids town U.S.A. 54 41.59N 91.39W
Cedros I. Mexico 56 28.15N115.15W
Ceduna Australia 44 32.07S133.42E
Celaya Mexico 56 20.32N100.48W
Celebes i. Indonesia 33 2.00S120.30E
Celebes Sea Indonesia 33 4.00N122.00E
Central d. U.K. 18 56.10N 4.00W
Central, Cordillera mts. Colombia 60 6.00N 75.00W
Central African Republic Africa 40 6.30N 20.00E
Centralia Ill. U.S.A. 54 38.32N 89.08W
Central Plain f. Rep. of Ire. 20 53.30N 8.00W
Central Russian Uplands U.S.S.R. 22 53.00N 37.00E
Central Siberian Plateau f. U.S.S.R. 29 66.00N108.00E
Central Sierras mts. Spain 21 40.55N 4.05W
Ceram i. Indonesia 33 3.10S129.30E
Cerro de Pasco Peru 60 10.43S 76.15W
Cessnock Australia 45 32.51S151.21E
Ceuta Spain 38 35.53N 5.19W
Cevennes mts. France 21 44.25N 4.05E
Chad Africa 38 13.00N 19.00E
Chad, L. Africa 38 13.30N 14.00E
Chamah, Gunung mtn. Malaysia 34 5.13N101.33E
Champaign U.S.A. 54 40.07N 88.14W
Champlain, L. U.S.A. 55 44.45N 73.20W
Chandeleur Is. U.S.A. 53 29.50N 88.50W
Changchun China 32 43.51N125.15E
Changde China 32 29.00N111.35E
Chang Jiang r. China 32 32.15N119.50E
Changsha China 32 28.09N112.59E
Channel Is. U.K. 20 49.28N 2.13W

Channel-Port-aux-Basques town Canada 51 47.35N 59.10W
Chapala, Lago de l. Mexico 56 20.00N103.00W
Chapayevsk U.S.S.R. 28 52.58N 49.44E
Chapleau Canada 54 47.50N 83.24W
Chardzhou U.S.S.R. 28 39.00N 63.34E
Chari r. Chad 38 13.00N 14.30E
Charleroi Belgium 20 50.25N 4.27E
Charleston S.C. U.S.A. 53 32.48N 79.58W
Charleston W.Va. U.S.A. 53 38.23N 81.20W
Charleville Australia 44 26.25S146.13E
Charlotte N.C. U.S.A. 53 35.05N 80.50W
Charlottetown Canada 51 46.14N 63.09W
Chartres France 21 48.27N 1.30E
Chatham Ont. Canada 54 42.24N 82.11W
Chatham Is. Pacific Oc. 47 43.00S176.00W
Chattahoochee r. U.S.A. 53 30.52N 84.57W
Chattanooga U.S.A. 53 35.01N 85.18W
Cheboksary U.S.S.R. 28 56.08N 47.12E
Cheboygan U.S.A. 54 45.40N 84.28W
Chelmsford U.K. 18 51.44N 0.28E
Chelyabinsk U.S.S.R. 28 55.10N 61.25E
Chelyuskin, C. U.S.S.R. 29 77.20N106.00E
Chen, Mt. U.S.S.R. 29 65.30N141.20E
Chenderoh, Tasik l. Malaysia 34 5.00N100.58E
Chengdu China 32 30.41N104.05E
Cherbourg France 20 49.38N 1.37W
Cheremkhovo U.S.S.R. 29 53.08N103.01E
Cherepovets U.S.S.R. 25 59.05N 37.55E
Cherkassy U.S.S.R. 22 49.27N 32.04E
Chernigov U.S.S.R. 22 51.30N 31.18E
Chernovtsy U.S.S.R. 22 48.19N 25.52E
Cherskogo Range mts. U.S.S.R. 29 65.50N143.00E
Chesapeake B. U.S.A. 53 38.00N 76.00W
Cheshire d. U.K. 18 53.14N 2.30W
Chester U.K. 18 53.12N 2.53W
Chester Penn. U.S.A. 55 39.50N 75.23W
Chetumal Mexico 57 18.30N 88.17W
Chetumal B. Mexico 57 18.30N 88.00W
Cheviot Hills U.K. 19 55.22N 2.24W
Cheyenne U.S.A. 52 41.08N104.50W
Chiang Mai Thailand 32 18.48N 98.59E
Chiapas d. Mexico 56 16.30N 93.00W
Chiba Japan 35 35.38N140.07E
Chibougamau Canada 53 49.56N 74.24W
Chicago U.S.A. 54 41.50N 87.45W
Chichagof I. U.S.A. 50 57.55N135.45W
Chichester U.K. 18 50.50N 0.47W
Chiclayo Peru 60 6.47S 79.47W
Chico U.S.A. 52 39.46N121.50W
Chicoutimi-Jonquière Canada 55 48.26N 71.06W
Chidley, C. Canada 51 60.30N 65.00W
Chihli, G. of China 32 38.40N119.00E
Chihuahua Mexico 56 28.40N106.06W
Chihuahua d. Mexico 56 28.40N104.58W
Chile S. America 61 33.00S 71.00W
Chillán Chile 61 36.37S 72.10W
Chillicothe Ohio U.S.A. 54 38.20N 83.00W
Chiloé I. Chile 61 43.00S 73.00W
Chilpancingo Mexico 56 17.33N 99.30W
Chimborazo mtn. Ecuador 60 1.10S 78.50W
Chimbote Peru 60 8.58S 78.34W
Chimkent U.S.S.R. 28 42.16N 69.25E
China Asia 32 35.00N 98.00E
Chinandega Nicaragua 57 12.35N 87.10W
Chinati Peak U.S.A. 52 30.05N104.30W
Chindwin r. Burma 31 21.30N 95.12E
Chinhoyi Zimbabwe 41 17.00S 30.10E
Chipata Zambia 41 13.37S 32.40E
Chippewa r. U.S.A. 54 44.23N 92.05W
Chippewa Falls town U.S.A. 54 44.56N 91.25W
Chirchik U.S.S.R. 28 41.28N 69.31E
Chiriqui mtn. Panama 57 8.49N 82.38W
Chirripo mtn. Costa Rica 57 9.31N 83.30W
Chistopol U.S.S.R. 28 55.11N 50.32E
Chita U.S.S.R. 29 52.03N113.35E
Chitral Pakistan 31 35.52N 71.58E
Chittagong Bangla. 31 22.20N 91.48E
Chokai san mtn. Japan 35 39.08N140.04E
Choke Mts. Ethiopia 40 11.00N 37.30E
Choluteca Honduras 57 13.16N 87.11W
Chongjin N. Korea 32 41.55N129.50E
Chongqing China 32 29.31N106.35E
Chott Djerid f. Tunisia 38 33.30N 8.30E
Chott ech Chergui f. Algeria 38 34.00N 0.30E
Chott Melrhir f. Algeria 38 34.15N 7.00E
Christchurch New Zealand 46 43.33S172.40E
Christmas I. Indian Oc. 33 10.00S106.00E
Christmas I. Pacific Oc. 47 2.00N157.00W
Chuckchee Pen. U.S.S.R. 29 66.00N174.30W
Chugoku sanchi mts. Japan 35 35.30N133.00E
Chuiquimula Guatemala 57 14.52N 89.50W
Chukai Malaysia 34 4.16N103.24E
Chuna r. U.S.S.R. 29 58.00N 94.00E
Churchill Canada 51 58.45N 94.00W
Churchill r. Man. Canada 51 58.20N 94.15W
Churchill r. Nfld. Canada 51 53.20N 60.00W
Churchill, C. Canada 51 58.50N 93.00W
Churchill L. Canada 50 56.00N108.00W
Churchill Peak mtn. Canada 50 58.10N125.00W

INDEX

Ciego de Avila Cuba 57 21.51N 78.47W
Ciénaga Colombia 60 11.11N 74.15W
Cienfuegos Cuba 57 22.10N 80.27W
Cimarron r. U.S.A. 53 36.15N 96.55W
Cincinnati U.S.A. 54 39.10N 84.30W
Ciudad Bolívar Venezuela 60 8.06N 63.36W
Ciudad Camargo Mexico 56 27.41N105.10W
Ciudad Guayana Venezuela 60 8.22N 62.40W
Ciudad Ixtepec Mexico 56 16.32N 95.10W
Ciudad Juárez Mexico 56 31.42N106.29W
Ciudad Madero Mexico 56 22.19N 97.50W
Ciudad Obregon Mexico 56 27.28N109.55W
Ciudad Victoria Mexico 56 23.43N 99.10W
Clare d. Rep. of Ire. 18 52.52N 9.00W
Clare U.S.A. 54 43.49N 84.47W
Claremont U.S.A. 55 43.23N 72.21W
Clarence r. New Zealand 46 42.10S173.55E
Clarksburg U.S.A. 54 39.16N 80.22W
Clayton N.Mex. U.S.A. 52 36.27N103.12W
Clearwater L. Canada 51 56.10N 74.30W
Clermont Ferrand France 21 45.47N 3.05E
Cleveland d. U.K. 18 54.37N 1.08W
Cleveland Ohio U.S.A. 54 41.30N 81.41W
Clinton Iowa U.S.A. 54 41.51N 90.12W
Clonmel Rep. of Ire. 19 52.21N 7.44W
Cloquet U.S.A. 54 46.40N 92.30W
Cloud Peak mtn. U.S.A. 54 44.23N107.11W
Clutha r. New Zealand 46 46.18S169.05E
Cluj Romania 22 46.47N 23.37E
Clwyd d. U.K. 18 53.07N 3.20W
Clyde r. U.K. 19 55.58N 4.31W
Coahuila d. Mexico 56 27.00N103.00W
Coast Mts. Canada 50 55.30N128.00W
Coast Range mts. U.S.A. 52 40.00N123.00W
Coats I. Canada 51 62.30N 83.00W
Coatzacoalcos Mexico 56 18.10N 94.25W
Cobalt Canada 55 47.24N 79.41W
Cobán Guatemala 56 15.28N 90.20W
Cobar Australia 45 31.32S145.51E
Cobija Bolivia 60 11.01S 68.45W
Cochabamba Bolivia 60 17.26S 66.10W
Cochin India 31 9.56N 76.15E
Cochrane Ont. Canada 54 49.04N 81.02W
Cockburn Australia 45 32.05S141.00E
Coco r. Honduras 57 14.58N 83.15W
Cocos Is. Indian Oc. 7 13.00S 96.00E
Cod, C. U.S.A. 55 42.08N 70.10W
Coff's Harbour Australia 45 30.19S153.05E
Coimbatore India 31 11.00N 76.57E
Coimbra Portugal 21 40.12N 8.25W
Colac Australia 45 38.22S143.38E
Colima Mexico 56 19.14N103.41W
Colima d. Mexico 56 19.05N104.00W
Coll i. U.K. 19 56.38N 6.34W
Colnett, C. Mexico 56 31.00N116.20W
Cologne W. Germany 20 50.56N 6.57E
Colombia S. America 60 5.00N 75.00W
Colombo Sri Lanka 31 6.55N 79.52E
Colon Panama 57 9.21N 79.54W
Colorado r. Argentina 61 39.50S 62.02W
Colorado r. Ariz. N. America 52 32.00N114.58W
Colorado d. U.S.A. 52 39.00N106.00W
Colorado r. Tex. U.S.A. 53 28.30N 96.00W
Colorado Plateau f. U.S.A. 52 35.45N112.00W
Colorado Springs town U.S.A. 52 38.50N104.40W
Columbia r. U.S.A. 52 46.10N123.30W
Columbia S.C. U.S.A. 53 34.00N 81.00W
Columbus Ga. U.S.A. 53 32.28N 84.59W
Columbus Ohio U.S.A. 54 39.59N 83.03W
Colville r. U.S.A. 50 70.06N151.30W
Colwyn Bay town U.K. 19 53.18N 3.43W
Comayagua Honduras 57 14.30N 87.39W
Commonwealth Territory d. Australia 45 35.00S151.00E
Como Italy 21 45.48N 9.04E
Como, L. Italy 21 46.05N 9.17E
Comodoro Rivadavia Argentina 61 45.50S 67.30W
Conakry Guinea 38 9.30N 13.43W
Concepción Chile 61 36.50S 73.03W
Concepción Paraguay 61 23.22S 57.26W
Conception, Pt. U.S.A. 52 34.27N120.26W
Conchos r. Mexico 56 29.34N104.30W
Concord N.H. U.S.A. 55 43.13N 71.34W
Concordia Argentina 61 31.25S 58.00W
Condobolin Australia 45 33.03S147.11E
Congo Africa 40 1.00S 16.00E
Connecticut d. U.S.A. 55 41.30N 72.50W
Connecticut r. U.S.A. 55 41.20N 72.19W
Constance, L. Europe 21 47.40N 9.30E
Constanţa Romania 22 44.10N 28.31E
Constantine Algeria 38 36.22N 6.38E
Cook, Mt. New Zealand 46 43.45S170.12E
Cook Is. Pacific Oc. 47 20.00S157.00W
Cook Str. New Zealand 46 41.15S174.30E
Cooktown Australia 44 15.29S145.15E
Coolah Australia 45 31.48S149.45E
Coolgardie Australia 44 31.01S121.12E
Cooma Australia 45 36.15S149.07E
Coonamble Australia 45 30.55S148.26E
Cooper Creek r. Australia 45 28.36S138.00E
Cootamundra Australia 45 34.41S148.03E

Copenhagen Denmark 24 55.43N 12.34E
Copiapó Chile 61 27.20S 70.23W
Coppermine r. Canada 50 67.54N115.10W
Coppermine town Canada 50 67.49N115.12W
Coquimbo Chile 61 30.00S 71.25W
Coral Sea Pacific Oc. 44 13.00S148.00E
Corangamite, L. Australia 45 38.10S143.25E
Córdoba Argentina 61 31.25S 64.11W
Cordoba Mexico 56 18.55N 96.55W
Córdoba Spain 21 37.53N 4.46W
Corfu i. Greece 23 39.35N 19.50E
Corinth Greece 23 37.56N 22.55E
Corinto Nicaragua 57 12.29N 87.14W
Cork Rep. of Ire. 19 51.54N 8.28W
Cork d. Rep. of Ire. 18 52.00N 8.40W
Corning N.Y. U.S.A. 55 42.10N 77.04W
Cornwall Canada 55 45.02N 74.45W
Cornwall d. U.K. 18 50.26N 5.00W
Cornwallis I. Canada 51 75.00N 95.00W
Coromandel Pen. New Zealand 46 36.45S175.30E
Coronation G. Canada 50 68.00N112.00W
Corpus Christi U.S.A. 53 27.47N 97.26W
Corrib, Lough Rep. of Ire. 19 53.26N 9.14W
Corrientes Argentina 61 27.30S 58.48W
Corse, Cap c. France 21 43.00N 9.21E
Corsica i. France 21 42.00N 9.10E
Corte France 21 42.18N 9.08E
Cortland N.Y. U.S.A. 55 42.36N 76.10W
Corumbá Brazil 61 19.00S 57.25W
Cosenza Italy 23 39.17N 16.14E
Coshocton U.S.A. 54 40.16N 81.53W
Costa Rica C. America 57 10.00N 84.00W
Cotonou Benin 38 6.24N 2.31E
Cotopaxi mtn. Ecuador 60 0.40S 78.30W
Cotswold Hills U.K. 19 51.50N 2.00W
Cottbus E. Germany 22 51.43N 14.21E
Coulonge r. Canada 55 45.55N 76.52W
Coventry U.K. 19 52.25N 1.31W
Covilhã Portugal 21 40.17N 7.30W
Covington Ohio U.S.A. 54 39.06N 84.21W
Cowal, L. Australia 45 33.36S147.22E
Cowan, L. Australia 44 32.00S122.00E
Cowra Australia 45 33.50S148.45E
Cozumel I. Mexico 57 20.30N 87.00W
Cracow Poland 22 50.03N 19.55E
Craiova Romania 22 44.18N 23.46E
Cranbrook Canada 52 49.29N115.48W
Crawley U.K. 19 51.07N 0.10W
Cree L. Canada 50 57.20N108.30W
Crete i. Greece 23 35.15N 25.00E
Crewe U.K. 19 53.06N 2.28W
Crimea pen U.S.S.R. 22 45.30N 34.00E
Cristóbal Colón mtn. Colombia 60 10.53N 73.48W
Cromwell New Zealand 46 45.03S169.14E
Crooked I. Bahamas 57 22.45N 74.00W
Crowsnest Pass Canada 52 49.40N114.41W
Crozet Is. Indian Oc. 7 46.27S 52.00E
Cruz, Cabo c. Cuba 57 19.52N 77.44W
Cuando r. Angola 41 18.30S 23.32E
Cuango r. Angola/Zaïre 40 3.20S 17.23E
Cuanza r. Angola 41 9.20S 13.09E
Cuba C. America 57 22.00N 79.00W
Cubango r. Angola/Botswana 41 18.30S 22.04E
Cúcuta Colombia 60 7.55N 72.31W
Cuenca Ecuador 60 2.54S 79.00W
Cuenca Spain 21 40.04N 2.07W
Cuernavaca Mexico 56 18.57N 99.15W
Cuiabá Brazil 60 15.32S 56.05W
Cuiabá r. Brazil 60 17.05S 56.35W
Cuito r. Angola 41 18.01S 20.50E
Culgoa r. Australia 45 29.54S145.31E
Culiacán Mexico 56 24.50N107.23W
Cumaná Venezuela 60 10.29N 64.12W
Cumberland r. U.S.A. 53 37.16N 88.25W
Cumberland Md. U.S.A. 55 39.40N 78.47W
Cumberland, L. U.S.A. 53 37.00N 85.00W
Cumberland Sd. Canada 51 65.00N 65.30W
Cumbria d. U.K. 18 54.40N 3.00W
Cunene r. Angola 41 17.15S 11.50E
Cunnamulla Australia 45 28.04S145.40E
Curaçao i. Neth. Antilles 57 12.15N 69.00W
Curicó Chile 61 35.00S 71.15W
Curitiba Brazil 61 25.24S 49.16W
Cuttack India 31 20.26N 85.56E
Cuzco Peru 60 13.32S 72.10W
Cwmbran U.K. 18 51.39N 3.01W
Cyclades is. Greece 23 37.00N 25.00E
Cyprus Asia 23 35.00N 33.00E
Cyrenaica f. Libya 39 31.00N 22.10E
Czechoslovakia Europe 22 49.10N 16.00E
Czestochowa Poland 22 50.49N 19.07E

D

Dardanelles str. Turkey 23 40.15N 26.30E
Da Hinggan Ling mts. China 32 50.00N122.10E
Dahlak Is. Ethiopia 40 15.45N 40.00E
Dakar Senegal 38 14.38N 17.27W
Dakhla W. Sahara 38 23.43N 15.57W
Dal r. Sweden 24 60.38N 17.05E
Dalby Australia 45 27.11S151.12E

Dallas Tex. U.S.A. 53 32.47N 96.48W
Dalmatia f. Yugo. 22 43.30N 17.00E
Daloa Ivory Coast 38 6.56N 6.28W
Damaraland f. Namibia 41 22.00S 17.00E
Damascus Syria 30 33.30N 36.19E
Dammam Saudi Arabia 30 26.23N 50.08E
Dampier Australia 44 20.45S116.50E
Danakil f. Ethiopia 41 13.00N 41.00E
Da Nang Vietnam 33 16.04N108.14E
Danbury Conn. U.S.A. 55 41.24N 73.26W
Dandenong Australia 45 37.59S145.14E
Danli Honduras 57 14.02N 86.30W
Danube r. Europe 22 45.26N 29.38E
Danville Ill. U.S.A. 54 40.09N 87.37W
Dar es Salaam Tanzania 40 6.51S 39.18E
Darfield New Zealand 46 43.29S172.07E
Darfur mts. Sudan 41 12.30N 24.00E
Dargaville New Zealand 46 35.57S173.53E
Darjeeling India 31 27.02N 88.20E
Darling r. Australia 45 34.05S141.57E
Darling Downs f. Australia 45 28.00S149.45E
Darlington U.K. 19 54.33N 1.33W
Darmstadt W. Germany 20 49.52N 8.30E
Dartmoor hills U.K. 19 50.33N 3.55W
Darwin Australia 44 12.23S130.44E
Dasht-e-Kavir des. Iran 30 34.40N 55.00E
Dasht-e-Lut des. Iran 30 31.30N 58.00E
Daugavpils U.S.S.R. 24 55.52N 26.31E
Dauphin Canada 52 51.09N100.05W
Davao Philippines 33 7.05N125.50E
Davenport U.S.A. 54 41.32N 90.36W
David Panama 57 8.26N 82.26W
Davis Str. N. America 51 66.00N 58.00W
Dawson Canada 50 64.04N139.24W
Dawson Creek town Canada 50 55.44N120.15W
Dayton Ohio U.S.A. 54 39.45N 84.10W
Daytona Beach town U.S.A. 53 29.11N 81.01W
De Aar R.S.A. 41 30.39S 24.01E
Dead Sea Jordan 30 31.25N 35.30E
Death Valley f. U.S.A. 52 36.00N116.45W
Debrecen Hungary 22 47.30N 21.37E
Decatur Ill. U.S.A. 54 39.51N 88.57W
Decatur Ind. U.S.A. 54 40.50N 84.57W
Deccan f. India 31 18.30N 77.30E
Děčín Czech. 22 50.48N 14.15E
Dee r. D. and G. U.K. 19 54.50N 4.05W
Dee r. Grampian U.K. 19 57.07N 2.04W
Dee r. Wales U.K. 19 53.13N 3.05W
Defiance U.S.A. 54 41.17N 84.21W
Dehra Dun India 31 30.19N 78.00E
Delaware d. U.S.A. 55 39.00N 75.30W
Delaware r. U.S.A. 55 39.15N 75.20W
Delaware B. U.S.A. 55 39.00N 75.05W
Delhi India 31 28.40N 77.14E
Delicias Mexico 56 28.10N105.30W
De Long Str. U.S.S.R. 29 70.00N178.00E
Demavend mtn. Iran 30 35.47N 52.04E
Den Helder Neth. 20 52.58N 4.46E
Deniliquin Australia 45 35.33S144.58E
Denizli Turkey 23 37.46N 29.05E
Denmark Australia 44 34.54S117.25E
Denmark Europe 24 56.00N 10.00E
Denver U.S.A. 52 39.45N104.58W
Derby W.A. Australia 44 17.19S123.38E
Derby U.K. 19 52.55N 1.28W
Derbyshire d. U.K. 18 52.55N 1.28W
Derg, Lough Tipperary Rep. of Ire. 19 52.57N 8.18W
Derna Libya 39 32.45N 22.39E
Derwent r. Australia 45 42.45S147.15E
Derwent r. N. Yorks. U.K. 19 53.45N 0.57W
Deseado Argentina 61 47.44S 65.56W
Des Moines Iowa U.S.A. 53 41.35N 93.35W
Desna r. U.S.S.R. 22 50.32N 30.37E
Dessye Ethiopia 41 11.05N 39.40E
Detroit U.S.A. 54 42.23N 83.05W
Devils Lake town U.S.A. 52 48.08N 98.50W
Devon d. U.K. 18 50.50N 3.40W
Devon I. Canada 51 75.00N 86.00W
Devonport Australia 45 41.09S146.16E
Dhaka Bangla. 31 23.42N 90.22E
Dieppe France 20 49.55N 1.05E
Digby Canada 53 44.37N 65.47W
Dijon France 21 47.20N 5.02E
Dikwa Nigeria 40 12.01N 13.55E
Dili Indonesia 33 8.35S125.35E
Dilolo Zaïre 41 10.39S 22.20E
Dingle B. Rep. of Ire. 19 52.05N 10.12W
Diourbel Senegal 38 14.30N 16.10W
Dipolog Philippines 33 8.34N123.28E
Diredawa Ethiopia 39 9.35N 41.50E
Disappointment, L. Australia 44 23.30S122.55E
Disaster B. Australia 45 37.20S149.58E
Disko i. Greenland 51 69.45N 53.00W
District of Columbia d. U.S.A. 55 38.55N 77.00W
Distrito Federal d. Mexico 56 19.20N 99.10W
Diu India 31 20.41N 70.59E
Dixon Entrance str. Canada/U.S.A. 50 54.10N133.30W
Djado Plateau f. Niger 38 22.00N 12.30E

Djelfa Algeria 38 34.43N 3.14E
Djibouti Africa 41 12.00N 42.50E
Djibouti town Djibouti 41 11.35N 43.11E
Dneprodzerzhinsk U.S.S.R. 22 48.30N 34.37E
Dnepropetrovsk U.S.S.R. 22 48.29N 35.00E
Dnestr r. U.S.S.R. 22 46.21N 30.20E
Dnieper r. U.S.S.R. 22 46.30N 32.25E
Dno U.S.S.R. 25 57.30N 30.00E
Dobruja f. Romania 22 44.30N 28.15E
Dodecanese is. Greece 23 37.00N 27.00E
Dodge City U.S.A. 52 37.45N100.02W
Dodoma Tanzania 40 6.10S 35.40E
Dog L. Canada 54 48.45N 89.30W
Doha Qatar 30 25.15N 51.34E
Dolomites mts. Italy 22 46.25N 11.50E
Dolomites mts. Italy 21 46.25N 11.50E
Dolores Argentina 61 36.23S 57.44W
Dolphin and Union Str. Canada 50 69.20N118.00W
Dominica Windward Is. 57 15.30N 61.30W
Dominican Republic C. America 57 18.00N 70.00W
Don r. England U.K. 19 53.41N 0.50W
Don r. U.S.S.R. 28 47.06N 39.16E
Doncaster U.K. 19 53.31N 1.09W
Donegal Rep. of Ire. 19 54.39N 8.06W
Donegal d. Rep. of Ire. 18 54.52N 8.00W
Donegal B. Rep. of Ire. 19 54.32N 8.18W
Donetsk U.S.S.R. 28 48.00N 37.50E
Donggala Indonesia 33 0.48S119.45E
Dongola Sudan 41 19.10N 30.27E
Dorchester U.K. 18 50.48N 2.25W
Dordogne r. France 21 44.59N 0.34W
Dore, Mont mtn. France 21 45.32N 2.49E
Dorset d. U.K. 18 50.48N 2.25W
Dortmund W. Germany 20 51.32N 7.27E
Douai France 20 50.22N 3.05E
Douala Cameroon 40 4.05N 9.43E
Doubs r. France 21 46.54N 5.02E
Doubtless B. New Zealand 46 35.10S173.30E
Douglas U.K. 19 54.09N 4.29W
Douro r. Portugal 21 41.10N 8.40W
Dover U.K. 19 51.07N 1.19E
Dover Del. U.S.A. 55 39.10N 75.32W
Dover, Str. of France/U.K. 20 51.00N 1.30E
Dovrefjell mts. Norway 24 62.05N 9.30E
Dovsk U.S.S.R. 22 53.07N 30.29E
Down d. U.K. 18 54.20N 6.00W
Dra, Wadi Morocco 38 28.40N 11.06W
Dragoman Pass Bulgaria/Yugo. 22 42.56N 22.52E
Drakensberg mts. R.S.A./Lesotho 41 30.00S 29.00E
Drammen Norway 24 49.45N 10.15E
Drava r. Yugo. 22 45.34N 18.56E
Dresden E. Germany 22 51.00N 13.45E
Dubai U.A.E. 30 25.13N 55.17E
Dubawnt r. Canada 51 62.50N102.00W
Dubawnt L. Canada 51 62.50N102.00W
Dubbo Australia 45 32.16S148.41E
Dublin Rep. of Ire. 19 53.21N 6.18W
Dublin d. Rep. of Ire. 18 53.20N 6.18W
Du Bois Penn. U.S.A. 55 41.06N 78.46W
Dubrovnik Yugo. 22 42.40N 18.07E
Dubuque U.S.A. 54 42.31N 90.41W
Dudinka U.S.S.R. 29 69.27N 86.13E
Dudley U.K. 19 52.30N 2.05W
Duero r. see Douro r. Spain 21
Duisburg W. Germany 20 51.26N 6.45E
Duluth U.S.A. 54 46.45N 92.10W
Dumfries U.K. 19 55.04N 3.37W
Dumfries and Galloway d. U.K. 18 55.10N 4.00W
Dundalk Rep. of Ire. 19 54.01N 6.25W
Dundalk B. Rep. of Ire. 19 53.55N 6.17W
Dundee U.K. 19 56.28N 3.00W
Dunedin New Zealand 46 45.52S170.30E
Dungun Malaysia 34 4.47N103.24E
Dungun r. Malaysia 34 4.47N103.26E
Dunkirk France 20 51.02N 2.23E
Dunkirk U.S.A. 55 42.29N 79.21W
Dun Laoghaire Rep. of Ire. 19 53.17N 6.09W
Dunstan Mts. New Zealand 46 44.45S169.45E
Durango Mexico 56 24.01N104.00W
Durango d. Mexico 56 24.01N104.00W
Durban R.S.A. 41 29.50S 30.59E
Durham U.K. 19 54.47N 1.34W
Durham d. U.K. 18 54.42N 1.45W
Durrës Albania 23 41.19N 19.27E
D'Urville I. New Zealand 46 40.45S173.50E
Dushanbe U.S.S.R. 28 38.38N 68.51E
Dusseldorf W. Germany 20 51.13N 6.47E
Dvina r. U.S.S.R. 24 57.03N 24.00E
Dyer, C. Canada 51 67.45N 61.45W
Dyfed d. U.K. 18 52.00N 4.17W
Dzerzhinsk R.S.F.S.R. U.S.S.R. 22 56.15N 43.30E
Dzhambul U.S.S.R. 28 42.50N 71.25E
Dzhankoi U.S.S.R. 22 45.40N 34.30E
Dzhugdzhur Range mts. U.S.S.R. 29 57.30N138.00E

E

Eabamet L. Canada 53 51.20N 87.30W
East C. New Zealand 46 37.45S178.30E
East China Sea Asia 32 29.00N125.00E
Easter I. Pacific Oc. 47 27.05S109.20W

INDEX

astern Ghats mts. India 31 16.30N 80.30E
astern Sayan mts. U.S.S.R. 29 53.30N 98.00E
ast European Plain f. Europe 25 56.00N 32.00E
ast London R.S.A. 41 33.00S 27.54E
astmain r. Canada 51 52.10N 78.30W
ast St. Louis U.S.A. 54 38.34N 90.04W
ast Siberian Sea U.S.S.R. 29 73.00N160.00E
ast Sussex d. U.K. 18 50.56N 0.12E
au Claire U.S.A. 54 44.50N 91.30W
bro r. Spain 21 40.40N 0.50E
chuca Australia 45 36.10S144.20E
cuador S. America 60 2.00S 78.00W
d Damer Sudan 41 17.37N 33.59E
den r. U.K. 19 54.57N 3.02W
dinburgh U.K. 19 55.57N 3.13W
dirne Turkey 23 41.40N 26.35E
dmonton Canada 50 53.34N113.25W
dmundston Canada 55 47.22N 68.20W
dward, L. Uganda/Zaïre 41 0.30S 29.30E
dwards Plateau f. U.S.A. 52 30.30N100.30W
ffingham U.S.A. 54 39.07N 88.33W
gmont, Mt. New Zealand 46 39.20S174.05E
gridir Turkey 23 37.52N 30.51E
gypt Africa 39 26.30N 29.30E
ighty Mile Beach f. Australia 44 19.00S121.00E
ildon Resr. Australia 45 37.10S146.00E
indhoven Neth. 20 51.26N 5.30E
El Aaiún W. Sahara 38 27.10N 13.11W
El Agheila Libya 38 30.15N 19.12E
El Alamein Egypt 39 30.50N 28.57E
El Aenam Algeria 38 36.20N 1.30E
Elba i. Italy 21 42.47N 10.17E
Elbe r. W. Germany 20 53.33N 10.00E
Elbert, Mt. U.S.A. 52 39.05N106.27W
Elbrus mtn. U.S.S.R. 28 43.21N 42.29E
Elburz Mts. Iran 30 36.00N 52.30E
Eldoret Kenya 41 0.31N 35.17E
Elephant Butte Resr. U.S.A. 52 33.25N107.10W
Elephant I. Atlantic Oc. 61 61.00S 55.00W
Eleuthera I. Bahamas 57 25.00N 76.00W
El Faiyûm Egypt 39 29.19N 30.50E
El Fasher Sudan 41 13.37N 25.22E
El Ferrol Spain 21 43.29N 8.14W
Elgin Ill. U.S.A. 54 42.03N 88.19W
El Gîza Egypt 39 30.01N 31.12E
El Goléa Algeria 38 30.35N 2.51E
Elgon, Mt. Uganda/Kenya 41 1.07N 34.35E
Elizabeth N.J. U.S.A. 55 40.40N 74.13W
El Jauf Libya 39 24.09N 23.19E
El Khârga Egypt 39 25.27N 30.32E
Elkins W.Va. U.S.A. 54 38.56N 79.53W
Elko U.S.A. 52 40.50N115.46W
Ellen, Mt. U.S.A. 52 38.06N110.50W
Ellesmere I. Canada 51 78.00N 82.00W
Ellsworth Land f. Antarctica 62 75.00S100.00W
El Muglad Sudan 41 11.01N 27.50E
El Obeid Sudan 41 13.11N 30.10E
El Paso U.S.A. 52 31.45N106.30W
El Qatrun Libya 38 24.55N 14.38E
El Salvador C. America 57 13.30N 89.00W
El Tigre Venezuela 60 8.44N 64.18W
Elvas Portugal 21 38.53N 7.10W
Ely Minn. U.S.A. 54 47.53N 91.52W
Emba r. U.S.S.R. 28 46.40N 53.30E
Emerson Canada 53 49.00N 97.00W
Emi Koussi mtn. Chad 38 19.58N 18.30E
Emory Peak mtn. U.S.A. 52 29.15N103.19W
Encarnación Paraguay 61 27.20S 55.50W
Endicott Mts. U.S.A. 50 68.00N152.00W
Engels U.S.S.R. 28 51.25N 46.07E
England d. U.K. 19 53.00N 2.00W
English Channel France/U.K. 20 50.15N 1.00E
En Nahud Sudan 41 12.41N 28.28E
Ennis Rep. of Ire. 18 52.51N 9.00W
Enschede Neth. 20 52.13N 6.55E
Ensenada Baja Calif. Norte Mexico 56 31.53N116.35W
Entebbe Uganda 41 0.05N 32.29E
Entre Rios f. Argentina 61 30.00S 58.00W
Enugu Nigeria 38 6.20N 7.29E
Epernay France 21 49.02N 3.58E
Equatorial Guinea Africa 40 1.30N 10.30E
Erciyaş, Mt. Turkey 23 38.33N 35.25E
Erciyaş, Mt. Turkey 23 38.33N 35.25E
Erebus, Mt. Antarctica 62 77.40S167.20E
Erfurt E. Germany 22 50.58N 11.02E
Ereğli Zonguldak Turkey 23 41.17N 31.26E
Erenhot China 32 43.48N112.00E
Erie U.S.A. 54 42.07N 80.06W
Erie, L. Canada/U.S.A 54 42.15N 81.00W
Erigavo Somali Rep. 39 10.40N 47.20E
Erne r. Rep. of Ire. 19 54.30N 8.17W
Er Rahad Sudan 41 12.42N 30.33E
Er Roseires Sudan 41 11.52N 34.23E
Esbjerg Denmark 55 55.28N 8.28E
Escanaba U.S.A. 54 45.47N 87.04W
Escondido r. Nicaragua 57 11.58N 83.45W
Escuintla Guatemala 56 14.18N 90.47W
Eskilstuna Sweden 24 59.22N 16.31E
Eskimo Point town Canada 51 61.10N 94.15W

Eskişehir Turkey 23 39.46N 30.30E
Esperance Australia 44 33.49S121.52E
Espoo Finland 24 60.13N 24.40E
Esquel Argentina 61 42.55S 71.20W
Essen W. Germany 20 51.27N 6.57E
Essequibo r. Guyana 60 6.48N 58.23W
Essex d. U.K. 18 51.46N 0.30E
Estevan Canada 50 49.09N103.00W
Estonia S.S.R. d. U.S.S.R. 24 58.45N 25.30E
Ethiopia Africa 39 10.00N 39.00E
Ethiopian Highlands Ethiopia 41 10.00N 37.00E
Etna, Mt. Italy 23 37.43N 14.59E
Etosha Pan f. Namibia 41 18.50S 16.30E
Euboea i. Greece 23 38.30N 23.50E
Eucla Australia 44 31.40S128.51E
Eufaula Resr. U.S.A. 53 35.15N 95.35W
Eugene U.S.A. 52 44.03N123.07W
Eugenia, Punta c. Mexico 56 27.50N115.05W
Euphrates r. Asia 30 31.00N 47.27E
Eureka Calif. U.S.A. 52 40.49N124.10W
Europe 8
Evans, L. Canada 53 50.55N 77.00W
Evanston Ill. U.S.A. 54 42.02N 87.41W
Everard, C. Australia 45 37.50S149.16E
Everest, Mt. Asia 31 27.59N 86.56E
Exe r. U.K. 19 50.40N 3.28W
Exeter U.K. 19 50.43N 3.31W
Exmoor hills U.K. 19 51.08N 3.45W
Exuma Is. Bahamas 57 24.00N 76.00W
Eyasi, L. Tanzania 40 3.40S 35.00E
Eyre, L. Australia 44 28.30S137.25E

F
Fairbanks U.S.A. 50 64.50N147.50W
Fair Isle U.K. 19 59.32N 1.38W
Fairmont W.Va. U.S.A. 54 39.28N 80.08W
Fairweather, Mt. U.S.A. 50 59.00N137.30W
Faisalabad Pakistan 31 31.25N 73.09E
Falkirk U.K. 19 56.00N 3.48W
Falkland Is. S. America 61 52.00S 60.00W
Fall River town U.S.A. 55 41.42N 71.08W
Faradofay Madagascar 41 25.00S 47.00E
Farason Is. Saudi Arabia 40 16.48N 41.54E
Farewell, C. Greenland 51 60.00N 44.20W
Farewell, C. New Zealand 46 40.30S172.35E
Fargo U.S.A. 53 46.52N 96.59W
Faro Portugal 21 37.01N 7.56W
Faroe Is. Europe 20 62.00N 7.00W
Fårösund Sweden 24 57.51N 19.05E
Faxaflói b. Iceland 24 64.30N 22.50W
Fdérik Mauritania 38 22.30N 12.30W
Fear, C. U.S.A. 53 33.51N 77.59W
Feilding New Zealand 46 40.10S175.25E
Feira Brazil 60 12.17S 38.53W
Fergana U.S.S.R. 28 40.23N 71.19E
Fermanagh d. U.K. 18 54.21N 7.40W
Ferrara Italy 21 44.49N 11.38E
Fethiye Turkey 23 36.37N 29.06E
Fez Morocco 38 34.05N 5.00W
Fianarantsoa Madagascar 41 21.26S 47.05E
Fife d. U.K. 18 56.20N 3.00W
Fiji Pacific Oc. 47 17.20S179.00E
Findlay U.S.A. 54 41.02N 83.40W
Finisterre, C. Spain 21 42.54N 9.16W
Finland Europe 24 64.30N 27.00E
Finland, G. of Finland/U.S.S.R. 24 60.00N 26.50E
Finlay r. Canada 50 56.30N124.40W
Firth of Clyde est. U.K. 19 55.35N 4.23W
Firth of Forth est. U.K. 19 56.05N 3.00W
Firth of Lorn est. U.K. 19 56.20N 5.40W
Firth of Tay est. U.K. 19 56.24N 3.08W
Fisher Str. Canada 51 63.00N 84.00W
Fishguard U.K. 19 51.59N 4.59W
Fitchburg U.S.A. 55 42.35N 71.50W
Fitzroy Crossing Australia 44 18.13S125.33E
Flagstaff U.S.A. 52 35.12N111.38W
Flaming Gorge Resr. U.S.A. 52 41.10N109.30W
Flathead L. U.S.A. 52 47.50N114.05W
Flattery, C. U.S.A. 52 48.23N124.43W
Flensburg W. Germany 20 54.47N 9.27E
Flinders r. Australia 44 17.30S140.45E
Flinders I. Tas. Australia 45 40.00S148.00E
Flinders Range mts. Australia 45 31.00S138.30E
Flin Flon Canada 50 54.47N101.51W
Flint U.S.A. 54 43.03N 83.40W
Flint r. Ga. U.S.A. 53 30.52N 84.35W
Florence Italy 21 43.46N 11.15E
Flores i. Indonesia 33 8.40S121.20E
Flores Sea Indonesia 33 7.00S121.00E
Florianópolis Brazil 61 27.35S 48.31W
Florida d. U.S.A. 53 29.00N 82.00W
Flushing Neth. 20 51.27N 3.35E
Foggia Italy 23 41.28N 15.33E
Folkestone U.K. 19 51.05N 1.11E
Fond du Lac U.S.A. 54 43.48N 88.27W
Fonseca, G. of Honduras 57 13.10N 87.30W
Fontainebleau France 21 48.24N 2.42E
Forbes Australia 45 33.24S148.03E
Forel, Mt. Greenland 51 67.00N 37.00E
Formentera i. Spain 21 38.41N 1.30E

Formosa see Taiwan Asia 32
Formosa Str. China/Taiwan 32 24.30N119.30E
Forrest Australia 44 30.49S128.03E
Fortaleza Brazil 60 3.45S 38.45W
Fort-de-France Martinique 57 14.36N 61.05W
Fort Frances Canada 54 48.37N 93.23W
Fort George Canada 51 53.50N 79.01W
Forth r. U.K. 19 56.06N 3.48W
Fort Lauderdale U.S.A. 53 26.08N 80.08W
Fort Liard Canada 50 60.14N123.28W
Fort Madison U.S.A. 54 40.38N 91.21W
Fort Peck Resr. U.S.A. 52 47.55N107.00W
Fort Polignac Algeria 38 26.40N 8.25E
Fort Portal Uganda 40 0.40N 30.17E
Fort Randall U.S.A. 50 55.10N162.47W
Fort Rupert Que. Canada 51 51.30N 79.45W
Fort Shevchenko U.S.S.R. 28 44.31N 50.15E
Fort Simpson Canada 50 61.46N121.15W
Fort Smith Canada 50 60.00N111.51W
Fort Smith d. Canada 50 63.00N115.00W
Fort Smith U.S.A. 53 35.22N 94.27W
Fort Wayne U.S.A. 54 41.05N 85.08W
Fort William U.K. 19 56.49N 5.07W
Fort Worth U.S.A. 53 32.45N 97.20W
Fort Yukon U.S.A. 50 66.35N145.20W
Fostoria U.S.A. 54 41.10N 83.25W
Foulwind, C. New Zealand 46 41.45S171.30E
Foveaux Str. New Zealand 46 46.40S168.00E
Foxe Basin b. Canada 51 67.30N 79.00W
Foxe Channel Canada 51 65.00N 80.00W
Foxton New Zealand 46 40.27S175.18E
Foyle r. U.K. 19 55.00N 7.20W
Foyle, Lough U.K. 19 55.00N 7.20W
France Europe 21 47.30N 2.30E
Francistown Botswana 41 21.12S 27.29E
Frankfort Ky. U.S.A. 53 38.11N 84.53W
Frankfurt W. Germany 20 50.06N 8.41E
Franklin Ind. U.S.A. 54 39.29N 86.02W
Franklin D. Roosevelt L. U.S.A. 52 47.55N118.20W
Franz Josef Land is. U.S.S.R. 28 81.00N 54.00E
Fraser r. B.C. Canada 50 49.00N123.00W
Fraser, Bukit hill Malaysia 34 3.42N101.40E
Frederick Md. U.S.A. 55 39.25N 77.25W
Fredericton Canada 55 45.57N 66.40W
Frederikshåb Greenland 51 62.05N 49.30W
Frederikshavn Denmark 24 57.28N 10.33E
Frederikstad Norway 24 59.15N 10.55E
Freeport Bahamas 57 26.40N 78.30W
Freetown Sierra Leone 38 8.30N 13.17W
Freiburg W. Germany 21 48.00N 7.52E
Fremantle Australia 44 32.07S115.44E
Frenchman's Cap mtn. Australia 45 42.27S145.54E
Fresno U.S.A. 52 36.41N119.57W
Frio, Cabo c. Brazil 61 22.50S 42.10W
Frisian Is. Neth. 20 53.30N 6.00E
Frobisher B. Canada 51 63.00N 66.45W
Frobisher Bay town Canada 51 63.45N 68.30W
Frohavet est. Norway 24 63.55N 9.05E
Frome, L. Australia 45 30.45S139.45E
Frunze U.S.S.R. 28 42.53N 74.46E
Fuerte r. Mexico 56 25.42N109.20W
Fuerteventura i. Canary Is. 38 28.20N 14.10W
Fujiyama mtn. Japan 35 35.23N138.42E
Fukui Japan 35 36.04N136.12E
Fukuoka Japan 35 33.39N130.21E
Fukushima Japan 35 37.44N140.28E
Fundy, B. of U.S.A. 55 45.00N 66.30W
Funen i. Denmark 24 55.15N 10.30E
Furnas Dam Brazil 61 20.40S 46.22W
Furneaux Group is. Australia 45 40.15S148.15E
Fushun China 32 41.50N123.55E
Futa Jalon f. Guinea 38 11.30N 12.30W
Fuzhou China 32 26.09N119.21E
Fyne, Loch U.K. 19 55.55N 5.23W

G
Gabes, G. of Tunisia 38 34.00N 11.00E
Gabon Africa 40 1.00S 12.00E
Gaborone Botswana 41 24.25S 25.55E
Gagnon Canada 51 51.56N 68.16W
Gairdner, L. Australia 44 31.30S136.00E
Galapagos Is. Ecuador 47 1.00S 91.00W
Galaţi Romania 22 45.27N 27.59E
Galena Alas. U.S.A. 50 64.45N157.00W
Galesburg U.S.A. 54 40.58N 90.22W
Gallinas, C. Colombia 60 12.27N 71.44W
Gallipoli Turkey 23 40.25N 26.31E
Gällivare Sweden 24 67.10N 20.40E
Galveston U.S.A. 53 29.17N 94.48W
Galveston B. U.S.A. 53 29.40N 94.40W
Galway Rep. of Ire. 19 53.17N 9.04W
Galway d. Rep. of Ire. 18 53.25N 9.00W
Galway B. Rep. of Ire. 19 53.12N 9.07W
Gambia Africa 38 13.30N 15.00W
Gambia r. Gambia 38 13.28N 15.55W
Gander Canada 51 48.58N 54.34W
Ganges r. India 31 23.30N 90.25E
Gannett Peak mtn. U.S.A. 52 43.10N109.38W
Ganzhou China 32 25.49N114.50E
Gao Mali 38 16.19N 0.09W

Gaoxiong Taiwan 32 22.40N120.18E
Garda, L. Italy 21 45.40N 10.40E
Garissa Kenya 41 0.27S 39.39E
Garonne r. France 21 45.00N 0.37W
Garoua Cameroon 40 9.17N 13.22E
Garrison Resr. U.S.A. 52 47.30N102.20W
Garry L. Canada 51 66.00N100.00W
Garvie Mts. New Zealand 46 45.15S169.00E
Gary U.S.A. 54 41.34N 87.20W
Garyarsa China 31 31.30N 80.40E
Gascoyne r. Australia 44 25.00S113.40E
Gaspé Canada 51 48.50N 64.30W
Gaspé Pen. Canada 55 48.30N 66.45W
Gatun L. Panama 57 9.20N 80.00W
Gauhati India 31 26.05N 91.55E
Gävle Sweden 24 60.41N 17.10E
Gawler Australia 45 34.38S138.44E
Geelong Australia 45 38.10S144.26E
Gemas Malaysia 34 2.34N102.37E
Geneina Sudan 41 13.27N 22.30E
Geneva Switz. 21 46.13N 6.09E
Geneva, L. Switz. 21 46.30N 6.30E
Genoa Italy 21 44.24N 8.54E
Genoa, G. of Italy 21 44.12N 8.55E
Gent Belgium 20 51.02N 3.42E
George r. Canada 51 58.30N 66.00W
George, L. N.S.W. Australia 45 35.07S149.22E
George, L. N.Y. U.S.A. 55 43.30N 73.30W
George Town Tas. Australia 45 41.04S146.48E
Georgetown Cayman Is. 57 19.20N 81.23W
Georgetown Guyana 60 6.46N 58.10W
George Town Malaysia 34 5.25N100.18E
Georgia d. U.S.A. 53 33.00N 83.00W
Georgia, Str. of Canada 52 49.15N123.45W
Georgian B. Canada 54 45.15N 80.45W
Georgia S.S.R. d. U.S.S.R. 28 42.30N 43.00E
Gera E. Germany 22 50.51N 12.11E
Geraldine New Zealand 46 44.05S171.15E
Geraldton Australia 44 28.49S114.36E
Gerlachovka mtn. Czech. 22 49.10N 20.05E
Gezira f. Sudan 41 14.30N 33.00E
Ghadames Libya 38 30.10N 9.30E
Ghana Africa 38 8.00N 1.00W
Ghanzi Botswana 41 21.42S 21.39E
Ghardaia Algeria 38 32.20N 3.40E
Ghat Libya 38 24.59N 10.11E
Gialo Libya 39 29.00N 21.30E
Gibraltar Europe 21 36.07N 5.22W
Gibraltar, Str. of Europe/Africa 21 36.00N 5.25W
Gibson Desert Australia 44 24.30S124.00E
Gifu Japan 35 35.27N136.50E
Gijón Spain 21 43.32N 5.40W
Gila r. U.S.A. 52 32.45N114.30W
Gilgandra Australia 45 31.42S148.40E
Gilgit Jammu & Kashmir 31 35.54N 74.20E
Gillingham Kent U.K. 19 51.24N 0.33E
Gimbala, Jebel mtn. Sudan 41 13.00N 24.20E
Gironde r. France 21 45.35N 1.00E
Gisborne New Zealand 46 38.41S178.02E
Gizhiga U.S.S.R. 29 62.00N160.34E
Gizhiga G. U.S.S.R. 29 61.00N158.00E
Glacier Peak mtn. U.S.A. 52 48.07N121.06W
Gladstone Qld. Australia 44 23.52S151.16E
Glåma r. Norway 24 59.15N 10.55E
Glasgow U.K. 19 55.52N 4.15W
Glendive U.S.A. 52 47.08N104.42W
Glen Innes Australia 45 29.42S151.45E
Glenrothes U.K. 18 56.12N 3.10W
Glens Falls town U.S.A. 55 43.17N 73.41W
Glittertind mtn. Norway 24 61.30N 8.20E
Gliwice Poland 22 50.17N 18.40E
Gloucester U.K. 19 51.52N 2.15W
Gloucestershire d. U.K. 18 51.50N 2.00W
Gobabis Namibia 41 22.30S 18.58E
Gobi des. Asia 32 45.00N108.00E
Godavari r. India 31 16.40N 82.15E
Goderich Canada 54 43.43N 81.43W
Godthåb Greenland 51 64.10N 51.40W
Goiânia Brazil 60 16.43S 49.18W
Golden B. New Zealand 46 40.45S172.50E
Golfito Costa Rica 57 8.42N 83.10W
Gombe Nigeria 40 10.17N 11.20E
Gomel U.S.S.R. 22 52.25N 31.00E
Gómez Palacio Mexico 56 25.39N103.30W
Gonaïves Haiti 57 19.29N 72.42W
Gonâve, G. of Haiti 57 19.20N 73.00W
Gondar Ethiopia 39 12.39N 37.29E
Gongga Shan mtn. China 32 29.30N101.30E
Good Hope, C. of R.S.A. 41 34.21S 18.28E
Goondiwindi Australia 45 28.30S150.17E
Goose L. U.S.A. 52 41.55N120.25W
Gorakhpur India 31 26.45N 83.23E
Gorki U.S.S.R. 28 56.20N 44.00E
Gorlovka U.S.S.R. 28 48.17N 38.05E
Gosford Australia 45 33.25S151.18E
Göta Canal Sweden 24 57.50N 11.50E
Göteborg Sweden 24 57.45N 12.00E
Gotland i. Sweden 24 57.30N 18.30E
Gottingen W. Germany 20 51.32N 9.57E

INDEX

Gough I. Atlantic Oc. 6 41.00S 10.00W
Gouin Resr. Canada 55 48.40N 74.45W
Goulburn Australia 45 34.47S149.43E
Governador Valadares Brazil 61 18.51S 42.00W
Gozo i. Malta 23 36.03N 14.16E
Graaff-Reinet R.S.A. 41 32.20S 24.31E
Gracias á Dios, Cabo c. Honduras/Nicaragua 57 15.00N 83.10W
Grafton Australia 45 29.40S152.56E
Grahamstown R.S.A. 41 33.18S 26.30E
Grampian d. U.K. 18 57.10N 3.00W
Grampian Highlands U.K. 19 56.55N 4.00W
Granada Nicaragua 57 11.58N 85.59W
Granada Spain 21 37.10N 3.35W
Granby Canada 55 45.23N 72.44W
Gran Canaria i. Canary Is. 38 28.00N 15.30W
Gran Chaco f. S. America 61 23.30S 60.00W
Grand r. Canada 54 42.53N 79.35W
Grand Bahama I. Bahamas 57 26.35N 78.00W
Grand Canyon f. U.S.A. 52 36.15N113.00W
Grand Cayman i. Cayman Is. 57 19.20N 81.30W
Grande, Bahía b. Argentina 61 50.45S 68.00W
Grande Prairie town Canada 50 55.10N118.52W
Grand Falls town N.B. Canada 55 47.02N 67.46W
Grand Falls town Nfld. Canada 51 48.57N 55.40W
Grand Forks U.S.A. 53 47.57N 97.05W
Grand Junction U.S.A. 52 39.04N108.33W
Grand Manan I. Canada 55 44.45N 66.45W
Grand Marais U.S.A. 54 47.45N 90.20W
Grand Rapids town Mich. U.S.A. 54 42.57N 85.40W
Grand Rapids town Minn. U.S.A. 54 47.13N 93.31W
Grand Teton mtn. U.S.A. 52 43.45N110.50W
Granite Peak mtn. U.S.A. 52 45.10N109.50W
Grants Pass town U.S.A. 52 42.26N123.20W
Grayling U.S.A. 54 44.40N 84.43W
Grays U.K. 19 51.29N 0.20E
Graz Austria 22 47.05N 15.27E
Great Abaco I. Bahamas 57 26.30N 77.00W
Great Artesian Basin f. Australia 44 26.30S143.02E
Great Australian Bight Australia 44 33.20S130.00E
Great Barrier I. New Zealand 46 36.15S175.30E
Great Barrier Reef f. Australia 44 16.30S146.30E
Great Basin f. U.S.A. 52 39.00N115.30W
Great Bear L. Canada 50 66.00N120.00W
Great Dividing Range mts. Australia 45 33.00S151.00E
Greater Antilles is. C. America 57 17.00N 70.00W
Greater London d. U.K. 18 51.31N 0.06W
Greater Manchester d. U.K. 18 53.30N 2.18W
Great Exuma i. Bahamas 57 23.00N 76.00W
Great Falls town U.S.A. 52 47.30N111.16W
Great Inagua I. Bahamas 57 21.00N 73.20W
Great Karoo f. R.S.A. 41 32.40S 23.00E
Great L. Australia 45 41.50S146.43E
Great Lakes N. America 8 47.00N 83.00W
Great Nama Land f. Namibia 41 25.30S 17.30E
Great Ouse r. U.K. 19 52.47N 0.23E
Great Rift Valley Africa 9 7.00S 33.00E
Great Salt L. U.S.A. 52 41.10N112.40W
Great Sandy Desert Australia 44 22.00S125.00E
Great Slave L. Canada 50 61.30N114.20W
Great Victoria Desert Australia 44 29.00S127.30E
Great Whale r. Canada 51 55.28N 77.45W
Great Yarmouth U.K. 19 52.40N 1.45E
Greece Europe 23 39.00N 22.00E
Greeley U.S.A. 52 40.26N104.43W
Green r. U.S.A. 52 38.20N109.53W
Green B. U.S.A. 54 45.00N 87.30W
Green Bay town U.S.A. 54 44.32N 88.00W
Greenland N. America 51 68.00N 45.00W
Green Mts. U.S.A. 55 43.30N 73.00W
Greenock U.K. 19 55.57N 4.45W
Greensboro N.C. U.S.A. 53 36.03N 79.50W
Greenville Maine U.S.A. 55 45.28N 69.36W
Greenville S.C. U.S.A. 53 34.52N 82.25W
Gregory, L. S.A. Australia 45 28.55S139.00E
Grenada i. Windward Is. 57 12.15N 61.45W
Grenoble France 21 45.11N 5.43E
Grey r. New Zealand 46 42.28S171.13E
Greymouth New Zealand 46 42.28S171.12E
Grey Range mts. Australia 45 28.30S142.15E
Griffith Australia 45 34.18S146.04E
Grim, C. Australia 45 40.45S144.45E
Grimsby U.K. 19 53.35N 0.05W
Grimsvötn mtn. Iceland 24 64.30N 17.10W
Grodno U.S.S.R. 22 53.40N 23.50E
Groningen Neth. 20 53.13N 6.35E
Groote Eylandt i. Australia 44 14.00S136.30E
Grootfontein Namibia 41 19.32S 18.05E
Gross Glockner mtn. Austria 22 47.05N 12.50E
Groundhog r. Canada 54 48.45N 82.00W
Groznyy U.S.S.R. 28 43.21N 45.42E
Guadalajara Mexico 56 20.30N103.20W
Guadalquivir r. Spain 21 36.50N 6.20W
Guadalupe Mexico 56 25.41N100.15W
Guadalupe I. Mexico 52 29.00N118.25W
Guadarrama, Sierra de mts. Spain 21 41.00N 3.50W
Guadeloupe i. Leeward Is. 57 16.20N 61.40W
Guadiana r. Portugal 21 37.10N 7.36W
Guajará Mirim Brazil 60 10.50S 65.21W
Guam Mariana Is. 47 13.30N144.40E

Guanajuato Mexico 56 21.00N101.16W
Guanajuato d. Mexico 56 21.00N101.00W
Guane Cuba 57 22.13N 84.07W
Guangzhou China 32 23.20N113.30E
Guantánamo Cuba 57 20.09N 75.14W
Guaporé r. Brazil 60 12.00S 65.15W
Guardafui, C. Somali Rep. 39 12.00N 51.30E
Guatemala C. America 57 15.40N 90.00W
Guatemala City Guatemala 56 14.38N 90.22W
Guaviare r. Colombia 60 4.30N 77.40W
Guayaquil Ecuador 60 2.13S 79.54W
Guayaquil, G. of Ecuador 60 2.30S 80.00W
Guaymas Mexico 56 27.59N110.54W
Guelph Canada 54 43.34N 80.16W
Guernsey i. U.K. 20 49.27N 2.35W
Guerrero d. Mexico 56 18.00N100.00W
Guiana S. America 60 4.00N 53.00W
Guiana Highlands S. America 60 4.00N 60.00W
Guilin China 32 25.20N110.10E
Guinea Africa 38 10.30N 10.30W
Guinea, G. of Africa 38 2.00N 1.00W
Guinea Bissau Africa 38 12.00N 15.30W
Güines Cuba 57 22.50N 82.02W
Güiria Venezuela 60 10.34N107.12E
Guiyang China 32 26.31N106.39E
Gujranwala Pakistan 31 32.06N 74.11E
Gulu Uganda 41 2.46N 32.21E
Gunnedah Australia 45 30.59S150.15E
Guntersville L. U.S.A. 53 34.35N 86.00W
Guryev U.S.S.R. 28 47.00N 52.00E
Guyana S. America 60 5.00N 59.00W
Gwabegar Australia 45 30.34S149.00E
Gwadar Pakistan 30 25.09N 62.21E
Gwai Zimbabwe 41 19.15S 27.42E
Gwalior India 31 26.12N 78.09E
Gwanda Zimbabwe 41 20.59S 29.00E
Gwent d. U.K. 18 51.44N 3.00W
Gweru Zimbabwe 41 19.25S 29.45E
Gwynedd d. U.K. 18 53.00N 4.00W
Gydanskiy Pen. U.S.S.R. 28 70.00N 78.30E
Györ Hungary 22 47.41N 17.40E

H

Haarlem Neth. 20 52.23N 4.38E
Hachinohe Japan 35 40.30N141.30E
Hadhramaut f. S. Yemen 30 16.30N 49.30E
Hagerstown U.S.A. 55 39.39N 77.44W
Haifa Israel 23 32.49N 34.59E
Haikou China 32 20.03N110.27E
Hail Saudi Arabia 30 27.31N 41.45E
Hainan i. China 33 19.00N121.00E
Haines Alas. U.S.A. 50 59.11N135.23W
Haiphong Vietnam 32 20.48N106.40E
Haiti C. America 57 19.00N 73.00W
Hakodate Japan 35 41.46N140.44E
Haliburton Highlands Canada 55 45.10N 78.30W
Halifax Canada 51 44.38N 63.35W
Halkett, C. U.S.A. 50 71.00N152.00W
Halle E. Germany 22 51.28N 11.58E
Hall's Creek town Australia 44 18.17S127.44E
Halmahera i. Indonesia 33 0.45N128.00E
Halmstad Sweden 24 56.41N 12.55E
Hälsingborg Sweden 24 56.05N 12.45E
Hamadān Iran 30 34.47N 48.33E
Hamamatsu Japan 35 34.42N137.42E
Hamburg W. Germany 20 53.33N 10.00E
Hamersley Range mts. Australia 44 22.00S118.00E
Hamhung N. Korea 32 39.54N127.35E
Hamilton Australia 45 37.45S142.04E
Hamilton Canada 54 43.15N 79.50W
Hamilton New Zealand 46 37.46S175.18E
Hamilton Ohio U.S.A. 54 39.23N 84.33W
Hammerfest Norway 24 70.40N 23.44E
Hammond U.S.A. 54 41.48N 87.37W
Hampshire d. U.K. 18 51.03N 1.20W
Hancock Mich. U.S.A. 54 47.08N 88.34W
Hangzhou China 32 30.14N120.08E
Hannibal Mo. U.S.A. 54 39.41N 91.20W
Hannover W. Germany 20 52.23N 9.44E
Hanoi Vietnam 32 21.01N105.52E
Han Shui r. China 32 30.32N114.20E
Hantengri Feng mtn. China 31 42.09N 80.12E
Haparanda Sweden 24 65.50N 24.10E
Haradh Saudi Arabia 30 24.12N 49.08E
Harar Ethiopia 39 9.20N 42.10E
Harare Zimbabwe 41 17.49S 31.04E
Harbin China 32 45.45N126.41E
Hardanger Fjord est. Norway 24 60.15N 6.25E
Hargeisa Somali Rep. 39 9.31N 44.02E
Hari r. Afghan. 30 35.42N 61.12E
Harlow U.K. 19 51.47N 0.08E
Harney Basin f. U.S.A. 52 43.20N119.00W
Harricanaw r. Canada 53 51.05N 79.45W
Harris i. U.K. 19 57.50N 6.55W
Harrisburg Penn. U.S.A. 55 40.17N 76.54W
Harrison, C. Canada 51 55.00N 58.00W
Hartford U.S.A. 55 41.45N 72.42W
Harwich U.K. 19 51.56N 1.18E
Harz Mts. E. Germany/W. Germany 20 51.40N 10.55E
Hassi Messaoud Algeria 38 31.43N 6.03E

Hastings New Zealand 46 39.39S176.52E
Hastings Minn. U.S.A. 54 44.43N 92.50W
Hatfield Australia 45 33.53S143.47E
Hatteras, C. U.S.A. 53 35.14N 75.31W
Haugesund Norway 24 59.25N 5.16E
Hauraki G. New Zealand 46 36.30S175.00E
Havana Cuba 57 23.07N 82.25W
Havant U.K. 19 50.52N 0.59W
Hawaii i. Hawaii U.S.A. 52 19.30N155.30W
Hawaiian Is. U.S.A. 47 21.00N157.00W
Hawea, L. New Zealand 46 44.30S169.15E
Hawera New Zealand 46 39.35S174.19E
Hawick U.K. 19 55.25N 2.47W
Hawke, C. Australia 45 32.12S152.33E
Hawke B. New Zealand 46 39.18S177.15E
Hay Australia 45 34.31S144.31E
Hayes r. Canada 51 57.00N 92.30W
Hay River town Canada 50 60.51N115.42W
Hazelton Canada 50 55.16N127.18W
Heard I. Indian Oc. 7 53.07S 73.20E
Hearst Canada 54 49.42N 83.40W
Hebrides is. U.K. 20 58.00N 7.00W
Hecate Str. Canada 50 53.00N131.00W
Hefei China 32 31.50N117.16E
Heidelberg W. Germany 20 49.25N 8.42E
Hejaz f. Saudi Arabia 30 26.00N 37.30E
Hekla, Mt. Iceland 24 64.00N 19.45W
Helena U.S.A. 52 46.35N112.00W
Helmand r. Asia 30 31.10N 61.20E
Helsinki Finland 24 60.08N 25.00E
Hempstead N.Y. U.S.A. 55 40.42N 73.37W
Hengyang China 32 26.52N112.35E
Henrietta Maria, C. Canada 51 55.00N 82.15W
Herat Afghan. 30 34.21N 62.10E
Hereford and Worcester d. U.K. 18 52.08N 2.30W
Hermon, Mt. Lebanon 23 33.24N 35.52E
Hermosillo Mexico 56 29.15N110.59W
Heron Bay town Canada 54 48.41N 86.26W
Hertford U.K. 18 51.48N 0.05W
Hertfordshire d. U.K. 18 51.51N 0.05W
Hidalgo d. Mexico 56 20.50N 98.30W
High Atlas mts. Morocco 38 32.00N 5.50W
Highland d. U.K. 18 57.30N 5.00W
Hiiumaa i. U.S.S.R. 24 58.50N 22.30E
Hikurangi mtn. New Zealand 46 37.50S178.10E
Hillston Australia 45 33.30S145.33E
Hilo Hawaii U.S.A. 52 19.42N155.04W
Himalaya mts. Asia 31 29.00N 84.00E
Hindmarsh, L. Australia 45 36.03S141.53E
Hindu Kush mts. Asia 31 36.40N 70.00E
Hirosaki Japan 35 40.34N140.28E
Hiroshima Japan 35 34.30N132.27E
Hispaniola i. C. America 57 19.00N 71.00W
Hitachi Japan 35 36.35N140.40E
Hitra i. Norway 24 63.30N 8.50E
Hobart Australia 45 42.54S147.18E
Ho Chi Minh City Vietnam 33 10.46N106.43E
Hodeida Yemen 30 14.50N 42.58E
Höfn Iceland 24 64.16N 15.10W
Hofsjökull mtn. Iceland 24 64.50N 19.00W
Hofuf Saudi Arabia 30 25.20N 49.34E
Hohhot China 32 40.42N111.38E
Hokitika New Zealand 46 42.42S170.59E
Hokkaido i. Japan 35 43.00N144.00E
Holbrook U.S.A. 52 34.58N110.00W
Holguín Cuba 57 20.54N 76.15W
Holstebro Denmark 24 56.22N 8.38E
Holyhead U.K. 19 53.18N 4.38W
Holyoke Mass. U.S.A. 55 42.12N 72.37W
Home B. Canada 51 69.00N 66.00W
Homer Alas. U.S.A. 50 59.40N151.37W
Homer Tunnel New Zealand 46 44.40S168.15E
Homs Syria 30 34.44N 36.43E
Hondo r. Mexico 57 18.33N 88.22W
Honduras C. America 57 14.30N 87.00W
Honduras, G. of Carib. Sea 57 16.20N 87.30W
Hong Kong Asia 32 23.00N113.00E
Hongshui He r. China 32 23.20N110.04E
Honiara Solomon Is. 47 9.28S159.52E
Honolulu Hawaii U.S.A. 52 21.19N157.50W
Honshu i. Japan 35 36.00N138.00E
Hood, Mt. U.S.A. 52 45.24N121.41W
Hoover Dam U.S.A. 52 36.01N114.45W
Hopetoun Vic. Australia 45 35.43S142.20E
Horn, C. S. America 61 55.47S 67.00W
Horsham Australia 45 36.45S142.15E
Horton r. Canada 50 70.00N127.00W
Houston Tex. U.S.A. 53 29.45N 95.25W
Howe, C. Australia 45 37.30S149.59E
Howland I. Pacific Oc. 47 0.48N176.38W
Howrah India 31 22.35N 88.20E
Hoy i. U.K. 19 58.51N 3.17W
Huambo Angola 41 12.47S 15.44E
Huancayo Peru 60 12.15S 75.12W
Huang He r. China 32 37.55N118.46E
Huanuco Peru 60 10.00S 76.11W
Huascaran mtn. Peru 60 9.20S 77.36W
Hubli India 31 15.20N 75.14E
Huddersfield U.K. 19 53.38N 1.49W
Hudson r. U.S.A. 55 40.45N 74.00W

Hudson B. Canada 51 58.00N 86.00W
Hudson Str. Canada 51 62.00N 70.00W
Hué Vietnam 33 16.28N107.35E
Huelva Spain 21 37.15N 6.56W
Huesca Spain 21 42.02N 0.25W
Hughenden Australia 44 20.50S144.10E
Huiarau Range mts. New Zealand 46 38.20S177.15E
Huixtla Mexico 56 15.09N 92.30W
Hull Canada 55 45.26N 75.45W
Humber r. U.K. 19 53.40N 0.12W
Humberside d. U.K. 18 53.48N 0.35W
Hume, L. Australia 45 36.05S147.10E
Humphreys Peak mtn. U.S.A. 52 35.21N111.41W
Hun Libya 38 29.06N 15.57E
Húnaflói b. Iceland 24 65.45N 20.50W
Hungary Europe 22 47.00N 19.00E
Huntington W.Va. U.S.A. 53 38.24N 82.26W
Huntly New Zealand 46 37.35S175.10E
Huntsville Tex. U.S.A. 53 30.43N 95.34W
Hurd, C. Canada 54 45.14N 81.44W
Huron, L. Canada/U.S.A. 54 45.00N 82.30W
Húsavik Iceland 24 66.03N 17.17W
Hvita r. Iceland 24 64.33N 21.45W
Hwange Zimbabwe 41 18.20S 26.29E
Hyderabad India 31 17.22N 78.26E
Hyndman Peak U.S.A. 52 43.46N113.55W

I

Iaşi Romania 22 47.09N 27.38E
Ibadan Nigeria 38 7.23N 3.56E
Ibagué Colombia 60 4.35N 75.30W
Ibarra Ecuador 60 0.23N 77.50W
Ibiza i. Spain 21 39.00N 1.23E
Iceland Europe 6 64.45N 18.00W
Idaho d. U.S.A. 52 45.00N115.00W
Idaho Falls town U.S.A. 52 43.30N112.01W
Idhi mtn. Greece 23 35.13N 24.45E
Iguala Mexico 56 18.21N 99.31W
Ihosy Madagascar 41 22.24S 46.08E
Iide yama mtn. Japan 35 37.50N139.42E
IJsselmeer l. Neth. 20 52.45N 5.20E
Ilebo Zaïre 40 4.20S 20.35E
Illinois d. U.S.A. 53 40.00N 89.00W
Illinois r. U.S.A. 54 38.56N 90.27W
Iloilo Philippines 33 10.45N122.33E
Ilorin Nigeria 38 8.32N 4.34E
Imandra, L. U.S.S.R. 25 67.30N 32.45E
Imphal India 31 24.47N 93.55E
Inari Finland 25 69.00N 28.00E
Inas, Gunung mtn. Malaysia 34 5.18N100.54E
Inchon S. Korea 32 37.30N126.38E
India Asia 31 22.00N 81.00E
Indiana d. U.S.A. 53 40.00N 86.00W
Indianapolis U.S.A. 54 39.45N 86.10W
Indian Harbour Canada 51 54.25N 57.20W
Indian Ocean 9
Indigirka r. U.S.S.R. 29 71.00N148.45E
Indonesia Asia 33 5.00S120.00E
Indore India 31 22.42N 75.54E
Indus r. Pakistan 31 24.00N 67.33E
Inebolu Turkey 23 41.57N 33.45E
Ingham Australia 44 18.43S146.12E
Inhambane Mozambique 41 23.51S 35.29E
Inn r. Europe 20 48.33N 13.26E
Inner Hebrides is. U.K. 19 56.50N 6.45W
Inner Mongolia d. China 32 43.00N112.00E
Innsbruck Austria 21 46.17N 11.25E
International Falls town U.S.A. 54 48.38N 93.26W
Inuvik Canada 50 68.16N133.40W
Inuvik d. Canada 50 67.00N130.00W
Invercargill New Zealand 46 46.26S168.21E
Inverell Australia 45 29.46S151.10E
Inverness U.K. 19 57.27N 4.15W
Ionian Is. Greece 23 38.45N 20.00E
Ionian Sea Med. Sea 23 38.30N 18.45E
Iowa d. U.S.A. 53 42.00N 93.00W
Iowa City U.S.A. 54 41.39N 91.31W
Ipoh Malaysia 34 4.36N101.05E
Ipswich Australia 45 27.38S152.40E
Ipswich U.K. 19 52.04N 1.09E
Iquique Chile 61 20.15S 70.08W
Iquitos Peru 60 3.51S 73.13W
Iráklion r. Greece 23 35.20N 25.08E
Iran Asia 30 33.00N 55.00E
Iranian Plateau f. Asia 9 33.00N 55.00E
Irapuato Mexico 56 20.40N101.40W
Iraq Asia 30 32.00N 44.00E
Iringa Tanzania 40 7.49S 35.39E
Irish Sea U.K./Rep. of Ire. 19 53.40N 4.30W
Irkutsk U.S.S.R. 29 52.18N104.15E
Irong, Gunung mtn. Malaysia 34 4.08N102.48E
Iron Gate f. Romania/Yugo. 22 44.40N 22.30E
Iron Mountain town U.S.A. 54 45.51N 88.05W
Ironwood U.S.A. 54 46.25N 90.08W
Irrawaddy r. Burma 33 17.45N 25.25E
Irrawaddy Delta Burma 31 16.30N 95.20E
Irtysh r. U.S.S.R. 28 61.00N 68.40E
Isabella, Cordillera mts. Nicaragua 57 13.30N 85.00W
Isafjördhur Iceland 24 66.05N 23.06W
Isar r. W. Germany 20 48.48N 12.57E

INDEX

Ascia Baidoa Somali Rep. 39 3.08N 43.34E
Ise Japan 35 34.29N136.41E
Isfahan Iran 30 32.42N 51.40E
Ishikari r. Japan 35 43.15N141.21E
Ishim r. U.S.S.R. 28 57.50N 71.00E
Isiolo Kenya 40 0.20N 37.36E
Isiro Zaïre 41 2.50S 27.40E
Islamabad Pakistan 31 33.40N 73.08E
Islands, B. of New Zealand 46 35.15S174.15E
Islay i. U.K. 19 55.45N 6.20W
Israel Asia 30 32.00N 35.00E
Issyk Kul l. U.S.S.R. 28 42.30N 77.10E
Istanbul Turkey 23 41.02N 28.58E
Istra pen. Yugo. 22 45.12N 13.55E
Itabuna Brazil 60 14.48S 39.18W
Ithaca U.S.A. 55 42.26N 76.30W
Ivalo Finland 25 68.41N 27.30E
Ivanhoe Australia 45 32.56S144.22E
Ivano-Frankovsk U.S.S.R. 22 48.55N 24.42E
Ivanovo R.S.F.S.R. U.S.S.R. 28 57.00N 41.00E
Ivory Coast Africa 38 7.00N 5.30W
Iwaki Japan 35 36.58N140.58E
Iwaki r. Japan 35 41.20N140.00E
Iwakuni Japan 35 34.10N132.09E
Izmir Turkey 23 38.24N 27.09E
Izmit Turkey 23 40.48N 29.55E

J
Jabalpur India 31 23.10N 79.59E
Jackson Mich. U.S.A. 54 42.15N 84.24W
Jackson Miss. U.S.A. 53 32.20N 90.11W
Jacksonville Fla. U.S.A. 53 30.20N 81.40W
Jacksonville Ill. U.S.A. 54 39.44N 90.14W
Jacobabad Pakistan 31 28.16N 68.30E
Jaffa, C. Australia 45 36.58S139.39E
Jaffna Sri Lanka 31 9.38N 80.02E
Jaghbub Libya 39 29.42N 24.38E
Jaipur India 31 26.53N 75.50E
Jakarta Indonesia 33 6.08S106.45E
Jalapa Mexico 56 19.45N 96.48W
Jalisco d. Mexico 56 21.00N103.00W
Jamaica C. America 57 18.00N 77.00W
Jamalpur Bangla. 31 24.54N 89.57E
Jambi Indonesia 33 1.36S103.39E
James r. S.Dak. U.S.A. 53 42.50N 97.15W
James B. Canada 51 52.00N 80.00W
Jamestown N.Dak. U.S.A. 52 46.54N 98.42W
Jamestown N.Y. U.S.A. 55 42.05N 79.15W
Jammu Jammu & Kashmir 31 32.44N 74.52E
Jammu and Kashmir Asia 31 33.30N 76.00E
Jamnagar India 31 22.28N 70.06E
Jamshedpur India 31 22.47N 86.12E
Janesville U.S.A. 54 42.42N 89.02W
Jan Mayen i. Arctic Oc. 6 71.00N 9.00W
Januária Brazil 60 15.28S 44.23W
Japan Asia 35 36.00N138.00E
Japan, Sea of Asia 35 40.00N135.00E
Japan Trench Pacific Oc. 9 30.00N145.00E
Japurá r. Brazil 60 3.00S 64.30W
Jardines de la Reina is. Cuba 57 20.30N 79.00W
Jarosław Poland 22 50.02N 22.24E
Jasper Canada 50 52.55N118.05W
Java i. Indonesia 33 7.30S110.00E
Javari r. Peru 60 4.30S 70.00W
Jayapura Indonesia 33 2.28S140.38E
Jebel al Akhdar mts. Oman 30 23.00N 57.50E
Jefferson, Mt. Nev. U.S.A. 52 38.47N116.58W
Jefferson City U.S.A. 54 38.33N 92.10W
Jelai r. Malaysia 34 4.05N102.19E
Jérémie Haiti 57 18.40N 74.09W
Jerez Spain 21 36.41N 6.08W
Jersey i. U.K. 20 49.13N 2.08W
Jersey City U.S.A. 55 40.44N 74.04W
Jerusalem Israel/Jordan 23 31.47N 35.13E
Jhansi India 31 25.27N 78.34E
Jiddah Saudi Arabia 30 21.30N 39.10E
Jilin China 32 43.53N126.35E
Jiménez Mexico 56 27.08N104.55W
Jimma Ethiopia 41 7.39N 36.47E
Jinan China 32 36.40N117.01E
Jinja Uganda 39 0.27N 33.14E
Jinotepe Nicaragua 57 11.50N 86.10W
Jinzhou China 32 41.06N121.05E
Jitra Malaysia 34 6.17N100.25E
João Pessoa Brazil 60 7.06S 34.53W
Jodhpur India 31 26.18N 73.08E
Johannesburg R.S.A. 41 26.11S 28.04E
Johnstown Penn. U.S.A. 55 40.20N 78.56W
Johor d. Malaysia 34 2.10N103.25E
Johor Bahru Malaysia 34 1.28N103.46E
Joliet U.S.A. 54 41.32N 88.05W
Joliette Canada 55 46.02N 73.27W
Jönköping Sweden 24 57.45N 14.10E
Jordan Asia 30 31.00N 36.00E
Joseph Bonaparte G. Australia 44 14.00S128.30E
Jotunheimen mts. Norway 24 61.30N 9.00E
Juan Fernandez Is. Chile 61 34.20S 80.00W
Juba r. Somali Rep. 39 0.20S 42.53E
Juba Sudan 41 4.50N 31.35E

Júcar r. Spain 21 39.10N 0.15W
Juchitán Mexico 56 16.27N 95.05W
Juiz de Fora Brazil 61 21.47S 43.23W
Julianehåb Greenland 51 60.45N 46.00W
Jumla Nepal 31 29.17N 82.10E
Junction City Kans. U.S.A. 53 39.02N 96.51W
Jundiaí Brazil 61 22.59S 47.00W
Juneau U.S.A. 50 58.20N134.20W
Junee Australia 45 34.51S147.40E
Junggar Pendi f. Asia 31 44.20N 86.30E
Jura i. U.K. 19 55.58N 5.55W
Jura Mts. France 21 46.55N 6.45E
Juruá r. Brazil 60 2.30S 65.40W
Juticalpa Honduras 57 14.45N 86.12W

K
K2 mtn. Asia 31 35.53N 76.32E
Kabalo Zaïre 40 6.02S 27.00E
Kabia i. Indonesia 33 6.07S120.28E
Kabul Afghan. 31 34.30N 69.10E
Kabwe Zambia 41 14.27S 28.25E
Kaduna Nigeria 38 10.28N 7.25E
Kafue r. Zambia 41 15.53S 28.50E
Kaga Bandoro C.A.R. 40 7.00N 19.10E
Kagoshima Japan 35 31.37N130.32E
Kaiapoi New Zealand 46 43.23S172.39E
Kaifeng China 32 34.46N114.22E
Kaikohe New Zealand 46 35.25S173.49E
Kaikoura New Zealand 46 42.24S173.41E
Kaikoura Range mts. New Zealand 46 42.00S173.40E
Kaimanawa Mts. New Zealand 46 39.10S176.15E
Kaipara Harbour est. New Zealand 46 36.30S174.00E
Kairouan Tunisia 38 35.40N 10.04E
Kaitaia New Zealand 46 35.08S173.18E
Kajaani Finland 25 64.14N 27.37E
Kajang Malaysia 34 2.59N101.46E
Kakinada India 31 16.59N 82.20E
Kalahari Desert Botswana 41 23.30S 23.00E
Kalámai Greece 23 37.02N 22.06E
Kalamazoo U.S.A. 54 42.17N 85.36W
Kalemie Zaïre 40 5.57S 29.10E
Kalgoorlie Australia 44 30.49S121.29E
Kalinin U.S.S.R. 25 56.47N 35.57E
Kaliningrad U.S.S.R. 24 54.40N 20.30E
Kalinkovichi U.S.S.R. 22 52.10N 29.13E
Kalisz Poland 22 51.46N 18.02E
Kallavesi l. Finland 25 62.45N 28.00E
Kalmar Sweden 24 56.39N 16.20E
Kaluga U.S.S.R. 25 54.31N 36.16E
Kama r. U.S.S.R. 28 55.30N 52.00E
Kamchatka Pen. U.S.S.R. 29 56.00N160.00E
Kamen mtn. U.S.S.R. 29 68.40N 94.20E
Kamenskoye U.S.S.R. 29 62.31N165.15E
Kamensk-Ural'skiy U.S.S.R. 28 56.29N 61.49E
Kamet mtn. China 31 31.03N 79.25E
Kamina Zaïre 41 8.46S 24.55E
Kamloops Canada 52 50.39N120.24W
Kampala Uganda 41 0.19N 32.35E
Kampar Malaysia 34 4.18N101.09E
Kampong Merchang Malaysia 34 5.02N103.16E
Kampot Kampuchea 33 10.37N104.11E
Kampuchea Asia 33 12.00N105.00E
Kananga Zaïre 40 5.53S 22.26E
Kanazawa Japan 35 36.35N136.40E
Kanchenjunga mtn. Asia 31 27.44N 88.11E
Kandahar Afghan. 31 31.36N 65.47E
Kandalaksha U.S.S.R. 25 67.09N 32.31E
Kandalakskaya G. U.S.S.R. 25 66.30N 34.00E
Kandy Sri Lanka 31 7.18N 80.43E
Kane U.S.A. 55 41.40N 78.48W
Kangar Malaysia 34 6.28N100.10E
Kangaroo I. Australia 45 35.45S137.30E
Kanin, C. U.S.S.R. 28 68.00N 43.30E
Kanin Pen. U.S.S.R. 28 68.00N 45.00E
Kankakee U.S.A. 54 41.08N 87.52W
Kankan Guinea 38 10.22N 9.11W
Kano Nigeria 38 12.00N 8.31E
Kanpur India 31 26.27N 80.14E
Kansas d. U.S.A. 52 38.00N 99.00W
Kansas City Mo. U.S.A. 53 39.02N 94.33W
Kansk U.S.S.R. 29 56.11N 95.20E
Kapiti I. New Zealand 46 40.50S174.50E
Kapuas r. Indonesia 33 0.13S109.12E
Kara U.S.S.R. 28 69.12N 65.00E
Kara Bogaz Gol B. U.S.S.R. 28 41.20N 53.40E
Karachi Pakistan 31 24.51N 67.02E
Karaganda U.S.S.R. 28 49.53N 73.07E
Karak Malaysia 34 3.25N102.03E
Karakoram Pass Asia 31 35.53N 77.51E
Karakoram Range mts. Jammu & Kashmir 31 35.30N 76.30E
Kara Kum des. U.S.S.R. 28 40.00N 60.00E
Karaman Turkey 23 37.11N 33.13E
Karamea Bight b. New Zealand 46 41.15S171.30E
Kara Nur l. Mongolia 32 48.10N 93.30E
Karasburg Namibia 41 28.00S 18.43E
Kara Sea U.S.S.R. 28 73.00N 65.00E
Karima Sudan 40 18.33N 31.51E
Karisimbi, Mt. Zaïre 40 1.31S 29.25E

Karkinitskiy, G. of U.S.S.R. 22 45.50N 32.45E
Karl Marx Stadt E. Germany 22 50.50N 12.55E
Karlskrona Sweden 24 56.10N 15.35E
Karlsruhe W. Germany 20 49.00N 8.24E
Karlstad Sweden 24 59.24N 13.32E
Karpáthos i. Greece 23 35.35N 27.08E
Karsakpay U.S.S.R. 28 47.47N 66.43E
Kasai r. Zaïre 40 3.10S 16.13E
Kasese Uganda 40 0.07N 30.06E
Kashi China 31 39.29N 76.02E
Kaskaskia r. U.S.A. 54 38.30N 89.15W
Kassala Sudan 41 15.24N 36.30E
Kassel W. Germany 20 51.18N 9.30E
Kataba Zambia 41 16.12S 25.00E
Katahdin, Mt. U.S.A. 55 45.55N 68.57W
Katherina, Gebel mtn. Egypt 39 28.30N 33.57E
Katherine Australia 44 14.29S132.20E
Katmandu Nepal 31 27.42N 85.19E
Katoomba Australia 45 33.42S150.23E
Katsina Nigeria 38 13.00N 7.32E
Kattegat str. Denmark/Sweden 24 57.00N 11.20E
Kauai i. Hawaii U.S.A. 52 22.05N159.30W
Kaunas U.S.S.R. 24 54.52N 23.55E
Kaura Namoda Nigeria 38 12.39N 6.38E
Kawagoe Japan 35 35.58N139.30E
Kawasaki Japan 35 35.30N139.45E
Kawerau New Zealand 46 38.05S176.42E
Kayes Mali 38 14.26N 11.28W
Kayseri Turkey 23 38.42N 35.28E
Kazachye U.S.S.R. 29 70.46N136.15E
Kazakhstan S.S.R. d. U.S.S.R. 28 49.00N 64.00E
Kazan U.S.S.R. 28 55.55N 49.10E
Kazbek mtn. U.S.S.R. 28 42.42N 44.30E
Kebbi r. Nigeria 38 11.24N 4.07E
Kebnekaise mtn. Sweden 24 67.55N 18.30E
Kedah d. Malaysia 34 6.00N100.30E
Kediri Indonesia 33 7.55S112.01E
Keele Peak mtn. Canada 50 63.15N130.50W
Keene U.S.A. 55 42.55N 72.17W
Keetmanshoop Namibia 41 26.36S 18.08E
Keewatin Canada 53 49.46N 94.30W
Keewatin d. Canada 51 65.00N 90.00W
Keflavík Iceland 24 64.01N 22.35W
Kelang Malaysia 34 3.01N101.27E
Kelantan d. Malaysia 34 4.55N102.00E
Kelantan r. Malaysia 34 6.10N102.14E
Kelloselkä Finland 25 66.57N 28.50E
Kelowna Canada 52 49.50N119.29W
Keluang Malaysia 34 2.01N103.18E
Kemerovo U.S.S.R. 28 55.25N 86.10E
Kemi r. Finland 24 65.47N 24.28E
Kempsey Australia 45 31.05S152.50E
Kempt, L. Canada 55 47.30N 74.15W
Kendari Indonesia 33 3.57S122.36E
Kenora Canada 53 49.47N 94.26W
Kenosha U.S.A. 54 42.34N 87.50W
Kent d. U.K. 18 51.12N 0.40E
Kentucky d. U.S.A. 53 38.00N 85.00W
Kentucky L. U.S.A. 53 36.15N 88.00W
Kenya Africa 40 1.00N 38.00E
Kenya, Mt. Kenya 41 0.10S 37.19E
Kerang Australia 45 35.42S143.59E
Kerguelen i. Indian Oc. 7 49.30S 69.30E
Kerinci, G. mtn. Indonesia 33 1.45S101.20E
Kermadec Is. Pacific Oc. 47 30.00S178.30W
Kermadec Trench Pacific Oc. 9 33.00S176.00W
Kermān Iran 30 30.18N 57.05E
Kermānshāh Iran 30 34.19N 47.04E
Keroh Malaysia 34 5.42N100.59E
Kerry d. Rep. of Ire. 18 52.07N 9.35W
Keweenaw B. U.S.A. 54 47.00N 88.15W
Keweenaw Pt. U.S.A. 54 47.23N 87.42W
Khabarovsk U.S.S.R. 29 48.32N135.08E
Khalkidhiki f. Greece 23 40.25N 23.27E
Khanka, L. U.S.S.R. 29 45.00N132.30E
Khanty-Mansiysk U.S.S.R. 28 61.00N 69.00E
Kharkov U.S.S.R. 22 50.00N 36.15E
Khartoum Sudan 41 15.33N 32.35E
Khatanga U.S.S.R. 29 71.50N102.31E
Khatangskiy G. U.S.S.R. 29 75.00N112.10E
Kherson U.S.S.R. 22 46.39N 32.38E
Khios i. Greece 23 38.23N 26.04E
Khmelnitskiy U.S.S.R. 22 49.25N 26.49E
Khöbsögöl Dalai l. Mongolia 32 51.00N100.30E
Khulna Bangla. 31 22.49N 89.34E
Khyber Pass Asia 31 34.06N 71.05E
Kicking Horse Pass Canada 52 51.28N116.23W
Kidal Mali 38 18.27N 1.25E
Kiel W. Germany 20 54.20N 10.08E
Kiel Canal W. Germany 20 53.54N 9.12E
Kiev U.S.S.R. 22 50.28N 30.29E
Kigali Rwanda 40 1.59S 30.05E
Kigoma Tanzania 40 4.52S 29.46E
Kii suido str. Japan 35 34.00N135.00E
Kildare d. Rep. of Ire. 18 53.10N 6.50W
Kilimanjaro, Mt. Tanzania 40 3.02S 37.20E
Kilkenny Rep. of Ire. 18 52.39N 7.16W
Kilkenny d. Rep. of Ire. 18 52.35N 7.15W
Killarney Rep. of Ire. 19 52.04N 9.32W
Kilmarnock U.K. 19 55.37N 4.30W

Kilosa Tanzania 40 6.49S 37.00E
Kimberley R.S.A. 41 28.44S 24.44E
Kimberley Plateau Australia 44 17.20S127.20E
Kinabalu mtn. Malaysia 33 6.10N116.40E
Kindu Zaïre 40 3.00S 25.56E
King Christian Ninth Land f. Greenland 51 68.20N 37.00W
King Frederik Sixth Coast f. Greenland 51 63.00N 44.00W
King I. Australia 45 39.50S144.00E
King Leopold Ranges mts. Australia 44 17.00S125.30E
King's Lynn U.K. 19 52.45N 0.25E
Kingston Australia 45 36.50S139.50E
Kingston Canada 55 44.14N 76.30W
Kingston Jamaica 57 17.58N 76.48W
Kingston N.Y. U.S.A. 55 41.55N 74.00W
Kingston upon Hull U.K. 19 53.45N 0.20W
Kingston upon Thames U.K. 18 51.25N 0.17W
Kingstown St. Vincent 57 13.12N 61.14W
Kinshasa Zaïre 40 4.18S 15.18E
Kipawa L. Canada 55 46.55N 79.00W
Kirensk U.S.S.R. 29 57.45N108.00E
Kirghizstan S. S. R. d. U.S.S.R. 28 42.00N 75.00E
Kirgiz Steppe f. U.S.S.R. 28 49.28N 57.07E
Kiribati Pacific Oc. 47 2.00S175.00E
Kirikkale Turkey 23 39.51N 33.32E
Kirkcaldy U.K. 19 56.07N 3.10W
Kirkland Lake town Canada 54 48.10N 80.02W
Kirknes Norway 25 69.44N 30.05E
Kirkwall U.K. 19 58.59N 2.58W
Kirov R.S.F.S.R. U.S.S.R. 28 58.38N 49.38E
Kirov R.S.F.S.R. U.S.S.R. 22 53.59N 34.20E
Kirovabad U.S.S.R. 28 40.39N 46.20E
Kirovograd U.S.S.R. 22 48.31N 32.15E
Kirovsk U.S.S.R. 25 67.37N 33.39E
Kisangani Zaïre 41 0.33N 25.14E
Kishinev U.S.S.R. 22 47.00N 28.50E
Kismayu Somali Rep. 39 0.25S 42.31E
Kisumu Kenya 41 0.03S 34.47E
Kitakyushu Japan 35 33.50N130.50E
Kitchener Canada 54 43.27N 80.30W
Kitgum Uganda 40 3.17N 32.54E
Kíthira i. Greece 23 36.15N 23.00E
Kitikmeot d. Canada 50 70.00N105.00W
Kitimat Canada 50 54.05N128.38W
Kittanning U.S.A. 55 40.49N 79.31W
Kitwe Zambia 41 12.50S 28.04E
Kivu, L. Rwanda/Zaïre 40 2.00S 29.10E
Kizil r. Turkey 30 41.45N 35.57E
Klaipeda U.S.S.R. 24 55.43N 21.07E
Klar r. Sweden 24 59.25N 13.25E
Klyuchevskaya mtn. U.S.S.R. 29 56.00N160.30E
Knoxville U.S.A. 53 36.00N 83.57W
Knysna R.S.A. 41 34.02S 23.03E
Kobe Japan 35 34.42N135.15E
Koblenz W. Germany 20 50.21N 7.36E
Kochi Japan 35 33.33N133.52E
Kodiak U.S.A. 50 57.49N152.30W
Kodiak I. U.S.A. 50 57.00N153.50W
Kofu Japan 35 35.44N138.34E
Kojonup Australia 44 33.50S117.05E
Kokand U.S.S.R. 28 40.30N 86.09W
Kokchetav U.S.S.R. 28 53.18N 69.25E
Kokkola Finland 24 63.50N 23.10E
Kokomo U.S.A. 54 40.30N 86.09W
Koksoak r. Canada 51 58.30N 68.15W
Kokstad R.S.A. 41 30.32S 29.25E
Kolaka Indonesia 33 4.04S121.38E
Kola Peninsula f. U.S.S.R. 25 67.00N 38.00E
Kolepom i. Indonesia 33 8.00S138.30E
Kolguyev i. U.S.S.R. 28 69.00N 49.00E
Kolomna U.S.S.R. 25 55.05N 38.45E
Kolyma r. U.S.S.R. 29 68.50N161.00E
Kolyma Range mts. U.S.S.R. 29 63.00N160.00E
Kommunizma, Peak mtn. U.S.S.R. 28 38.59N 72.01E
Komsomolets i. U.S.S.R. 29 80.20N 96.00E
Komsomolsk-na-Amur U.S.S.R. 29 50.32N136.59E
Kongur mtn. China 31 38.40N 75.30E
Konosha U.S.S.R. 25 60.58N 40.08E
Konotop U.S.S.R. 22 51.15N 33.14E
Konstanz W. Germany 21 47.40N 9.10E
Konya Turkey 23 37.51N 32.30E
Korbu, Gunung mtn. Malaysia 34 4.42N101.18E
Korčula i. Yugo. 22 42.56N 16.53E
Korea B. North Korea 32 39.30N123.40E
Korea Str. Asia 32 35.00N129.20E
Kōriyama Japan 35 37.23N140.22E
Korosten U.S.S.R. 22 51.00N 28.30E
Koryak Range mts. U.S.S.R. 29 62.20N171.00E
Kos i. Greece 23 36.48N 27.10E
Kosciusko, Mt. Australia 45 36.28S148.17E
Košice Czech. 22 48.44N 21.15E
Kosti Sudan 41 13.11N 32.38E
Kostroma U.S.S.R. 28 57.46N 41.10E
Kota India 31 25.11N 75.58E
Kota Bharu Malaysia 34 6.07N102.15E
Kota Kinabalu Malaysia 33 5.59N116.04E
Kota Tinggi Malaysia 34 1.45N103.54E
Kotelnyy i. U.S.S.R. 29 75.30N141.00E
Kotka Finland 24 60.26N 26.55E
Kotlas U.S.S.R. 28 61.15N 46.28E
Kotuy r. U.S.S.R. 29 71.40N103.00E

INDEX

Kovrov U.S.S.R. 25 56.23N 41.21E
Kowloon Hong Kong 32 22.19N114.12E
Koyukuk r. U.S.A. 50 64.50N157.30W
Kragujevac Yugo. 22 44.01N 20.55E
Krasnodar U.S.S.R. 28 45.02N 39.00E
Krasnovodsk U.S.S.R. 28 40.01N 53.00E
Krasnoyarsk U.S.S.R. 29 56.05N 92.46E
Krefeld W. Germany 20 51.20N 6.32E
Kremenchug U.S.S.R. 22 49.00N 33.25E
Kristiansand Norway 24 58.08N 7.59E
Kristiansund Norway 24 63.15N 7.55E
Kristinestad Finland 24 56.02N 14.10E
Krivoy Rog U.S.S.R. 22 47.55N 33.24E
Kroonstad R.S.A. 41 27.38S 27.12E
Kuala Brang Malaysia 34 5.04N103.01E
Kuala Kangsar Malaysia 34 4.47N100.56E
Kuala Krai Malaysia 34 5.32N102.12E
Kuala Kuba Baharu Malaysia 34 3.33N101.37E
Kuala Lipis Malaysia 34 4.11N102.03E
Kuala Lumpur Malaysia 34 3.08N101.42E
Kuala Pilah Malaysia 34 2.44N102.15E
Kuala Selangor Malaysia 34 3.20N101.06E
Kuala Trengganu Malaysia 34 5.20N103.08E
Kuantan Malaysia 34 3.50N103.19E
Kuantan r. Malaysia 34 3.50N103.19E
Kuching Malaysia 33 1.32N110.20E
Kudat Malaysia 33 6.45N116.47E
Kulai Malaysia 34 1.39N103.36E
Kulim Malaysia 34 5.22N100.33E
Kumagaya Japan 35 36.09N139.22E
Kumamoto Japan 35 32.50N130.42E
Kumasi Ghana 38 6.45N 1.35W
Kunashir i. U.S.S.R. 35 44.25N146.00E
Kungur U.S.S.R. 28 57.27N 56.50E
Kunlun Shan mts. China 31 36.40N 88.00E
Kunming China 32 25.04N102.04E
Kuopio Finland 25 62.51N 27.30E
Kupang Indonesia 33 10.13S123.38E
Kurdistan f. Asia 30 37.00N 43.30E
Kurgan U.S.S.R. 28 55.20N 65.20E
Kuria Muria Is. Oman 30 17.30N 56.00E
Kuril Is. U.S.S.R. 29 46.00N150.30E
Kuril Trench Pacific Oc. 9 46.00N150.00E
Kuri san mtn. Japan 35 33.08N131.10E
Kursk U.S.S.R. 22 51.45N 36.14E
Kushiro Japan 35 42.58N144.24E
Kuskokwim Mts. U.S.A. 50 62.50N156.00W
Kustanay U.S.S.R. 28 53.15N 63.40E
Kuwait Asia 30 29.00N 47.00E
Kuwait town Kuwait 30 29.20N 48.00E
Kuybyshev U.S.S.R. 28 53.10N 50.15E
Kuybyshev Resr. U.S.S.R. 28 55.00N 49.00E
Kwangju S. Korea 32 35.07N126.52E
Kwekwe Zimbabwe 41 18.50S 29.46E
Kyle of Lochalsh town U.K. 19 57.17N 5.43W
Kyoga, L. Uganda 40 1.30N 33.00E
Kyoto Japan 35 35.04N135.50E
Kyushu i. Japan 35 32.00N130.00E
Kyushu sanchi mts. Japan 35 32.20N131.20E
Kyzyl U.S.S.R. 29 51.42N 94.28E
Kyzyl Kum des. U.S.S.R. 28 42.00N 64.30E
Kzyl Orda U.S.S.R. 28 44.52N 65.28E

L

La Barca Mexico 56 20.2N102.33W
Labé Guinea 38 11.17N 12.11W
Labis Malaysia 34 2.22N103.01E
La Blanquilla i. Venezuela 57 11.53N 64.38W
Labrador f. Canada 51 54.00N 61.30W
La Ceiba Honduras 57 15.45N 86.45W
Lachlan r. Australia 45 34.21S143.58E
La Coruña Spain 21 43.22N 8.24W
La Crosse Wisc. U.S.A. 54 43.48N 91.04W
Ladoga, L. U.S.S.R. 25 61.00N 32.00E
Ladysmith R.S.A. 41 28.32S 29.47E
Lae P.N.G. 44 6.45S146.30E
Lafayette Ind. U.S.A. 54 40.25N 86.54W
Lågen r. Norway 24 60.10N 11.28E
Lagos Mexico 56 21.21N101.55W
Lagos Nigeria 38 6.27N 3.28E
La Grande r. Canada 51 53.50N 79.00W
La Habana see Havana Cuba 57
Lahat Indonesia 33 3.46S103.32E
Lahore Pakistan 31 31.34N 74.22E
Lake Charles town U.S.A. 53 30.13N 93.13W
Lake District f. U.K. 19 54.30N 3.10W
Lakeland town U.S.A. 53 28.02N 81.59W
Lakewood Ohio U.S.A. 54 41.29N 81.50W
Lakshadweep Is. Indian Oc. 31 11.00N 72.00E
Lambaréné Gabon 40 0.41S 10.13E
Lamu Kenya 40 2.20S 40.54E
La Nao, Cabo de Spain 21 38.42N 0.15E
Lancang Jiang r. see Mekong r. China 32
Lancashire d. U.K. 18 53.53N 2.30W
Lancaster U.K. 19 54.03N 2.48W
Lancaster Penn. U.S.A. 55 40.01N 76.19W
Lancaster Sd. Canada 51 74.00N 85.00W
Landes f. France 21 44.00N 1.00W
Land's End c. U.K. 19 50.03N 5.45W
Langanes c. Iceland 24 66.30N 14.30W

Langkawi i. Malaysia 34 6.23N 99.48E
Lansing U.S.A. 54 42.44N 84.34W
Lanzarote i. Canary Is. 38 29.00N 13.55W
Lanzhou China 32 36.01N103.46E
Laois d. Rep. of Ire. 18 53.00N 7.20W
La Oroya Peru 60 11.36S 75.54W
Laos Asia 33 16.00N103.00E
La Palma i. Canary Is. 38 28.50N 18.00W
La Paz Bolivia 60 16.30S 68.10W
La Paz Mexico 56 24.10N110.17W
La Perouse Str. U.S.S.R. 29 45.50N142.30E
Lapland f. Finland/Sweden 24 68.10N 24.00E
La Plata Argentina 61 34.52S 57.55W
La Plata, Rio de est. S. America 61 35.15S 56.45W
Laptev Sea U.S.S.R. 29 74.30N125.00E
Laramie Range mts. U.S.A. 52 42.00N105.30W
Larch r. Canada 51 57.40N 69.30W
Laredo U.S.A. 52 27.32N 99.22W
La Rioja Argentina 61 29.26S 66.50W
Lárisa Greece 23 39.36N 22.24E
Larnaca Cyprus 23 34.54N 33.39E
Larne U.K. 19 54.51N 4.49W
La Rochelle France 21 46.10N 1.10W
La Romana Dom. Rep. 57 18.27N 68.57W
Larut Hills Malaysia 34 5.00N100.54E
La Salle U.S.A. 54 41.20N 89.06W
Lashio Burma 32 22.58N 97.48E
Las Palmas Canary Is. 38 28.08N 15.27W
Las Perlas, Archipelago de Panama 57 8.45N 79.30W
La Spezia Italy 21 44.07N 9.49E
Las Vegas Nev. U.S.A. 52 36.10N115.10W
La Tuque Canada 55 47.26N 72.47W
Latvia S.S.R. d. U.S.S.R. 24 57.00N 25.00E
Launceston Australia 45 41.25S147.07E
Laurel Del. U.S.A. 55 38.22N 75.34W
Laurentides Mts. Canada 55 47.40N 71.40W
Lausanne Switz. 21 46.32N 6.39E
La Vega Dom. Rep. 57 19.15N 70.33W
Laverton Australia 44 28.49S122.25E
Lavumisa R.S.A. 41 27.00S 32.00E
Lawit, Gunung mtn. Malaysia 34 5.26N102.36E
Lawrence Mass. U.S.A. 55 42.41N 71.12W
Lawrenceville Ill. U.S.A. 54 38.44N 87.42W
Leaf r. Canada 51 58.47N 70.06W
Lebanon Asia 30 34.00N 36.00E
Lebir r. Malaysia 34 5.32N102.11E
Lecce Italy 23 40.21N 18.11E
Ledang, Gunung mtn. Malaysia 34 2.22N102.36E
Leech L. U.S.A. 53 47.10N 94.30W
Leeds U.K. 19 53.48N 1.34W
Leeuwin, C. Australia 44 34.00S115.00E
Leeward Is. C. America 57 18.00N 61.00W
Legges Tor mtn. Australia 45 41.32S147.41E
Leghorn Italy 21 43.33N 10.18E
Le Havre France 20 49.30N 0.06E
Leicester U.K. 19 52.39N 1.09W
Leicestershire d. U.K. 18 52.40N 1.10W
Leigh Creek town Australia 45 30.31S138.25E
Leipzig E. Germany 22 51.20N 12.20E
Leitrim d. Rep. of Ire. 18 54.08N 8.00W
Le Mans France 21 48.00N 0.10E
Lemmon U.S.A. 52 45.56N102.00W
Lena r. U.S.S.R. 29 72.00N127.10E
Leninabad U.S.S.R. 28 40.14N 69.30E
Leninakan U.S.S.R. 28 40.47N 43.49E
Leningrad U.S.S.R. 25 59.55N 30.25E
Leninogorsk U.S.S.R. 28 50.23N 83.32E
Leninsk Kuznetskiy U.S.S.R. 28 54.44N 86.13E
León Mexico 56 21.10N101.42W
León Nicaragua 57 12.24N 86.52W
León Spain 21 42.35N 5.34W
Leonora Australia 44 28.54S121.20E
Lérida Spain 21 41.37N 0.38E
Lerwick U.K. 19 60.09N 1.09W
Les Cayes Haiti 57 18.15N 73.46W
Lesotho Africa 41 29.00S 28.00E
Lesser Antilles is. C. America 57 13.00N 65.00W
Lesser Slave L. Canada 50 55.30N115.00W
Lésvos i. Greece 23 39.10N 26.16E
Lethbridge Canada 52 49.43N112.43W
Leticia Colombia 60 4.09S 69.57W
Lévêque, C. Australia 44 16.25S123.00E
Levin New Zealand 46 40.37S175.18E
Lévis Canada 55 46.47N 71.12W
Lewes U.K. 18 50.53N 0.02E
Lewis i. U.K. 19 58.10N 6.40W
Lewis Pass f. New Zealand 46 42.30S172.15E
Lewiston Maine U.S.A. 55 44.05N 70.15W
Lewistown Penn. U.S.A. 55 40.37N 77.36W
Lexington Ky. U.S.A. 53 38.02N 84.30W
Lhasa China 31 29.41N 91.10E
Liaoyuan China 32 42.50N125.08E
Liard r. Canada 50 61.56N120.35W
Libenge Zaïre 40 3.39N 18.39E
Liberia Africa 38 6.30N 9.30W
Liberia Costa Rica 57 10.39N 85.28W
Libreville Gabon 40 0.30N 9.25E
Libya Africa 38 26.30N 17.00E
Libyan Desert Africa 39 25.00N 26.10E
Lichinga Mozambique 41 13.09S 35.17E

Liechtenstein Europe 21 47.10N 9.30E
Liège Belgium 20 50.38N 5.35E
Liepāja U.S.S.R. 24 56.30N 21.00E
Lifford Rep. of Ire. 18 54.50N 7.31W
Ligurian Sea Med. Sea 21 43.00N 8.30E
Likasi Zaïre 41 11.00S 26.50E
Lille France 20 50.39N 3.05E
Lillehammer Norway 24 61.06N 10.27E
Lilongwe Malaŵi 41 13.58S 33.49E
Lima Peru 60 12.06S 77.03W
Lima Ohio U.S.A. 54 40.43N 84.06W
Limassol Cyprus 23 34.40N 33.03E
Limerick Rep. of Ire. 19 52.40N 8.37W
Limerick d. Rep. of Ire. 18 52.30N 8.40W
Lim Fjord str. Denmark 24 56.55N 9.10E
Límnos i. Greece 23 39.55N 25.14E
Limoges France 21 45.50N 1.15E
Límon Costa Rica 57 10.00N 83.01W
Limpopo r. Mozambique 41 25.14S 33.33E
Linares Mexico 56 24.54N 99.38W
Linares Spain 21 38.05N 3.38W
Lincoln New Zealand 46 43.38S172.29E
Lincoln U.K. 19 53.14N 0.32W
Lincoln Maine U.S.A. 55 45.23N 68.30W
Lincoln Nebr. U.S.A. 53 40.49N 96.41W
Lincolnshire d. U.K. 18 53.14N 0.32W
Lindesnes c. Norway 24 58.00N 7.05E
Lindi Tanzania 41 10.00S 39.41E
Line Is. Pacific Oc. 47 0.00 158.00W
Lingayen Philippines 33 16.02N121.14E
Linköping Sweden 24 58.25N 15.35E
Linz Austria 22 48.18N 14.18E
Lions, G. of France 21 43.12N 4.15E
Lipari Is. Italy 23 38.35N 14.45E
Lipetsk U.S.S.R. 28 52.37N 39.36E
Lira Uganda 40 2.15N 32.53E
Lisala Zaïre 41 2.08N 21.37E
Lisbon Portugal 21 38.44N 9.08W
Lisburn U.K. 19 54.30N 6.03W
Lisburne, C. U.S.A. 50 69.00N165.50W
Lismore N.S.W. Australia 45 28.48S153.17E
Lithgow Australia 45 33.30S150.09E
Lithuania S.S.R. d. U.S.S.R. 24 55.00N 23.50E
Little Cayman i. Cayman Is. 57 19.40N 80.00W
Little Inagua i. Bahamas 57 21.30N 73.00W
Little Rock town U.S.A. 53 34.42N 92.17W
Livermore, Mt. U.S.A. 52 30.39N104.11W
Liverpool Canada 51 44.03N 64.43W
Liverpool U.K. 19 53.25N 2.59W
Liverpool Plains f. Australia 45 31.20S150.00E
Liverpool Range mts. Australia 45 31.45S150.45E
Livingstone Zambia 41 17.40S 25.50E
Ljubljana Yugo. 22 46.04N 14.28E
Ljungan r. Sweden 24 61.15N 17.08E
Llandrindod Wells U.K. 18 52.15N 3.23W
Llanos f. Colombia/Venezuela 60 5.30N 72.00W
Lloydminster Canada 50 53.18N110.00W
Lobito Angola 41 12.20S 13.34E
Łódź Poland 22 51.49N 19.28E
Lofoten is. Norway 24 68.15N 13.50E
Logan, Mt. Canada 50 60.45N140.00W
Logansport U.S.A. 54 40.45N 86.25W
Logone r. Cameroon/Chad 38 12.10N 15.00E
Loire r. France 21 47.17N 2.00W
Loja Ecuador 60 3.59S 79.16W
Lolland i. Denmark 24 54.50N 11.30E
Lomé Togo 38 6.10N 1.21E
Lomond, Loch U.K. 19 56.07N 4.36W
London Canada 54 42.58N 81.15W
London U.K. 19 51.32N 0.06W
Londonderry U.K. 19 55.00N 7.21W
Londonderry d. U.K. 18 55.00N 7.00W
Londonderry, C. Australia 44 13.58S126.55E
Londrina Brazil 61 23.30S 51.13W
Long Beach town Calif. U.S.A. 52 33.57N118.15W
Longford Rep. of Ire. 18 53.44N 7.48W
Longford d. Rep. of Ire. 18 53.42N 7.45W
Long I. Bahamas 57 23.00N 75.00W
Long I. U.S.A. 55 40.50N 73.20W
Long L. Canada 54 49.40N 86.45W
Longlac town Canada 51 49.47N 86.34W
Long Pt. Canada 54 42.33N 80.04W
Longs Peak U.S.A. 52 40.16N105.37W
Lookout, C. U.S.A. 53 34.34N 76.34W
Lopez, C. Gabon 40 0.36S 8.45E
Lop Nur l. China 32 40.30N 90.30E
Lopphavet est. Norway 24 70.30N 21.00E
Lorain U.S.A. 54 41.28N 82.11W
Lorca Spain 21 37.40N 1.41W
Lord Howe I. Pacific Oc. 47 31.33S159.06E
Lorient France 21 47.45N 3.21W
Los Angeles U.S.A. 52 34.00N118.17W
Los Mochis Mexico 56 25.45N108.57W
Los Roques is. Venezuela 57 12.00N 67.00W
Lot r. France 21 44.17N 0.22E
Lothian d. U.K. 18 55.50N 3.00W
Louisiana d. U.S.A. 53 31.00N 92.30W
Louisville Ky. U.S.A. 53 38.13N 85.45W
Louth d. Rep. of Ire. 18 53.55N 6.30W
Lowell U.S.A. 55 42.38N 71.19W
Lower California pen. Mexico 52 30.00N115.00W

Lower Hutt New Zealand 46 41.13S174.55E
Lower Lough Erne U.K. 19 54.28N 7.48W
Lower Tunguska r. U.S.S.R. 29 65.50N 88.00E
Loyalty Is. Pacific Oc. 47 21.00S167.30E
Lualaba r. Zaïre 40 0.18N 25.32E
Luanda Angola 41 8.50S 13.20E
Luang Prabang Laos 32 19.53N102.10E
Luapula r. Zaïre/Zambia 41 9.25S 28.36E
Lubango Angola 41 14.52S 13.30E
Lubbock U.S.A. 52 33.35N101.53W
Lübeck W. Germany 20 53.52N 10.40E
Lublin Poland 22 51.18N 22.31E
Lubumbashi Zaïre 41 11.44S 27.29E
Lucknow India 31 26.50N 80.54E
Lüda China 32 38.49N121.48E
Lüderitz Namibia 41 26.38S 15.10E
Ludgate Canada 54 45.54N 80.32W
Ludhiana India 31 30.56N 75.52E
Ludington U.S.A. 54 43.58N 86.27W
Ludwigshafen W. Germany 20 49.29N 8.27E
Luena Angola 41 11.46S 19.55E
Luga U.S.S.R. 25 58.42N 29.49E
Lugo Spain 21 43.00N 7.33W
Luizhou China 32 24.19N109.12E
Lule r. Sweden 24 65.40N 21.48E
Luleå Sweden 24 65.35N 22.10E
Lulua r. Zaïre 40 5.03S 21.07E
Lumut Malaysia 34 4.13N100.37E
Lund Sweden 24 55.42N 13.10E
Luoyang China 32 34.48N112.25E
Lurgan U.K. 19 54.28N 6.21W
Lusaka Zambia 41 15.20S 28.14E
Lusambo Zaïre 40 5.00S 23.26E
Luton U.K. 19 51.53N 0.25W
Luvua r. Zaïre 40 6.45S 27.00E
Luxembourg Europe 20 49.50N 6.15E
Luxembourg town Lux. 20 49.37N 6.08E
Luxor Egypt 39 24.41N 32.24E
Luzern Switz. 21 47.03N 8.17E
Luzon i. Philippines 33 17.50N121.00E
Luzon Str. Pacific Oc. 33 19.00N121.00E
Lvov U.S.S.R. 22 49.50N 24.00E
Lyell, Mt. U.S.A. 52 37.45N119.18W
Lyme B. U.K. 19 50.40N 2.55W
Lynn Lake town Canada 51 56.51N101.01W
Lyon France 21 45.46N 4.50E
Lyubertsy U.S.S.R. 25 55.38N 37.58E

M

Ma'ān Jordan 30 30.11N 35.43E
Maas r. Neth. 20 51.44N 4.42E
Macao Asia 32 22.11N113.33E
Macapá Brazil 60 0.01N 51.01W
Macdonnell Ranges mts. Australia 44 23.30S132.00E
Maceió Brazil 60 9.34S 35.47W
Mackay Australia 44 21.10S149.10E
Mackay, L. Australia 44 22.30S128.58E
Mackenzie r. Canada 50 69.20N134.00W
Mackenzie King I. Canada 50 77.30N112.00W
Mackenzie Mts. Canada 50 64.00N130.00W
Mackinaw City U.S.A. 54 45.47N 84.43W
Maclean Australia 45 29.27S153.14E
Mâcon France 21 46.18N 4.50E
Macon Ga. U.S.A. 53 32.47N 83.37W
Macquarie r. Australia 45 41.08S146.52E
Madagascar Africa 41 18.00S 47.00E
Madang P.N.G. 44 5.14S145.45E
Madawaska r. Canada 55 45.35N 76.25W
Madeira i. Atlantic Oc. 38 32.45N 17.00W
Madeira r. Brazil 60 3.50S 58.30W
Madison Wisc. U.S.A. 54 43.04N 89.22W
Madras India 31 13.05N 80.18E
Madre de Dios r. Bolivia 60 11.00S 66.30W
Madre del Sur, Sierra mts. Mexico 56 17.00N100.00W
Madre Lagoon Mexico 56 25.00N 97.30W
Madre Occidental, Sierra mts. Mexico 56 24.00N103.00W
Madre Oriental, Sierra mts. Mexico 56 24.00N 99.00W
Madrid Spain 21 40.25N 3.43W
Madurai India 31 9.55N 78.07E
Maebashi Japan 35 36.30N139.04E
Maestra, Sierra mts. Cuba 57 20.10N 76.30W
Mafia I. Tanzania 40 7.50S 39.50E
Mafikeng R.S.A. 41 25.52S 25.36E
Magadan U.S.S.R. 29 59.38N150.50E
Magadi Kenya 40 2.00S 36.18E
Magangue Colombia 60 9.14N 74.46W
Magdalena r. Colombia 60 10.56N 74.58W
Magdeburg E. Germany 22 52.08N 11.36E
Magellan's Str. Chile 61 53.00S 71.00W
Magnitogorsk U.S.S.R. 28 53.28N 59.06E
Mahajanga Madagascar 41 15.43S 46.19E
Mahia Pen. New Zealand 46 39.10S177.50E
Mahón Spain 21 39.55N 4.18E
Maidstone U.K. 18 51.17N 0.32E
Maiduguri Nigeria 38 11.53N 13.16E
Main r. W. Germany 20 50.00N 8.19E
Main Barrier Range mts. Australia 45 31.25S141.25E
Mai Ndombe l. Zaïre 40 2.00S 18.20E
Maine d. U.S.A. 55 45.00N 69.00W
Mainland i. Orkney Is. U.K. 19 59.00N 3.10W

INDEX

Mainland i. Shetland Is. U.K. 19 60.15N 1.22W
Mainz W. Germany 20 50.00N 8.16E
Maitland Australia 45 32.33S151.33E
Maizuru Japan 35 35.30N135.20E
Majorca i. Spain 21 39.35N 3.00E
Makassar Str. Indonesia 33 3.00S118.00E
Makeyevka U.S.S.R. 28 47.55N 38.05E
Makgadikgadi Salt Pan f. Botswana 41 20.50S 25.45E
Makhachkala U.S.S.R. 28 42.59N 47.30E
Makran f. Iran 30 26.30N 61.20E
Makurdi Nigeria 38 7.44N 8.35E
Malabo Equat. Guinea 40 3.45N 8.48E
Malacca, Straits of Indonesia/Malaysia 34 2.00N102.00E
Málaga Spain 21 36.43N 4.25W
Malakál Sudan 39 9.31N 31.40E
Malange Angola 41 9.36S 16.21E
Mälaren l. Sweden 24 59.30N 17.00E
Malawi Africa 41 12.00S 34.00E
Malawi, L. Africa 41 12.00S 34.30E
Malaysia Asia 33 4.00N107.00E
Maldives Indian Oc. 31 6.20N 73.00E
Mali Africa 38 16.00N 3.00W
Malin Head Rep. of Ire. 18 55.23N 7.24W
Mallaig U.K. 19 57.00N 5.50W
Malmö Sweden 24 55.35N 13.00E
Malta Europe 23 35.55N 14.25E
Malta Channel Med. Sea 23 36.20N 14.45E
Mamore r. Bolivia 60 12.00S 65.15W
Mamudju Indonesia 33 2.41S118.55E
Man, Isle of U.K. 19 54.15N 4.30W
Managua Nicaragua 57 12.06N 86.18W
Managua, L. Nicaragua 57 12.10N 86.30W
Manama Bahrain 30 26.12N 50.36E
Mananjary Madagascar 41 21.13S 48.20E
Manapouri, L. New Zealand 46 45.30S167.00E
Manaus Brazil 60 3.06S 60.00W
Manchester U.K. 19 53.30N 2.15W
Manchester Conn. U.S.A. 55 41.47N 72.31W
Manchester N.H. U.S.A. 55 42.59N 71.28W
Manchurian Plain f. China 32 45.00N125.00E
Mandalay Burma 32 21.57N 96.04E
Mangalore India 31 12.54N 74.51E
Mango Togo 38 10.23N 0.30E
Mangoche Malawi 41 14.29S 35.05E
Mangoky r. Madagascar 41 21.29S 43.41E
Mangyshlak Pen. U.S.S.R. 28 44.00N 52.30E
Manicouagane r. Canada 51 49.00N 68.13W
Manila Philippines 33 14.36N121.59E
Manistee r. U.S.A. 54 44.17N 85.45W
Manistique U.S.A. 54 45.58N 86.17W
Manitoba d. Canada 51 54.00N 96.00W
Manitoba, L. Canada 52 51.35N 99.00W
Manitou Is. U.S.A. 54 45.05N 86.05W
Manitoulin I. Canada 54 45.50N 82.15W
Manitowoc U.S.A. 54 44.04N 87.40W
Manizales Colombia 60 5.03N 75.32W
Mannheim W. Germany 20 49.30N 8.28E
Manokwari Indonesia 33 0.53S134.05E
Mansel I. Canada 51 62.00N 80.00W
Mansfield Ohio U.S.A. 54 40.46N 82.31W
Manukau Harbour est. New Zealand 46 37.10S174.00E
Manyoni Tanzania 40 5.46S 34.50E
Manzanillo Cuba 57 20.21N 77.21W
Manzhouli China 32 49.36N117.28E
Maoke Range mts. Indonesia 33 4.00S137.30E
Mappi Indonesia 33 7.06S139.23E
Maputo Mozambique 41 25.58S 32.35E
Maracaibo Venezuela 60 10.44N 71.37W
Maracaibo, L. Venezuela 57 10.00N 71.30W
Maracay Venezuela 60 10.20N 67.28W
Maradi Niger 38 13.29N 7.10E
Marahuaca, Cerro mtn. Venezuela 60 4.20N 65.30W
Marajó I. Brazil 60 1.00S 49.30W
Maran Malaysia 34 3.36N102.46E
Marañón r. Peru 60 4.00S 73.30W
Marble Bar Australia 44 21.16S119.45E
Marburg W. Germany 20 50.49N 8.36E
Marcus I. Pacific Oc. 47 24.00N153.45E
Marcy, Mt. U.S.A. 55 44.07N 73.56W
Mar del Plata Argentina 61 38.00S 57.32W
Mariana Is. Pacific Oc. 47 9.00S139.00W
Mariana Trench Pacific Oc. 9 19.00N148.00E
Maribor Yugo. 22 46.35N 15.40E
Marie-Galante i. Guadeloupe 57 15.54N 61.11W
Mariental Namibia 41 24.36S 17.59E
Marília Brazil 61 22.13S 50.20W
Marinette U.S.A. 54 45.06N 87.38W
Maringá Brazil 61 23.36S 52.02W
Marion Ohio U.S.A. 54 40.35N 83.08W
Markha r. U.S.S.R. 29 63.37N119.00E
Marmagao India 31 15.26N 73.50E
Marmara, Sea of Turkey 23 40.45N 28.15E
Maroua Cameroon 40 10.35N 14.20E
Marquesas Is. Pacific Oc. 47 9.00S139.00W
Marquette U.S.A. 54 46.33N 87.23W
Marrakesh Morocco 38 31.49N 8.00W
Marromeu Mozambique 41 18.20S 35.56E
Marsabit Kenya 40 2.20N 37.59E
Marseille France 21 43.18N 5.22E
Marshall Is. Pacific Oc. 47 8.00N172.00E

Marshfield U.S.A. 54 44.40N 90.11W
Martaban, G. of Burma 31 15.10N 96.30E
Martha's Vineyard i. U.S.A. 55 41.25N 70.35W
Martinique i. Windward Is. 57 14.40N 61.00W
Martin Pt. U.S.A. 50 70.10N143.50W
Martinsburg W.Va. U.S.A. 55 39.28N 77.59W
Marton New Zealand 46 40.04S175.25E
Maryborough Qld. Australia 44 25.32S152.36E
Maryborough Vic. Australia 45 37.05S143.47E
Maryland d. U.S.A. 53 39.00N 76.30W
Maseru Lesotho 41 29.18S 27.48E
Mashhad Iran 30 36.16N 59.34E
Mashonaland f. Zimbabwe 41 17.00S 30.00E
Masira I. Oman 30 20.30N 58.50E
Mask, Lough Rep. of Ire. 19 53.38N 9.22W
Massachusetts d. U.S.A. 55 42.48S146.30E
Massawa Ethiopia 41 15.36N 39.29E
Massif Central mts France 21 45.00N 3.30E
Masterton New Zealand 46 40.57S175.39E
Masvingo Zimbabwe 41 20.10S 30.49E
Matabeleland f. Zimbabwe 41 19.50S 28.00E
Matadi Zaïre 40 5.50S 13.36E
Matagorda B. U.S.A. 53 28.30N 96.20W
Matakana I. New Zealand 46 37.35S176.15E
Matamata New Zealand 46 37.49S175.46E
Matamoros Coahuila Mexico 56 25.33N103.15W
Matamoros Tamaulipas Mexico 56 25.50N 97.31W
Matanzas Cuba 57 23.04N 81.35W
Matapan, C. Greece 23 36.22N 22.28E
Mataura r. New Zealand 46 46.34S168.45E
Matawin r. Canada 55 46.56N 72.55W
Matehuala Mexico 56 23.40N100.40W
Matlock U.K. 18 53.08N 1.32W
Mato Grosso town Brazil 60 15.05S 59.57W
Mato Grosso, Planalto do f. Brazil 60 15.00S 55.00W
Matsue Japan 35 35.29N133.00E
Matsumoto Japan 35 36.18N137.58E
Matsuyama Japan 35 33.50N132.47E
Maui i. Hawaii U.S.A. 52 20.45N156.15W
Maumee r. U.S.A. 54 41.34N 83.41W
Maun Botswana 41 19.52S 23.40E
Mauritania Africa 38 20.00N 10.00W
Mauritius Indian Oc. 7 20.10S 58.00E
May, C. U.S.A. 55 38.55N 74.55W
Mayaguana I. Bahamas 57 22.30N 73.00W
Maya Mts. Belize 57 16.30N 89.00W
Maydena Australia 45 42.48S146.30E
Mayo d. Rep. of Ire. 18 53.47N 9.20W
Mayo Landing Canada 50 63.45N135.45W
Mayor I. New Zealand 46 37.15S176.15E
Mazatenango Guatemala 56 14.31N 91.30W
Mazatlán Mexico 56 23.11N106.25W
Mbabane Swaziland 41 26.19S 31.08E
Mbala Zambia 41 8.50S 31.24E
Mbandaka Zaïre 40 0.03N 18.28E
Mbarara Uganda 40 0.36S 30.56E
Mbeya Tanzania 41 8.54S 33.29E
Mbinda Congo 40 2.11S 12.55E
McClintock Channel Canada 51 71.20N102.00W
McClure Str. Canada 50 74.30N116.00W
McConaughy, L. U.S.A. 52 41.20N102.00W
McKinley, Mt. U.S.A. 50 63.00N151.00W
Mead, L. U.S.A. 52 36.10N114.25W
Meath d. Rep. of Ire. 18 53.35N 6.40W
Mecca Saudi Arabia 30 21.26N 39.49E
Medan Indonesia 33 3.35N 98.39E
Medellín Colombia 60 6.15N 75.36W
Medenine Tunisia 38 33.24N 10.25E
Medicine Hat Canada 52 50.03N110.41W
Medina Saudi Arabia 30 24.30N 39.35E
Mediterranean Sea 38 37.00N 15.00E
Medvezhyegorsk U.S.S.R. 25 62.56N 34.28E
Meekatharra Australia 44 26.35S118.30E
Mega Ethiopia 40 4.07N 38.16E
Meknès Morocco 38 33.53N 5.37W
Mekong r. Asia 33 10.00N106.20E
Melaka Malaysia 34 2.11N102.16E
Melaka d. Malaysia 34 2.18N102.20E
Melanesia Pacific Oc. 47 1.00N150.00E
Melbourne Australia 45 37.45S144.58E
Melilla Spain 38 35.17N 2.57W
Melitopol U.S.S.R. 22 46.51N 35.22E
Melville, C. Australia 44 14.02S144.30E
Melville I. Australia 44 11.30S131.00E
Melville I. Canada 50 75.30N110.00W
Melville Pen. Canada 51 68.00N 84.00W
Memphis Tenn. U.S.A. 53 35.05N 90.00W
Menado Indonesia 33 1.30N124.58E
Mendocino, C. U.S.A. 52 40.26N124.24W
Mendoza Argentina 61 33.00S 68.52W
Menindee Australia 45 32.23S142.30E
Menongue Angola 41 14.40S 17.41E
Mentakab Malaysia 34 3.28N102.20E
Mentawai Is. Indonesia 33 2.00S 98.00E
Merapoh Malaysia 34 4.41N102.00E
Mercedes San Luis Argentina 61 34.00S 65.00W
Mergui Archipelago is. Burma 33 12.00N 98.00E
Mérida Mexico 57 20.59N 89.39W
Meridian U.S.A. 53 32.21N 88.42W
Merowe Sudan 41 18.30N 31.49E

Mersey r. U.K. 19 53.22N 2.37W
Merseyside d. U.K. 18 53.28N 3.00W
Mersin Turkey 23 36.47N 34.37E
Mersing Malaysia 34 2.25N103.50E
Merthyr Tydfil U.K. 19 51.45N 3.23W
Mesopotamia f. Iraq 30 33.30N 44.30E
Messina Italy 23 38.13N 15.34E
Meta r. Venezuela 60 6.10N 67.30W
Metz France 20 49.07N 6.11E
Meuse r. see Maas France 20
Mexicali Mexico 56 32.26N115.30W
Mexico C. America 56 20.00N100.00W
México d. Mexico 56 19.45N 99.30W
Mexico Mo. U.S.A. 54 39.10N 91.53W
Mexico, G. of N. America 56 25.00N 90.00W
Mexico City Mexico 56 19.25N 99.10W
Mezen U.S.S.R. 25 65.50N 44.20E
Mezen r. U.S.S.R. 25 65.50N 44.20E
Miami r. U.S.A. 54 39.07N 84.43W
Miami Fla. U.S.A. 53 25.45N 80.10W
Michigan d. U.S.A. 54 44.50N 85.20W
Michigan, L. U.S.A. 54 44.00N 87.00W
Michigan City U.S.A. 54 41.43N 86.54W
Michipicoten Harbour town Canada 54 47.57N 84.55W
Michipicoten I. Canada 54 47.45N 85.45W
Michoacán d. Mexico 56 19.20N101.00W
Micronesia Pacific Oc. 47 13.00N160.00E
Middlesbrough U.K. 19 54.34N 1.13W
Mid Glamorgan d. U.K. 18 51.38N 3.25W
Midway Is. Pacific Oc. 47 28.00N178.00W
Mikkeli Finland 25 61.44N 27.15E
Milan Italy 21 45.28N 9.10E
Mildura Australia 45 34.14S142.13E
Miles City U.S.A. 52 46.24N105.48W
Milford Haven town U.K. 19 51.43N 5.02W
Milford Sound New Zealand 46 44.41S167.56E
Milk r. U.S.A. 52 47.55N106.15W
Mille Lacs, Lac des Canada 54 48.50N 90.30W
Mille Lacs L. U.S.A. 53 46.15N 93.40W
Millicent Australia 45 37.36S140.22E
Milos i. Greece 23 36.40N 24.36E
Milwaukee U.S.A. 54 43.03N 87.56W
Minatitlán Mexico 56 17.59N 94.32W
Mindanao i. Philippines 33 7.30N125.00E
Mindoro i. Philippines 33 13.00N121.00E
Minna Nigeria 38 9.39N 6.32E
Minneapolis U.S.A. 53 45.00N 93.15W
Minnesota d. U.S.A. 53 46.00N 95.00W
Miño r. Spain 21 41.50N 8.52W
Minorca i. Spain 21 40.00N 4.00E
Minot U.S.A. 52 48.16N101.19W
Minsk U.S.S.R. 22 53.51N 27.30E
Mirim, L. Brazil 61 33.10S 53.30W
Miskolc Hungary 22 48.07N 20.47E
Misoöl i. Indonesia 33 1.50S130.10E
Missinaibi r. Canada 53 50.50N 81.12W
Mississippi d. U.S.A. 53 33.00N 90.00W
Mississippi r. U.S.A. 53 28.55N 89.05W
Mississippi Delta U.S.A. 53 29.00N 89.10W
Missouri d. U.S.A. 53 39.00N 93.00W
Missouri r. U.S.A. 53 38.40N 90.20W
Mistassini, L. Canada 53 50.45N 73.40W
Misurata Libya 38 32.24N 15.04E
Mitchell r. Qld. Australia 44 15.12S141.40E
Mitchell, Mt. U.S.A. 53 35.57N 82.16W
Miyazaki Japan 35 31.58N131.50E
Mobile U.S.A. 53 30.40N 88.05W
Mobile B. U.S.A. 53 30.30N 87.50W
Moçambique town Mozambique 41 15.00S 40.47E
Moçamedes Angola 41 15.10S 12.10E
Modena Italy 21 44.39N 10.55E
Mogadishu Somali Rep. 39 2.02N 45.21E
Mogilev U.S.S.R. 22 53.54N 30.20E
Mohawk r. U.S.A. 55 42.50N 73.40W
Moisie r. Canada 51 50.15N 66.00W
Mold U.K. 18 53.10N 3.08W
Mollendo Peru 60 17.20S 72.10W
Molokai i. Hawaii U.S.A. 52 21.20N157.00W
Molopo r. R.S.A. 41 28.30S 20.07E
Moluccas is. Indonesia 33 4.00S128.00E
Mombasa Kenya 40 4.04S 39.40E
Monaco Europe 21 43.40N 7.25E
Monaghan Rep. of Ire. 18 54.15N 6.58W
Monaghan d. Rep. of Ire. 18 54.10N 7.00W
Monclova Mexico 56 26.55N101.20W
Moncton Canada 53 46.10N 64.50W
Monga Zaïre 41 4.05N 22.56E
Mongolia Asia 32 47.00N105.00E
Monongahela r. U.S.A. 54 40.26N 80.00W
Monroe Mich. U.S.A. 54 41.56N 83.21W
Monrovia Liberia 38 6.20N 10.46W
Montana d. U.S.A. 52 47.00N110.00W
Montauban France 21 44.01N 1.20E
Montauk Pt. U.S.A. 55 41.04N 71.51W
Montbéliard France 21 47.40N 6.40E
Monte Carlo Monaco 21 43.44N 7.25E
Montego Bay town Jamaica 57 18.27N 77.56W
Monterey Calif. U.S.A. 52 36.35N121.55W
Monterey B. U.S.A. 52 36.45N122.00W
Montería Colombia 60 8.45N 75.54W

Monterrey Mexico 56 25.40N100.20W
Montes Claros Brazil 60 16.45S 43.52W
Montevideo Uruguay 61 34.55S 56.10W
Montgomery Ala. U.S.A. 53 32.22N 86.20W
Mont Joli town Canada 55 48.34N 68.05W
Mont Laurier town Canada 46 46.33N 75.31W
Montluçon France 21 46.20N 2.36E
Montmagny Canada 55 46.58N 70.34W
Montpelier Vt. U.S.A. 55 44.16N 72.34W
Montpellier France 21 43.36N 3.53E
Montreal Canada 55 45.30N 73.36W
Montserrat i. Leeward Is. 57 16.45N 62.14W
Monza Italy 21 45.35N 9.16E
Moora Australia 44 30.40S116.01E
Moore, L. Australia 44 29.30S117.30E
Moosehead L. U.S.A. 55 45.45N 69.45W
Moose Jaw Canada 52 50.23N105.35W
Mopti Mali 38 14.29N 4.10W
Moradabad India 31 28.50N 78.45E
Moray Firth est. U.K. 19 57.35N 4.00W
Morden Canada 51 49.15N 98.10W
Morecambe B. U.K. 19 54.05N 3.00W
Moree Australia 45 29.29S149.53E
Morelia Mexico 56 19.40N101.11W
Morelos d. Mexico 56 18.40N 99.00W
Morgan Australia 45 34.02S139.40E
Morioka Japan 35 39.43N141.10E
Morocco Africa 38 31.00N 5.00W
Morogoro Tanzania 40 6.47S 37.40E
Morón Cuba 57 22.08N 78.39W
Morpeth U.K. 18 55.10N 1.40W
Morrinsville New Zealand 46 37.39S175.32E
Morwell Australia 45 38.14S146.25E
Moscow U.S.S.R. 25 55.45N 37.42E
Mosel r. W. Germany 20 50.23N 7.38E
Mosgiel New Zealand 46 45.53S170.22E
Moshi Tanzania 40 3.23S 37.21E
Mosjøen Norway 24 65.50N 13.10E
Mosquitia Plain f. Honduras 57 15.00N 84.00W
Mosquito Coast f. Nicaragua 57 13.00N 84.00W
Mosquitos, G. of Panama 57 9.00N 81.00W
Mossoró Brazil 60 5.10S 37.20W
Mosul Iraq 30 36.21N 43.08E
Motagua r. Guatemala 57 15.56N 87.45W
Motala Sweden 24 58.34N 15.05E
Motherwell U.K. 19 55.48N 4.00W
Motueka New Zealand 46 41.08S173.01E
Moulmein Burma 33 16.30N 97.40E
Mount Barker town W.A. Australia 44 34.36S117.37E
Mount Gambier town Australia 45 37.51S140.50E
Mount Hagen town P.N.G. 44 5.54S144.13E
Mount Isa town Australia 44 20.50S139.29E
Mount Magnet town Australia 44 28.06S117.50E
Mount Newman town Australia 44 23.20S119.40E
Mourne Mts. U.K. 19 54.10N 6.02W
Moyale Kenya 40 3.31N 39.04E
Mozambique Africa 41 18.00S 35.00E
Mozambique Channel Indian Oc. 41 19.00S 40.00E
Mpanda Tanzania 40 6.21S 31.01E
Mpika Zambia 41 11.52S 31.30E
Mtwara Tanzania 41 10.17S 40.11E
Muar Malaysia 34 2.01N102.34E
Muar r. Malaysia 34 2.20N102.32E
Muchinga Mts. Zambia 41 12.15S 31.00E
Muda r. Malaysia 34 5.35N100.20E
Mudanjiang China 32 43.36N129.42E
Mudgee Australia 45 32.37S149.36E
Mukalla S. Yemen 30 14.34N 49.09E
Mulhacén mtn. Spain 21 37.04N 3.22W
Mulhouse France 21 47.45N 7.21E
Mull i. U.K. 19 56.28N 5.56W
Mullingar Rep. of Ire. 18 53.31N 7.21W
Mull of Galloway c. U.K. 19 54.39N 4.52W
Multan Pakistan 31 30.10N 71.36E
Mungbere Zaïre 40 2.40N 28.25E
Munich W. Germany 21 48.08N 11.35E
Munku Sardyk mtn. Mongolia 32 51.45N100.30E
Münster W. Germany 20 51.58N 7.37E
Muonio r. Finland/Sweden 24 67.13N 23.30E
Murallón mtn. Argentina/Chile 61 49.48S 73.26W
Murchison r. Australia 44 27.30S114.10E
Murcia Spain 21 37.59N 1.08W
Murmansk U.S.S.R. 25 68.59N 33.08E
Murom U.S.S.R. 25 55.04N 42.04E
Muroran Japan 35 42.21N140.59E
Murray r.S.A. Australia 45 35.23S139.20E
Murray Bridge town Australia 45 35.10S139.17E
Murrumbidgee r. Australia 45 34.38S143.10E
Murupara New Zealand 46 38.27S176.42E
Murwillumbah Australia 45 28.20S153.24E
Murzuq Libya 38 25.56N 13.57E
Musala mtn. Bulgaria 23 42.11N 23.35E
Muscat Oman 30 23.36N 58.37E
Musgrave Ranges mts. Australia 44 26.30S131.10E
Muskegon U.S.A. 54 43.13N 86.15W
Muskegon r. U.S.A. 54 43.15N 86.00W
Muskingum r. U.S.A. 54 39.25N 81.25W
Muskogee U.S.A. 53 35.45N 95.21W
Muswellbrook Australia 45 32.17S150.55E
Mutare Zimbabwe 41 18.50S 32.40E

INDEX

Muzaffarpur India 31 26.07N 85.23E
Mvuma Zimbabwe 41 19.16S 30.40E
Mwanza Tanzania 40 2.30S 32.54E
Mweru, L. Zäire/Zambia 41 9.00S 28.40E
Myitkyina Burma 32 25.24N 97.25E
Myösa l. Norway 24 60.50N 10.50E
Mysore India 31 12.18N 76.37E
Mytishchi U.S.S.R. 25 55.45N 37.47E

N

Naas Rep. of Ire. 19 53.13N 6.41W
Naberezhnyye Chelny U.S.S.R. 28 55.42N 52.20E
Nagano Japan 35 36.39N138.10E
Nagaoka Japan 35 37.30N138.50E
Nagapattinam India 31 10.45N 79.50E
Nagasaki Japan 35 32.45N129.52E
Nagercoil India 31 8.11N 77.30E
Nagoya Japan 35 35.08N136.53E
Nagpur India 31 21.10N 79.12E
Nain Canada 51 56.30N 61.45W
Nairobi Kenya 40 1.17S 36.50E
Nakhodka U.S.S.R. 29 42.53N132.54E
Naknek U.S.A. 50 58.45N157.00W
Nakuru Kenya 40 0.16S 36.04E
Nalut Libya 38 31.53N 10.59E
Namangan U.S.S.R. 28 40.59N 71.41E
Namib Desert Namibia 41 23.30S 15.00E
Namibia Africa 41 22.00S 17.00E
Nampula Mozambique 41 15.09S 39.14E
Namur Belgium 20 50.28N 4.52E
Nanaimo Canada 52 49.08N123.58W
Nanchang China 32 28.37N115.57E
Nancy France 21 48.42N 6.12E
Nanga Parbat mtn. Jammu & Kashmir 31 35.10N 74.35E
Nanjing China 32 32.02N118.52E
Nanning China 32 22.48N108.18E
Nantes France 21 47.14N 1.35W
Nantucket I. U.S.A. 55 41.16N 70.00W
Nantucket Sd. U.S.A. 55 41.30N 70.15W
Napier New Zealand 46 39.29S176.58E
Naples Italy 23 40.50N 14.14E
Naracoorte Australia 45 36.58S140.46E
Narayanganj Bangla. 31 23.36N 90.28E
Narbonne France 21 43.11N 3.00E
Nares Str. Canada 51 79.00N 75.00W
Narodnaya mtn. U.S.S.R. 28 65.00N 61.00E
Narooma Australia 45 36.15S150.06E
Narrabri Australia 45 30.20S149.49E
Narrandera Australia 45 34.36S146.34E
Narran L. Australia 45 29.40S147.25E
Narrogin Australia 44 32.58S117.10E
Narromine Australia 45 32.17S148.20E
Narvik Norway 24 68.26N 17.25E
Naryan Mar U.S.S.R. 28 67.37N 53.02E
Nashville U.S.A. 53 36.10N 86.50W
Näsijärvi l. Finland 24 61.30N 23.50E
Nasik India 31 20.00N 73.52E
Nassau Bahamas 57 25.03N 77.20W
Nasser, L. Egypt/Sudan 39 22.40N 32.00E
Natal Brazil 60 5.46S 35.15W
Natal d. R.S.A. 41 28.30S 30.30E
Natron, L. Tanzania 40 2.18S 36.05E
Nauru Pacific Oc. 47 0.31S166.56E
Navan Rep. of Ire. 18 53.39N 6.42W
Navlya U.S.S.R. 22 52.51N 34.30E
Navojoa Mexico 56 27.06N109.26W
Navrongo Ghana 38 10.51N 1.03W
Náxos i. Greece 23 37.03N 25.30E
Nayarit d. Mexico 56 21.30N104.00W
Nazas r. Mexico 56 25.34N103.25W
N'Djamena Chad 38 12.10N 14.59E
Ndola Zambia 41 12.58S 28.39E
Neagh, Lough U.K. 19 54.36N 6.25W
Nebraska d. U.S.A. 52 41.30N100.00W
Nebrodi Mts. Italy 23 37.53N 14.32E
Neches r. U.S.A. 53 29.55N 93.50W
Negelli Ethiopia 40 5.20N 39.36E
Negeri Sembilan d. Malaysia 34 2.45N102.10E
Negoiu mtn. Romania 22 45.36N 24.32E
Negra, C. Peru 60 6.06S 81.09W
Negro r. Argentina 61 41.00S 62.48W
Negro r. Brazil 60 3.30S 60.00W
Negros i. Philippines 33 10.00N123.00E
Neijiang China 32 29.29N105.03E
Neiva Colombia 60 2.58N 75.15W
Nejd d. Saudi Arabia 30 25.00N 45.00E
Nellore India 31 14.29N 80.00E
Nelson Canada 50 49.29N117.17W
Nelson r. Canada 51 57.00N 93.20W
Nelson New Zealand 46 41.18S173.17E
Nelson U.S.A. 52 35.30N113.16W
Nelson, C. Australia 45 38.27S141.35E
Nelspruit R.S.A. 41 25.27S 30.58E
Nemuro Japan 35 43.22N145.36E
Nemuro kaikyo str. Japan 35 44.40N145.50E
Nenana U.S.A. 50 64.35N149.20W
Nene r. U.K. 19 52.49N 0.12E
Nenggiri r. Malaysia 34 5.23N102.00E
Nepal Asia 31 29.00N 83.00E

Ness, Loch U.K. 19 57.16N 4.30W
Netherlands Europe 20 52.10N 6.00E
Netherlands Antilles S. America 57 12.30N 69.00W
Neuquén Argentina 61 38.55S 68.55W
Neuse r. U.S.A 53 35.04N 77.04W
Nevada d. U.S.A. 52 39.00N117.00W
Nevers France 21 47.00N 3.09E
New Amsterdam Guyana 60 6.18N 57.00W
Newark N.J. U.S.A. 55 40.44N 74.11W
New Bedford U.S.A. 55 41.38N 70.55W
Newberry Mich. U.S.A. 54 46.22N 85.30W
New Britain i. P.N.G. 44 6.00S150.00E
New Brunswick d. Canada 51 47.00N 66.00W
New Brunswick U.S.A. 55 40.29N 74.27W
Newburgh U.S.A. 55 41.30N 74.00W
New Caledonia i. Pacific Oc. 47 22.00S165.00E
Newcastle Australia 45 32.55S151.46E
Newcastle upon Tyne U.K. 19 54.58N 1.36W
New Delhi India 31 28.37N 77.13E
New England Range mts. Australia 45 30.00S152.00E
Newfoundland d. Canada 51 55.00N 60.00W
Newfoundland i. Canada 51 48.30N 56.00W
New Guinea i. Austa. 44 6.00S142.00E
New Hampshire d. U.S.A. 55 43.50N 71.45W
New Hanover i. Pacific Oc. 44 2.00S150.00E
New Haven U.S.A. 55 41.18N 72.55W
New Ireland i. P.N.G. 44 2.30S151.30E
New Jersey d. U.S.A. 55 39.50N 74.45W
New London Conn. U.S.A. 55 41.21N 72.06W
New Mexico d. U.S.A. 52 34.00N106.00W
New Norfolk Australia 45 42.46S147.02E
New Orleans U.S.A. 53 30.00N 90.03W
New Plymouth New Zealand 46 39.03S174.04E
Newport U.K. 18 50.43N 1.18W
Newport Gwent U.K. 19 51.34N 2.59W
Newport R.I. U.S.A. 55 41.30N 71.19W
Newport News U.S.A. 53 36.59N 76.26W
New Providence i. Bahamas 57 25.03N 77.25W
New Siberian Is. U.S.S.R. 29 76.00N144.00E
New South Wales d. Australia 45 33.45S147.00E
Newtown St. Boswells U.K. 18 55.35N 2.40W
New York U.S.A. 55 40.40N 73.50W
New York d. U.S.A. 55 42.50N 75.50W
New Zealand Austa. 46 41.00S175.00E
Ngaoundéré Cameroon 40 7.20N 13.35E
Ngaruawahia New Zealand 46 37.40S175.09E
Ngaruroro r. New Zealand 46 39.34S176.54E
Ngauruhoe mtn. New Zealand 46 39.10S175.35E
N'Guigmi Niger 38 14.00N 13.06E
Nguru Nigeria 40 12.53N 10.30E
Nha Trang Vietnam 33 12.15N109.10E
Niagara Falls town U.S.A. 55 43.06N 79.04W
Niamey Niger 38 13.32N 2.05E
Nicaragua C. America 57 13.00N 85.00W
Nicaragua, L. Nicaragua 57 11.30N 85.30W
Nice France 21 43.42N 7.16E
Nicobar Is. India 31 8.00N 94.00E
Nicosia Cyprus 23 35.11N 33.23E
Nicoya, G. of Costa Rica 57 9.30N 85.00W
Nicoya Pen. Costa Rica 57 10.30N 85.30W
Niger Africa 38 17.00N 9.30E
Niger r. Nigeria 38 4.15N 6.05E
Niger Delta Nigeria 38 5.30N 6.30E
Nigeria Africa 38 9.00N 7.30E
Niigata Japan 35 37.58N139.02E
Nikolayev U.S.S.R. 22 46.57N 32.00E
Nikolayevsk-na-Amur U.S.S.R. 29 53.20N140.44E
Nikopol U.S.S.R. 22 47.34N 34.25E
Nile r. Egypt 39 31.30N 30.25E
Nilgiri Hills India 31 11.30N 77.30E
Nîmes France 21 43.50N 4.21E
Ninety Mile Beach f. Australia 45 38.07S147.30E
Ninety Mile Beach f. New Zealand 46 34.45S173.00E
Ningbo China 32 29.56N121.32E
Niobrara r. U.S.A. 52 42.45N 98.10W
Nioro Mali 38 15.12N 9.35W
Nipigon Canada 54 49.02N 88.26W
Nipigon, L. Canada 53 48.40N 88.30W
Nipissing, L. Canada 54 46.15N 79.45W
Niš Yugo. 22 43.20N 21.54E
Niterói Brazil 61 22.45S 43.06W
Nith r. U.K. 19 55.00N 3.35W
Nizamabad India 31 18.40N 78.05E
Nizhneudinsk U.S.S.R. 29 54.55N 99.00E
Nizhnevartovsk U.S.S.R. 28 60.57N 76.40E
Nizhniy Tagil U.S.S.R. 28 58.00N 60.00E
Nkhotakota Malawi 41 12.55S 34.19E
Nobeoka Japan 35 32.36N131.40E
Nogales Mexico 56 31.20N111.00W
Nome U.S.A. 50 64.30N165.30W
Nordvik U.S.S.R. 29 73.40N110.50E
Norfolk d. U.K. 18 52.40N 1.00E
Norfolk Va. U.S.A. 53 36.54N 76.18W
Norfolk I. Pacific Oc. 47 28.58S168.03E
Norilsk U.S.S.R. 29 69.21N 88.02E
Normandy f. France 21 49.00N 0.00
Normanton Australia 44 17.40S141.05E
Norman Wells Canada 50 65.19N126.46W
Norris L. U.S.A. 53 36.20N 83.55W
Norristown U.S.A. 55 40.07N 75.20W

Norrköping Sweden 24 58.35N 16.10E
Norseman Australia 44 32.15S121.47E
Northallerton U.K. 18 54.20N 1.26W
Northam Australia 44 31.41S116.40E
North America 8
Northampton U.K. 19 52.14N 0.54W
Northamptonshire d. U.K. 18 52.18N 0.55W
North Bay town Canada 55 46.20N 79.28W
North C. New Zealand 46 34.28S173.00E
North Canadian r. U.S.A. 53 35.30N 95.45W
North Cape Norway 24 71.10N 25.45E
North Carolina d. U.S.A. 53 35.30N 79.00W
North Channel str. Canada 54 46.05N 83.00W
North Channel U.K. 19 55.15N 5.52W
North China Plain f. China 32 35.00N115.30E
North Dakota d. U.S.A. 52 47.00N100.00W
North Dvina r. U.S.S.R. 28 64.40N 40.50E
Northern Ireland d. U.K. 19 54.40N 6.45W
Northern Territory d. Australia 44 20.00S133.00E
North Frisian Is. W. Germany 20 54.30N 8.00E
North German Plain f. W. Germany 20 53.00N 11.00E
North I. New Zealand 46 39.00S175.00E
North Korea Asia 32 40.00N127.00E
North Platte U.S.A. 52 41.09N100.45W
North Platte r. U.S.A. 52 41.09N100.55W
North Pt. U.S.A. 54 45.02N 83.17W
North Sea Europe 20 57.00N 2.00E
North Sporades is. Greece 23 39.00N 24.00E
North Taranaki Bight b. New Zealand 46 38.45S174.15E
North Uist i. U.K. 19 57.35N 7.20W
Northumberland d. U.K. 18 55.20N 2.00W
Northway U.S.A. 50 62.58N142.00W
North West Highlands U.K. 19 57.30N 5.15W
North West Territories d. Canada 51 66.00N 95.00W
North Yorkshire d. U.K. 18 54.14N 1.14W
Norton Sound b. U.S.A. 50 63.50N164.00W
Norway Europe 24 65.00N 13.00E
Norwich U.K. 19 52.38N 1.17E
Nossob r. R.S.A./Botswana 41 26.54S 20.39E
Nottingham U.K. 19 52.57N 1.10W
Nottinghamshire d. U.K. 18 53.10N 1.00W
Nouadhibou Mauritania 38 20.54N 17.01W
Nouakchott Mauritania 38 18.09N 15.58W
Noumea New Caledonia 47 22.16S166.27E
Novara Italy 21 45.27N 8.37E
Nova Scotia d. Canada 51 45.00N 64.00W
Novaya Siberia i. U.S.S.R. 29 75.20N148.00E
Novaya Zemlya i. U.S.S.R. 28 74.00N 56.00E
Novgorod U.S.S.R. 25 58.30N 31.20E
Novi Sad Yugo. 22 45.16N 19.52E
Novokazalinsk U.S.S.R. 28 45.48N 62.06E
Novokuznetsk U.S.S.R. 28 53.45N 87.12E
Novorossiysk U.S.S.R. 28 44.44N 37.46E
Novosibirsk U.S.S.R. 28 55.04N 82.55E
Novy Port U.S.S.R. 28 67.38N 72.33E
Nowra Australia 45 34.54S150.36E
Nubian Desert Sudan 39 21.00N 34.00E
Nueces r. U.S.A. 53 27.55N 97.30W
Nueva Gerona Cuba 57 21.53N 82.49W
Nuevitas Cuba 57 21.34N 77.18W
Nuevo Laredo Mexico 56 27.30N 99.30W
Nuevo León d. Mexico 56 26.00N 99.00W
Nu Jiang r. see Salween r. China 32
Nuku'alofa Tonga 47 21.07S175.12W
Nullarbor Plain f. Australia 44 31.30S128.00E
Nunivak I. U.S.A. 50 60.00N166.30W
Nurnberg W. Germany 20 49.27N 11.05E
Nuuk see Godthåb Greenland 51
Nyala Sudan 41 12.01N 24.50E
Nylstroom R.S.A. 41 24.42S 28.24E
Nymagee Australia 45 32.05S146.20E
Nyngan Australia 45 31.34S147.14E

O

Oahe Resr. U.S.A. 52 45.45N100.20W
Oahu i. Hawaii U.S.A. 52 21.30N158.00W
Oakland Calif. U.S.A. 52 37.50N122.15W
Oakville Canada 55 43.27N 79.41W
Oamaru New Zealand 46 45.07S170.58E
Oaxaca Mexico 56 17.05N 96.41W
Oaxaca d. Mexico 56 17.30N 97.00W
Ob r. U.S.S.R. 28 66.50N 69.00E
Ob, G. of U.S.S.R. 28 68.30N 74.00E
Oban U.K. 19 56.26N 5.28W
Obbia Somali Rep. 39 5.20N 48.30E
Obihiro Japan 35 42.55N143.00E
Occidental, Cordillera mts. Colombia 60 6.00N 76.15W
Ocean I. Pacific Oc. 47 0.52S169.35E
Oceania 9
Ocotlán Mexico 56 20.21N102.42W
October Revolution i. U.S.S.R. 29 79.30N 96.00E
Odádhahraun mts. Iceland 24 65.00N 17.30W
Odawara Japan 35 35.20N139.08E
Odense Denmark 24 55.24N 10.25E
Oder r. Poland 22 53.30N 14.26E
Odessa Tex. U.S.A. 52 31.50N102.23W
Odessa U.S.S.R. 22 46.30N 30.46E
Ofanto r. Italy 23 41.22N 16.12E
Offaly d. Rep. of Ire. 18 53.15N 7.30W

Ogaki Japan 35 35.25N136.36E
Ogbomosho Nigeria 38 8.05N 4.11E
Ogden Utah U.S.A. 52 41.14N111.59W
Ogdensburg U.S.A. 55 44.42N 75.31W
Ogeechee r. U.S.A. 53 32.54N 81.05W
Ogója Nigeria 40 6.40N 8.45E
Ogoki r. Canada 53 51.00N 84.30W
Ogooué r. Gabon 40 1.00S 9.05E
Ohio d. U.S.A. 54 40.10N 82.20W
Ohio r. U.S.A. 53 37.07N 89.10W
Oil City U.S.A. 55 41.26N 79.44W
Oise r. France 21 49.00N 2.10E
Oka r. U.S.S.R. 25 56.09N 43.00E
Okahandja Namibia 41 21.59S 16.58E`
Okanogan r. U.S.A. 52 47.45N120.05W
Okavango Basin f. Botswana 41 19.30S 22.30E
Okayama Japan 35 34.40N133.54E
Okazaki Japan 35 34.58N137.10E
Okeechobee, L. U.S.A. 53 27.00N 80.45W
Okefenokee Swamp f. U.S.A. 53 30.40N 82.40W
Okha U.S.S.R. 29 53.35N142.50E
Okhotsk U.S.S.R. 29 59.20N143.15E
Okhotsk, Sea of U.S.S.R. 29 55.00N150.00E
Oki gunto is. Japan 35 36.10N133.10E
Oklahoma d. U.S.A. 53 35.00N 97.00W
Oklahoma City U.S.A. 53 35.28N 97.33W
Öland i. Sweden 24 56.50N 16.50E
Olbia Italy 21 40.55N 9.29E
Old Crow Canada 50 67.34N139.43W
Oldenburg W. Germany 20 53.08N 8.13E
Oldham U.K. 19 53.33N 2.08W
Olean U.S.A. 55 42.05N 78.26W
Olekma r. U.S.S.R. 29 60.20N120.30E
Olekminsk U.S.S.R. 29 60.25N120.00E
Olenek U.S.S.R. 29 68.38N112.15E
Olenek r. U.S.S.R. 29 73.00N120.00E
Olenekskiy G. U.S.S.R. 29 74.00N120.00E
Olga U.S.S.R. 29 43.46N135.14E
Olomouc Czech. 22 49.38N 17.15E
Olsztyn Poland 22 53.48N 20.29E
Olympia U.S.A. 52 47.03N122.53W
Olympus, Mt. Greece 23 40.04N 22.20E
Olympus, Mt. U.S.A. 52 47.49N123.42W
Omaha U.S.A. 53 41.15N 96.00W
Oman Asia 30 22.00N 57.00E
Oman, G. of Asia 30 25.00N 58.00E
Omdurman Sudan 41 15.37N 32.59E
Omolon r. U.S.S.R. 29 68.50N158.30E
Omono r. Japan 35 39.44N140.05E
Omsk U.S.S.R. 28 55.00N 73.22E
Omuta Japan 35 33.02N130.26E
Onega U.S.S.R. 25 63.59N 38.11E
Onega, L. U.S.S.R. 25 62.00N 35.30E
Oneida L. U.S.A. 55 43.13N 75.55W
Oneonta U.S.A. 55 42.28N 75.04W
Onitsha Nigeria 38 6.10N 6.47E
Ontaki san mtn. Japan 35 35.55N137.29E
Ontario d. Canada 51 50.00N 85.00W
Ontario, L. N. America 55 43.40N 78.00W
Ontonagon U.S.A. 54 46.52N 89.18W
Oporto Portugal 21 41.09N 8.37W
Opotiki New Zealand 46 38.00S177.18E
Oradea Romania 22 47.03N 21.55E
Oran Algeria 38 35.45N 0.38W
Orange Australia 45 33.19S149.10E
Orange r. R.S.A. 41 28.38S 16.38E
Orange, C. Brazil 60 4.25N 51.32W
Orange Free State d. R.S.A. 41 28.00S 28.00E
Orbost Australia 45 37.42S148.30E
Orchila i. Venezuela 57 11.52N 66.10W
Ord r. Australia 44 15.30S128.30E
Ordzhonikidze U.S.S.R. 28 43.02N 44.43E
Örebro Sweden 24 59.17N 5.13E
Oregon d. U.S.A. 52 44.00N120.00W
Orekhovo-Zuyevo U.S.S.R. 25 55.47N 39.00E
Orekhovo-Zuyevo U.S.S.R. 28 55.47N 39.00E
Orel U.S.S.R. 22 52.58N 36.04E
Ore Mts. E. Germany 22 50.30N 12.50E
Orenburg U.S.S.R. 28 51.50N 55.00E
Ore Sund str. Denmark 24 56.00N 12.30E
Oriental, Cordillera mts. Colombia 60 6.00N 74.00W
Orinoco r. Venezuela 60 9.00N 61.30W
Orinoco Delta f. Venezuela 60 9.00N 61.30W
Oristano Italy 21 39.53N 8.36E
Orizaba Mexico 56 18.51N 97.08W
Orkney Is. U.K. 19 59.00N 3.00W
Orlando U.S.A. 53 28.33N 81.21W
Orléans France 21 47.54N 1.54E
Orsha U.S.S.R. 25 54.30N 30.23E
Orsk U.S.S.R. 28 51.13N 58.35E
Oruro Bolivia 60 18.05S 67.00W
Osaka Japan 35 34.40N135.30E
Osh U.S.S.R. 28 40.37N 72.49E
Oshawa Canada 55 43.53N 78.51W
Oshogbo Nigeria 38 7.50N 4.35E
Oslo Norway 24 59.56N 10.45E
Oslo Fjord est. Norway 24 59.30N 10.30E
Osnabrück W. Germany 20 52.17N 8.03E
Ossa, Mt. Australia 45 41.52S146.04E
Ostend Belgium 20 51.33N 2.55E

INDEX

Östersund Sweden **24** 63.10N 14.40E
Ostrava Czech. **22** 49.50N 18.15E
Osumi gunto *is.* Japan **35** 30.30N131.00E
Osumi kaikyo *str.* Japan **35** 31.30N131.00E
Oswego U.S.A. **55** 43.27N 76.31W
Otago Pen. New Zealand **46** 45.48S170.45E
Otaru Japan **35** 43.14N140.59E
Otranto, Str. of Med. Sea **23** 40.10N 19.00E
Ottawa Canada **55** 45.25N 75.43W
Ottawa *r.* Canada **55** 45.23N 73.55W
Ottawa Is. Canada **51** 59.50N 80.00W
Otway, C. Australia **45** 38.51S143.34E
Ouachita *r.* U.S.A. **53** 33.10N 92.10W
Ouachita Mts. U.S.A. **53** 34.40N 94.30W
Ouagadougou Burkina Faso **38** 12.20N 1.40W
Ouargla Algeria **38** 32.00N 5.16E
Oudtshoorn R.S.A. **41** 33.35S 22.11E
Oujda Morocco **38** 34.41N 1.45W
Oulu Finland **24** 65.02N 25.27E
Oulujärvi *l.* Finland **25** 64.30N 27.00E
Ouse *r.* Humber. U.K. **19** 53.41N 0.42W
Outer Hebrides *is.* U.K. **19** 57.40N 7.35W
Outjo Namibia **41** 20.08S 16.08E
Ouyen Australia **45** 35.06S142.22E
Oviedo Spain **21** 43.21N 5.50W
Ovruch U.S.S.R. **22** 51.20N 28.50E
Owen Falls Uganda **39** 0.30N 33.05E
Owen Sound *town* Canada **54** 44.34N 80.56W
Owen Stanley Range *mts.* P.N.G. **44** 9.30S148.00E
Oxford U.K. **19** 51.48N 1.15W
Oxfordshire *d.* U.K. **18** 51.46N 1.20W
Oymyakon U.S.S.R. **29** 63.30N142.44E
Oyster B. Australia **45** 42.10S148.10E
Ozark Plateau U.S.A. **53** 36.00N 93.35W

P

Paamiut *see* Frederikshåb Greenland **51**
Pachuca Mexico **56** 20.10N 98.44W
Pacific Ocean **47**
Padang Indonesia **33** 0.55S100.21E
Padang, Pulau *i.* Indonesia **34** 1.15N102.20E
Padang Besar Malaysia **34** 6.39N100.16E
Padre I. U.S.A. **53** 27.00N 97.20W
Padua Italy **21** 45.27N 11.52E
Paeroa New Zealand **46** 37.23S175.41E
Pahang *d.* Malaysia **34** 3.30N102.30E
Pahang *r.* Malaysia **34** 3.30N103.24E
Paihia New Zealand **46** 35.16S174.05E
Päijänne *l.* Finland **24** 61.30N 25.30E
Painesville U.S.A. **54** 41.43N 81.15W
Paisley U.K. **19** 55.50N 4.26W
Pakanbaru Indonesia **33** 0.33N101.20E
Pakistan Asia **31** 28.00N 67.00E
Pakse Laos **33** 15.05N105.50E
Pakwach Uganda **39** 2.17N 31.28E
Palana U.S.S.R. **29** 59.05N159.59E
Palawan *i.* Philippines **33** 9.30N118.30E
Palembang Indonesia **33** 2.59S104.50E
Palencia Spain **21** 42.01N 4.34W
Palermo Italy **23** 38.09N 13.22E
Palliser, C. New Zealand **46** 41.35S175.15E
Palma Spain **21** 39.36N 2.39E
Palmas, C. Liberia **38** 4.30N 7.55W
Palmerston North New Zealand **46** 40.20S175.39E
Palmira Colombia **60** 3.33N 76.17W
Pamir *mts.* U.S.S.R. **28** 38.00N 73.30E
Pampas *f.* Argentina **61** 35.00S 63.00W
Pamplona Spain **21** 42.49N 1.39W
Panama C. America **57** 9.00N 80.00W
Panama, G. of Panama **57** 8.30N 79.00W
Panama City Panama **57** 8.57N 79.30W
Panay *i.* Philippines **33** 11.10N122.30E
Pangnirtung Canada **51** 66.05N 65.45W
Papeete Tahiti **47** 17.32S149.34W
Paphos Cyprus **23** 34.45N 32.25E
Papua, G. of P.N.G. **44** 8.50S145.00E
Papua New Guinea Oceania **44** 6.00S144.00E
Paraguay *r.* Argentina **61** 27.30S 58.50W
Paraguay S. America **61** 23.00S 58.00W
Parakou Benin **38** 9.23N 2.40E
Paramaribo Surinam **60** 5.50N 55.14W
Paraná Argentina **61** 31.45S 60.30W
Paraná *r.* Argentina **61** 34.00S 58.30W
Paraparaumu New Zealand **46** 40.55S175.00E
Paris France **21** 48.52N 2.20E
Parkersburg U.S.A. **55** 39.17N 81.33W
Parkes Australia **45** 33.10S148.13E
Park Falls *town* U.S.A. **54** 45.57N 90.28W
Parma Italy **21** 44.48N 10.18E
Parnaíba *r.* Brazil **60** 3.00S 42.00W
Parnassós *mtn.* Greece **23** 38.33N 22.35E
Pärnu U.S.S.R. **24** 58.28N 24.30E
Paroo *r.* Australia **45** 31.30S143.34E
Parral Mexico **56** 26.58N105.40W
Parramatta Australia **45** 33.50S150.57E
Parry, C. Greenland Canada **51** 76.50N 71.00W
Parry Is. Canada **51** 76.00N102.00W
Parry Sound *town* Canada **54** 45.21N 80.03W
Pasadena Calif. U.S.A. **52** 34.10N118.09W
Pasir Mas Malaysia **34** 6.02N102.08E

Pasir Puteh Malaysia **34** 5.50N102.24E
Paso de Bermejo *f.* Argentina **61** 32.50S 70.00W
Paso Socompa *f.* Chile **61** 24.27S 68.18W
Passau W. Germany **20** 48.35N 13.28E
Pasto Colombia **60** 1.12N 77.17W
Patagonia *f.* Argentina **61** 45.00S 68.00W
Paterson U.S.A. **55** 40.55N 74.10W
Patna India **31** 25.37N 85.12E
Patos, L. Brazil **61** 31.00S 51.10W
Pátras Greece **23** 38.15N 21.45E
Patras, G. of Med. Sea **23** 38.15N 21.35E
Pattani Thailand **34** 6.53N101.15E
Pattani *r.* Thailand **34** 6.54N101.15E
Patuca *r.* Honduras **57** 15.50N 84.18W
Pau France **21** 43.18N 0.22W
Pavia Italy **21** 45.10N 9.10E
Pavlodar U.S.S.R. **28** 52.21N 76.59E
Pawtucket U.S.A. **55** 41.53N 71.23W
Peace *r.* Canada **50** 59.00N111.26W
Peace River *town* Canada **50** 56.15N117.18W
Peale, Mt. U.S.A. **52** 38.26N109.14W
Pearl *r.* U.S.A. **53** 30.15N 89.25W
Pechenga U.S.S.R. **25** 69.28N 31.04E
Pechora *r.* U.S.S.R. **28** 68.10N 54.00E
Pechora G. U.S.S.R. **28** 69.00N 56.00E
Pecos *r.* U.S.A. **52** 29.45N101.25W
Pécs Hungary **22** 46.05N 18.14E
Peel *r.* Canada **50** 68.13N135.00W
Pegasus B. New Zealand **46** 43.15S173.00E
Pegu Burma **33** 17.18N 96.31E
Peipus, L. U.S.S.R. **25** 58.30N 27.30E
Pekan Malaysia **34** 3.30N103.24E
Pelabuhan Kelang Malaysia **34** 2.59N101.24E
Pelee, Pt. Canada **54** 41.45N 82.09W
Pelly *r.* Canada **50** 62.50N137.35W
Pelotas Brazil **61** 31.45S 52.20W
Pematangsiantar Indonesia **33** 2.59N 99.01E
Pemba Mozambique **41** 13.00S 40.30E
Pemba *i.* Tanzania **40** 5.00S 39.45E
Pennines *hills* U.K. **19** 55.40N 2.20W
Pennsylvania *d.* U.S.A. **55** 41.00N 75.45W
Penny Highland *mtn.* Canada **51** 67.10N 66.50W
Penobscot *r.* U.S.A. **55** 44.34N 68.48W
Penonome Panama **57** 8.30N 80.20W
Pensacola U.S.A. **53** 30.30N 87.12W
Penticton Canada **50** 49.29N119.38W
Pentland Firth *str.* U.K. **19** 58.40N 3.00W
Penza U.S.S.R. **28** 53.11N 45.00E
Penzance U.K. **19** 50.07N 5.32W
Penzhina, G. of U.S.S.R. **29** 61.00N163.00E
Peoria Ill. U.S.A. **54** 40.43N 89.38W
Perak *d.* Malaysia **34** 4.55N101.10E
Perak *r.* Malaysia **34** 3.57N100.53E
Pereira Colombia **60** 4.47N 75.46W
Peribonca *r.* Canada **53** 48.50N 72.00W
Périgueux France **21** 45.12N 0.44E
Perim *i.* S. Yemen **30** 12.40N 43.24E
Perlis *d.* Malaysia **34** 6.30N100.15E
Perm U.S.S.R. **28** 58.01N 56.10E
Perpignan France **21** 42.42N 2.54E
Perth Australia **45** 31.58S115.49E
Perth U.K. **19** 56.24N 3.28W
Perth Amboy U.S.A. **55** 40.32N 74.17W
Peru S. America **60** 10.00S 75.00W
Peru Ind. U.S.A. **54** 40.45N 86.04W
Peru-Chile Trench Pacific Oc. **61** 23.00S 71.30W
Perugia Italy **22** 43.06N 12.24E
Pescara Italy **22** 42.28N 14.13E
Peshawar Pakistan **31** 34.01N 71.40E
Petaling Jaya Malaysia **34** 3.06N101.40E
Petatlán Mexico **56** 17.31N101.16W
Peterborough S.A. Australia **45** 33.00S138.51E
Peterborough Canada **55** 44.19N 78.20W
Petropavlovsk U.S.S.R. **28** 54.53N 69.13E
Petropavlovsk Kamchatskiy U.S.S.R. **29** 53.03N158.43E
Petrópolis Brazil **61** 22.30S 43.02W
Petrovsk Zabaykal'skiy U.S.S.R. **29** 51.20N108.55E
Petrozavodsk U.S.S.R. **25** 61.46N 34.19E
Philadelphia Penn. U.S.A. **55** 40.00N 75.10W
Philippines Asia **33** 12.00N125.00E
Philippine Sea Pacific Oc. **47** 20.00N135.00E
Philippine Trench Pacific Oc. **9** 8.45N127.20E
Phnom Penh Kampuchea **33** 11.35N104.55E
Phoenix Ariz. U.S.A. **52** 33.30N111.55W
Phoenix Is. Pacific Oc. **47** 3.30S172.00W
Phuket Thailand **33** 8.00N 98.28E
Plave *r.* Italy **21** 45.33N 12.45E
Pic *r.* Canada **54** 48.35N 86.17W
Pickwick L. *resr.* U.S.A. **53** 35.00N 88.10W
Picton New Zealand **46** 41.17S174.02E
Piedras Negras Mexico **56** 28.40N100.32W
Pielinen *l.* Finland **25** 63.20N 29.50E
Pierre U.S.A. **52** 44.23N100.20W
Pietermaritzburg R.S.A. **41** 29.36S 30.23E
Pikes Peak *mtn.* U.S.A. **52** 38.50N105.03W
Pilcomayo *r.* Argentina/Paraguay **61** 25.15S 57.43W
Pinang, Pulau *i.* Malaysia **34** 5.26N100.14E
Pinar del Rio Cuba **57** 22.24N 83.42W

Pindus Mts. Albania/Greece **23** 39.40N 21.00E
Pines, I. of Cuba **57** 21.40N 82.40W
Pinnaroo Australia **45** 35.18S140.54E
Piqua U.S.A. **54** 40.08N 84.14W
Piracicaba Brazil **61** 22.20S 47.40W
Piraeus Greece **23** 37.56N 23.38E
Pisa Italy **21** 43.43N 10.24E
Pitcairn I. Pacific Oc. **47** 25.04S130.06W
Pittsburgh U.S.A. **54** 40.26N 80.00W
Piura Peru **60** 5.15S 80.38W
Plain of Lombardy *f.* Italy **21** 45.10N 9.00E
Platinum U.S.A. **50** 59.00N161.50W
Platte *r.* U.S.A. **53** 41.05N 96.50W
Plattsburgh U.S.A. **55** 44.42N 73.29W
Plauen E. Germany **22** 50.29N 12.08E
Plenty, B. of New Zealand **46** 37.40S176.50E
Pleven Bulgaria **22** 43.25N 24.39E
Plovdiv Bulgaria **23** 42.09N 24.45E
Plymouth U.K. **19** 50.23N 4.09W
Plymouth Mass. U.S.A. **55** 41.58N 70.40W
Plzen Czech. **20** 49.25N 13.22E
Plzeň Czech. **22** 49.45N 13.23E
Po *r.* Italy **21** 44.51N 12.30E
Pobeda, Mt. U.S.S.R. **29** 65.20N145.50E
Pocatello U.S.A. **52** 42.53N112.26W
Podolsk U.S.S.R. **25** 55.23N 37.32E
Pointe-à-Pitre Guadeloupe **57** 16.14N 61.32W
Pointe Noire Congo **40** 4.46S 11.53E
Poitiers France **21** 46.35N 0.20E
Poland Europe **22** 52.45N 19.00E
Polotsk U.S.S.R. **25** 55.30N 28.43E
Poltava U.S.S.R. **22** 49.35N 34.35E
Polynesia *is.* Pacific Oc. **47** 20.00S157.00W
Ponce Puerto Rico **57** 18.00N 66.40W
Pond Inlet *str.* Canada **51** 72.30N 75.00W
Ponta Grossa Brazil **61** 25.07S 50.00W
Pontiac Mich. U.S.A. **54** 42.39N 83.18W
Pontianak Indonesia **33** 0.05S109.16E
Pontian Kechil Malaysia **34** 1.28N103.25E
Poole U.K. **19** 50.43N 1.59W
Poopó, L. Bolivia **61** 19.00S 67.00W
Popocatépetl *mtn.* Mexico **56** 19.02N 98.38W
Porcupine *r.* U.S.A. **50** 66.25N145.20W
Porirua New Zealand **46** 41.08S174.50E
Poronaysk U.S.S.R. **29** 49.13N142.55E
Port Adelaide Australia **45** 34.52S138.30E
Portage Wisc. U.S.A. **54** 43.33N 89.29W
Portage la Prairie *town* Canada **52** 50.01N 98.20W
Port Alfred R.S.A. **41** 33.36S 27.00E
Port Antonio Jamaica **57** 18.10N 76.27W
Port Arthur Australia **45** 43.08S147.50E
Port Arthur U.S.A. **53** 29.55N 93.56W
Port Augusta Australia **45** 32.30S137.46E
Port-au-Prince Haiti **57** 18.33N 72.20W
Port Austin U.S.A. **54** 44.04N 82.59W
Port Burwell Canada **54** 42.39N 80.47W
Port Cartier Canada **51** 50.03N 66.46W
Port Chalmers New Zealand **46** 45.49S170.37E
Port Dickson Malaysia **34** 2.31N101.49E
Port Elizabeth R.S.A. **41** 33.57S 25.34E
Port Harcourt Nigeria **38** 4.43N 7.05E
Port Hedland Australia **44** 20.24S118.36E
Port Huron U.S.A. **54** 42.59N 82.28W
Portland Vic. Australia **45** 38.21S141.38E
Portland Ind. U.S.A. **54** 40.25N 84.58W
Portland Maine U.S.A. **55** 43.41N 70.18W
Portland Oreg. U.S.A. **52** 45.32N122.40W
Port Laoise Rep. of Ire. **18** 53.03N 7.20W
Port Lincoln Australia **44** 34.43S135.49E
Port Macquarie Australia **45** 31.28S152.25E
Port Moresby P.N.G. **44** 9.30S147.07E
Port of Spain Trinidad **57** 10.38N 61.31W
Porto Novo Benin **38** 6.30N 2.47E
Pôrto Velho Brazil **60** 8.45S 63.54W
Port Phillip B. Australia **45** 38.05S144.50E
Port Pirie Australia **45** 33.11S138.01E
Portree U.K. **19** 57.24N 6.12W
Port Said Egypt **39** 31.17N 32.18E
Portsmouth U.K. **19** 50.48N 1.06W
Portsmouth N.H. U.S.A. **55** 43.03N 70.47W
Portsmouth Ohio U.S.A. **54** 38.45N 82.59W
Port Sudan Sudan **41** 19.39N 37.01E
Port Talbot U.K. **19** 51.35N 3.48W
Portugal Europe **21** 39.30N 8.00W
Port Weld Malaysia **34** 4.50N100.38E
Posadas Argentina **61** 27.25S 55.48W
Poso Indonesia **33** 1.23S120.45E
Potenza Italy **23** 40.40N 15.47E
Potiskum Nigeria **40** 11.40N 11.03E
Potomac *r.* U.S.A. **55** 38.35N 77.00W
Potosí Bolivia **61** 19.34S 65.45W
Potsdam E. Germany **22** 52.24N 13.04E
Powder *r.* U.S.A. **52** 46.40N105.15W
Powell, L. U.S.A. **52** 37.30N110.45W
Powys *d.* U.K. **18** 52.26N 3.26W
Poza Rica Mexico **56** 20.34N 97.26W
Poznań Poland **22** 52.25N 16.53E

Prague Czech. **22** 50.05N 14.26E
Prato Italy **21** 43.52N 11.06E
Presque Isle *town* Maine U.S.A. **55** 46.42N 68.01W
Preston U.K. **19** 53.46N 2.42W
Pretoria R.S.A. **41** 25.43S 28.11E
Prieska R.S.A. **41** 29.40S 22.43E
Prince Albert Canada **50** 53.13N105.45W
Prince Alfred C. Canada **50** 74.30N125.00W
Prince Charles I. Canada **51** 67.50N 76.00W
Prince Edward I. Canada **53** 46.15N 64.00W
Prince Edward Is. Indian Oc. **7** 46.38S 37.55E
Prince Edward Island *d.* Canada **51** 46.30N 63.30W
Prince George Canada **50** 53.55N122.49W
Prince of Wales, C. U.S.A. **50** 66.00N168.30W
Prince of Wales I. Canada **51** 73.00N 99.00W
Prince of Wales I. U.S.A. **50** 55.00N132.30W
Prince Patrick I. Canada **50** 77.00N120.00W
Prince Rupert Canada **50** 54.09N130.20W
Princeton U.S.A. **54** 38.21N 87.33W
Principe *i.* São Tomé & Príncipe **38** 1.37N 7.27E
Pripet *r.* U.S.S.R. **22** 51.08N 30.30E
Pripet Marshes *f.* U.S.S.R. **22** 52.15N 28.00E
Priština Yugo. **22** 42.39N 21.10E
Progreso Mexico **57** 21.20N 89.40W
Prokopyevsk U.S.S.R. **28** 53.55N 86.45E
Prome Burma **32** 18.50N 95.14E
Providence U.S.A. **55** 41.50N 71.25W
Provo U.S.A. **52** 40.15N111.40W
Prut *r.* Romania/U.S.S.R. **22** 45.29N 28.14E
Przhevalsk U.S.S.R. **28** 42.31N 78.22E
Pskov U.S.S.R. **25** 57.48N 28.00E
Pucallpa Peru **60** 8.21S 74.33E
Puebla Mexico **56** 19.03N 98.10W
Puebla *d.* Mexico **56** 18.30N 98.00W
Pueblo U.S.A. **52** 38.17N104.38W
Puerto Armuelles Panama **57** 8.19N 82.15W
Puerto Barrios Guatemala **57** 15.41N 88.32W
Puerto Cabezas Nicaragua **57** 14.02N 83.24W
Puerto Cortés Honduras **57** 15.50N 87.55W
Puerto Juárez Mexico **57** 21.26N 86.51W
Puerto Montt Chile **61** 41.28S 73.00W
Puerto Natales Chile **61** 51.41S 72.15W
Puerto Penasco Mexico **56** 31.20N113.35W
Puerto Plata Dom. Rep. **57** 19.48N 70.41W
Puerto Quepos Costa Rica **57** 9.28N 84.10W
Puerto Rico C. America **57** 18.20N 66.30W
Pukaki, L. New Zealand **46** 44.00S170.10E
Pukekohe New Zealand **46** 37.12S174.56E
Pulaski N.Y. U.S.A. **55** 43.34N 76.06W
Pulau Pinang *d.* Malaysia **34** 5.20N100.15E
Pune India **31** 18.34N 73.58E
Puno Peru **60** 15.53S 70.03W
Punta Arenas *town* Chile **61** 53.10S 70.56W
Puntarenas Costa Rica **57** 10.00N 84.50W
Puntjak Jaya *mtn.* Indonesia **33** 4.00S137.15E
Pur *r.* U.S.S.R. **28** 67.30N 75.30E
Purus *r.* Brazil **60** 3.15S 61.30W
Pusan S. Korea **32** 35.05N129.02E
Putaruru New Zealand **46** 38.03S175.47E
Putoran Mts. U.S.S.R. **29** 68.30N 96.00E
Putumayo *r.* Brazil **60** 3.00S 67.30W
Puysegur Pt. New Zealand **46** 46.10S166.35E
Pya, L. U.S.S.R. **25** 66.00N 31.00E
Pyasina *r.* U.S.S.R. **29** 73.10N 84.55E
Pyongyang N. Korea **32** 39.00N125.47E
Pyramid L. U.S.A. **52** 40.00N119.35W
Pyrénées *mts.* France/Spain **21** 42.40N 0.30E

Q

Qaanaaq *see* Thule Greenland **51**
Qamdo China **32** 31.11N 97.18E
Qaqortoq *see* Julianehåb Greenland **51**
Qatar Asia **30** 25.20N 51.10E
Qattara Depression *f.* Egypt **39** 29.40N 27.30E
Qena Egypt **39** 26.08N 32.42E
Qilian Shan *mts.* China **32** 38.00N100.00E
Qinghai Hu *l.* China **32** 36.40N100.00E
Qiqihar China **32** 47.23N124.00E
Quanzhou China **32** 24.30N117.40E
Qu'Appelle *r.* Canada **52** 49.40N 99.40W
Queanbeyan Australia **45** 35.24S149.17E
Quebec Canada **55** 46.50N 71.15W
Québec *d.* Canada **51** 51.00N 70.00W
Queen Charlotte Is. Canada **50** 53.00N132.30W
Queen Charlotte Str. Canada **50** 51.00N129.00W
Queen Elizabeth Is. Canada **51** 78.30N 99.00W
Queen Mary Land *f.* Antarctica **62** 74.00S 90.00E
Queen Maud G. Canada **51** 68.30N101.00W
Queen Maud Land Antarctica **62** 74.00S 10.00E
Queensland *d.* Australia **44** 23.30S144.00E
Queenstown New Zealand **46** 45.03S168.41E
Quelimane Mozambique **41** 17.53S 36.57E
Querétaro Mexico **56** 20.38N100.23W
Querétaro *d.* Mexico **56** 21.03N100.00W
Quetta Pakistan **31** 30.15N 67.00E
Quezaltenango Guatemala **56** 14.50N 91.30W
Quezon City Phil. **33** 14.39N121.01E
Quill Lakes Canada **52** 51.50N104.10W
Quincy Ill. U.S.A. **54** 39.55N 91.22W
Quincy Mass. U.S.A. **55** 42.14N 71.00W

INDEX

Quingdao China 32 36.04N120.22E
Qui Nhon Vietnam 33 13.47N109.11E
Quintana Roo d. Mexico 57 19.00N 88.00W
Quirigua ruins Guatemala 57 15.20N 89.25W
Quito Ecuador 60 0.14S 78.30W
Quorn Australia 45 32.20S138.02E
Quseir Egypt 39 26.04N 34.15E

R

Rabat Morocco 38 34.02N 6.51W
Racine U.S.A. 54 42.42N 87.50W
Radom Poland 22 51.26N 21.10E
Rainier, Mt. U.S.A. 52 46.52N121.45W
Rainy L. Canada/U.S.A. 54 48.40N 93.15W
Raipur India 31 21.16N 81.42E
Rajkot India 31 22.18N 70.53E
Rakaia r. New Zealand 46 43.52S172.13E
Raleigh U.S.A. 53 35.46N 78.39W
Rama Nicaragua 57 12.09N 84.15W
Rancagua Chile 61 34.10S 70.45W
Ranchi India 31 23.22N 85.20E
Randers Denmark 24 56.28N 10.03E
Rangiora New Zealand 46 43.18S172.38E
Rangitaiki r. New Zealand 46 37.55S176.50E
Rangoon Burma 33 16.45N 96.20E
Rangsang, Pulau i. Indonesia 34 1.00N103.00E
Rann of Kutch f. India 31 23.50N 69.50E
Rapid City U.S.A. 52 44.06N103.14W
Ras al Hadd c. Oman 30 22.32N 59.49E
Ras Dashan mtn. Ethiopia 41 13.20N 38.10E
Rasht Iran 30 37.18N 49.38E
Raub Malaysia 34 3.47N101.52E
Ravenna Italy 21 44.25N 12.12E
Rawalpindi Pakistan 31 33.40N 73.08E
Rawlinna Australia 44 31.00S125.21E
Reading U.K. 19 51.27N 0.57W
Reading U.S.A. 55 40.20N 75.55W
Recife Brazil 60 8.06S 34.53W
Red r. Canada 53 49.55N 97.10W
Red r. U.S.A. 53 31.00N 91.30W
Redang, Pulau i. Malaysia 34 5.47N103.00E
Red Basin f. China 32 31.00N105.00E
Red Bluff U.S.A. 52 40.11N122.16W
Red Deer Canada 50 52.15N113.48W
Red Deer r. Canada 52 50.55N110.00W
Red L. U.S.A. 53 48.00N 95.00W
Red Sea Africa/Asia 39 20.00N 39.00E
Regensburg W. Germany 20 49.01N 12.07E
Reggane Algeria 38 26.30N 0.30E
Reggio Italy 21 44.40N 10.37E
Reggio Calabria Italy 23 38.07N 15.38E
Regina Canada 52 50.30N104.38W
Reims France 20 49.15N 4.02E
Reindeer L. Canada 50 57.00N102.20W
Reinosa Mexico 56 26.09N 97.10W
Renmark Australia 45 34.10S140.45E
Rennes France 21 48.06N 1.40W
Reno U.S.A. 52 39.32N119.49W
Republican r. U.S.A. 53 39.05N 94.50W
Republic of Ireland Europe 19 53.00N 8.00N
Republic of South Africa Africa 41 30.00S 25.00E
Resistencia Argentina 61 27.28S 59.00W
Resolute Canada 51 74.40N 95.00W
Resolution I. New Zealand 46 45.40S166.30E
Revilla Gigedo Is. Mexico 56 19.00N111.00W
Reykjavik Iceland 24 64.09N 21.58W
Rhine r. Europe 20 51.52N 6.03E
Rhinelander U.S.A. 54 45.39N 89.23W
Rhode Island d. U.S.A. 55 43.30N 71.35W
Rhodes i. Greece 23 36.12N 28.00E
Rhodope Mts. Bulgaria 23 41.35N 24.35E
Rhondda U.K. 19 51.39N 3.30W
Rhône r. France 21 43.25N 4.45E
Rhum i. U.K. 19 57.00N 6.20W
Ribble r. U.K. 19 53.45N 2.44W
Ribeirão Prêto Brazil 61 21.09S 47.48W
Richelieu r. Canada 55 46.02N 73.03W
Richmond New Zealand 46 41.20S173.10E
Richmond R.S.A. 41 31.24S 23.56E
Richmond Ind. U.S.A. 54 39.50N 84.51W
Richmond Va. U.S.A. 53 37.34N 77.27W
Riga U.S.S.R. 24 56.53N 24.08E
Riga, G. of U.S.S.R. 24 57.30N 23.50E
Rijeka Yugo. 22 45.20N 14.25E
Rimini Italy 22 44.04N 12.34E
Rimouski Canada 55 48.27N 68.32W
Riobamba Ecuador 60 1.44S 78.40W
Rio Branco Brazil 60 10.00S 67.49W
Rio de Janeiro Brazil 61 22.50S 43.17W
Rio Gallegos Argentina 61 51.35S 69.15W
Rio Grande town Brazil 61 32.03S 52.18W
Rio Grande r. Mexico/U.S.A. 56 25.57N 97.09W
Rio Grande r. Nicaragua 57 12.48N 83.30W
Rivas Nicaragua 57 11.26N 85.50W
Riverina f. Australia 45 35.00S146.00E
Riverton New Zealand 46 46.21S168.01E
Riviera f. France 21 43.45N 7.30E
Rivière-du-Loup town Canada 55 47.49N 69.32W
Riyadh Saudi Arabia 30 24.39N 46.44E
Rizzuto, C. Italy 23 38.53N 17.06E

Roanoke r. U.S.A. 53 36.00N 76.35W
Roberval Canada 55 48.31N 72.16W
Robson, Mt. Canada 50 53.00N119.09W
Rocha Uruguay 61 34.30S 54.22W
Rochester N.Y. U.S.A. 55 43.12N 77.37W
Rock r. U.S.A. 54 41.30N 90.35W
Rockford U.S.A. 54 42.16N 89.06W
Rockhampton Australia 44 23.22S150.32E
Rockland Maine U.S.A. 55 44.06N 69.08W
Rocklands Resr. Australia 45 37.13S141.52E
Rocky Mts. N. America 8 45.00N110.00W
Rokan r. Indonesia 34 1.51N100.58E
Romain, C. U.S.A. 53 33.01N 79.23W
Romaine r. Canada 51 50.20N 63.45W
Roman Romania 22 46.55N 26.56E
Romania Europe 22 46.20N 24.40E
Romano, C. U.S.A. 53 25.50N 81.42W
Rome Italy 21 41.54N 12.29E
Rome N.Y. U.S.A. 55 43.13N 75.28W
Rompin r. Malaysia 34 2.49N103.29E
Roof Butte mtn. U.S.A. 52 36.29N109.05W
Roosevelt r. Brazil 60 5.00S 60.30W
Roper r. Australia 44 14.40S135.30E
Roraima, Mt. Guyana 60 5.45N 61.00W
Rosa, Monte mtn. Switz./Italy 21 45.56N 7.51E
Rosario Argentina 61 33.00S 60.40W
Roscommon Rep. of Ire. 18 53.38N 8.13W
Roscommon d. Rep. of Ire. 18 53.38N 8.11W
Roscrea Rep. of Ire. 19 52.57N 7.49W
Roseau Dominica 57 15.18N 61.23W
Roseburg U.S.A. 52 43.13N123.21W
Ross Dependency Antarctica 62 75.00S170.00W
Ross Ice Shelf Antarctica 62 85.00S175.00W
Ross Sea Antarctica 62 76.00S170.00W
Rostock E. Germany 22 54.06N 12.09E
Rostov R.S.F.S.R. U.S.S.R. 28 47.10N 39.45E
Roti i. Indonesia 33 10.30S123.10E
Roto Australia 45 33.04S145.27E
Rotorua New Zealand 46 38.07S176.17E
Rotorua, L. New Zealand 46 38.00S176.00E
Rotterdam Neth. 20 51.55N 4.29E
Rouen France 20 49.26N 1.05E
Round Mt. Australia 45 30.26S152.15E
Rovno U.S.S.R. 22 50.39N 26.10E
Royale, I. U.S.A. 54 48.00N 88.45W
Royal Tunbridge Wells U.K. 19 51.09N 0.16E
Ruahine Range mts. New Zealand 46 40.00S176.00E
Ruapehu mtn. New Zealand 46 39.20S175.30E
Ruapuke I. New Zealand 46 46.45S168.30E
Rub al Khali des. Saudi Arabia 30 20.20N 52.30E
Rubtsovsk U.S.S.R. 28 51.29N 81.10E
Rufiji r. Tanzania 40 8.03S 39.19E
Rugby U.K. 19 52.23N 1.16W
Rügen i. E. Germany 22 54.30N 13.30E
Ruhr r. W. Germany 20 51.27N 6.41E
Rukwa, L. Tanzania 40 8.00S 32.20E
Rupat, Pulau i. Indonesia 34 1.50N101.35E
Rupert r. Canada 53 51.25N 78.45W
Ruse Bulgaria 22 43.50N 25.59E
Russian S.F.S.R. d. U.S.S.R. 28 62.00N 80.00E
Rustavi U.S.S.R. 28 41.34N 45.03E
Rutland U.S.A. 55 43.37N 72.59W
Ruvuma r. Mozambique/Tanzania 41 10.30S 40.30E
Ruwenzori Range mts. Uganda/Zaïre 41 0.30N 30.00E
Rwanda Africa 40 2.00S 30.00E
Ryazan U.S.S.R. 28 54.37N 39.43E
Ryazan U.S.S.R. 25 54.37N 39.43E
Rybinsk Resr. U.S.S.R. 25 58.30N 38.25E
Ryukyu Is. Japan 32 26.30N125.00E
Rzhev U.S.S.R. 25 56.15N 34.18E

S

Saarbrucken W. Germany 20 49.15N 6.58E
Saaremaa i. U.S.S.R. 24 58.30N 22.30E
Saba i. Leeward Is. 57 17.42N 63.26W
Sabadell Spain 21 41.33N 2.07E
Sabah d. Malaysia 33 5.00N117.00E
Sabak Malaysia 34 3.46N100.58E
Sabinas Hidalgo Mexico 56 26.33N100.10W
Sabine r. U.S.A. 53 30.00N 93.50W
Sable, C. Canada 51 43.30N 65.50W
Sable I. Canada 51 44.00N 60.00W
Sache China 31 38.27N 77.16E
Sacramento U.S.A. 52 38.32N121.30W
Sacramento r. U.S.A. 52 38.05N122.00W
Sacramento Mts. U.S.A. 52 34.00N105.40W
Sadiya India 31 27.49N 95.38E
Sado i. Japan 35 38.00N138.20E
Saginaw U.S.A. 54 43.25N 83.54W
Saginaw B. U.S.A. 54 43.80N 83.30W
Saglouc Canada 51 62.10N 75.40W
Saguenay r. Canada 55 48.10N 69.43W
Sahara des. Africa 38 18.00N 12.00E
Saharan Atlas mts. Algeria 38 34.20N 2.00E
Saimaa l. Finland 25 61.20N 28.00E
St. Andrews U.K. 19 56.20N 2.48W
St. Ann's Bay town Jamaica 57 18.26N 77.12W
St. Arnaud Australia 45 36.40S143.20E
St. Barthelemy i. Leeward Is. 57 17.55N 62.50W
St. Boniface Canada 51 49.54N 97.07W

St. Brieuc France 21 48.31N 2.45W
St. Catharines Canada 55 43.10N 79.15W
St. Clair, L. Canada 54 42.25N 82.35W
St. Cloud U.S.A. 53 45.34N 94.10W
St. Croix r. U.S.A. 54 44.43N 92.47W
St. David's Head U.K. 19 51.55N 5.19W
St. Elias, Mt. U.S.A. 50 60.20N141.00W
Sainte Marie, C. Madagascar 41 25.36S 45.00E
St. Étienne France 21 45.26N 4.25E
St. Gallen Switz. 21 47.25N 9.23E
St. George Australia 45 28.03S148.30E
St. George's Grenada 57 12.04N 61.44W
St. George's Channel U.K./Rep. of Ire. 19 52.00N 5.50W
St. Gotthard Pass Switz. 21 46.30N 8.55E
St. Helena i. Atlantic Oc. 6 16.00S 6.00W
St. Helens U.K. 19 53.28N 2.43W
St. Helens, Mt. U.S.A. 52 46.20N122.00W
St. Jérôme Canada 55 45.47N 74.01W
St. John Canada 53 45.16N 66.03W
St. John r. Canada 51 45.30N 66.05W
St. John, L. Canada 55 48.40N 72.00W
St. John's Antigua 57 17.07N 61.51W
St. John's Canada 51 47.34N 52.41W
St. Joseph Mo. U.S.A. 53 39.45N 94.51W
St. Joseph, L. Canada 53 51.00N 91.05W
St. Kilda i. U.K. 19 57.49N 8.34W
St. Kitts-Nevis Leeward Is. 57 17.20N 62.45W
St. Lawrence r. Canada 55 48.45N 68.30W
St. Lawrence, G. of Canada 51 48.00N 62.00W
St. Lawrence I. U.S.A. 50 63.00N170.00W
St. Leonard Canada 55 47.10N 67.55W
St. Louis Senegal 38 16.01N 16.30W
St. Louis U.S.A. 54 38.40N 90.15W
St. Lucia Windward Is. 57 14.05N 61.00W
St. Marc Haiti 57 19.08N 72.41W
St. Martin i. Leeward Is. 57 18.05N 63.05W
St. Marys Australia 45 41.33S148.12E
St. Maurice r. Canada 55 46.20N 72.30W
St. Nazaire France 21 47.18N 2.12W
St. Paul i. Indian Oc. 7 38.44S 77.30E
St. Paul Minn. U.S.A. 54 45.00N 93.10W
St. Petersburg U.S.A. 53 27.45N 82.40W
St. Pierre and Miquelon is. N. America 51 47.00N 56.15W
St. Quentin France 20 49.51N 3.17E
St. Stephen Canada 55 45.12N 67.18W
St. Vincent, C. Portugal 21 37.01N 8.59W
St. Vincent and the Grenadines Windward Is. 57 13.00N 61.15W
Sakai Japan 35 34.37N135.28E
Sakarya r. Turkey 23 41.08N 30.36E
Sakata Japan 35 38.55N139.51E
Sakhalin i. U.S.S.R. 29 50.00N143.00E
Salado r. La Pampa Argentina 61 36.15S 66.45W
Salado r. Santa Fé Argentina 61 31.40S 60.41W
Salado r. Mexico 56 26.46N 98.55W
Salala Oman 30 17.00N 54.04E
Salamanca Spain 21 40.58N 5.40W
Salar de Uyuni f. Bolivia 61 20.30S 67.45W
Sale Australia 45 38.06S147.06E
Salekhard U.S.S.R. 28 66.33N 66.35E
Salem India 31 11.38N 78.08E
Salem Ill. U.S.A. 54 38.37N 88.58W
Salem Oreg. U.S.A. 52 44.57N123.01W
Salerno Italy 23 40.41N 14.45E
Salima Malaŵi 41 13.50S 34.29E
Salina Cruz Mexico 56 16.11N 95.12W
Salisbury U.K. 19 51.04N 1.48W
Salmon r. U.S.A. 52 45.50N116.50W
Salmon River Mts. U.S.A. 52 44.30N114.30W
Salta Argentina 61 24.46S 65.28W
Salt Desert see Dasht-e-Kavir Iran 30
Saltillo Mexico 56 25.30N101.00W
Salt Lake City U.S.A. 52 40.45N111.55W
Salton Sea f. U.S.A. 52 33.25N115.45W
Salūm Egypt 39 31.31N 25.09E
Salvador Brazil 60 12.58S 38.20W
Salween r. Burma 33 16.30N 97.33E
Salzburg Austria 21 47.54N 13.03E
Salzburg Austria 21 47.48N 13.02E
Samana Dom. Rep. 57 19.14N 69.20W
Samar i. Philippines 33 11.45N125.15E
Samarinda Indonesia 33 0.30S117.09E
Samarkand U.S.S.R. 28 39.40N 66.57E
Sámos i. Greece 23 37.44N 26.45E
Samsun Turkey 30 41.17N 36.22E
San Mali 38 13.21N 4.57W
San'a Yemen 30 15.23N 44.14E
Sanaga r. Cameroon 40 3.35N 9.40E
San Ambrosio i. Chile 61 26.28S 79.53W
San Antonio Tex. U.S.A. 52 29.25N 98.30W
San Antonio, C. Cuba 57 21.50N 84.57W
San Antonio, Punta c. Mexico 56 29.45N115.41W
San Antonio Oeste Argentina 61 40.45S 64.58W
San Bernardino U.S.A. 52 34.07N117.18W
San Blas, C. U.S.A. 53 29.40N 85.25W
San Carlos Argentina 61 41.11S 71.23W
San Cristóbal Dom. Rep. 57 18.27N 70.07W
San Cristóbal Venezuela 60 7.46N 72.15W
Sancti Spiritus Cuba 57 21.55N 79.28W
Sanday i. U.K. 19 59.15N 2.33W
Sandgate Australia 45 27.18S153.00E

San Diego U.S.A. 52 32.45N117.10W
Sandusky Ohio U.S.A. 54 41.27N 82.42W
Sandy L. Ont. Canada 53 53.00N 93.00W
San Felipe Mexico 56 31.03N114.52W
San Felix i. Chile 61 26.23S 80.05W
San Fernando Trinidad 57 10.16N 61.28W
San Fernando Venezuela 60 7.53N 67.17W
San Francisco U.S.A. 52 37.45N122.27W
San Francisco, C. Ecuador 60 0.38N 80.08W
San Francisco de Macoris Dom. Rep. 57 19.19N 70.15W
Sangihe Is. Indonesia 33 2.45N125.20E
Sangre de Cristo Mts. U.S.A. 52 37.00N105.00W
San Jorge, G. of Argentina 61 46.00S 66.00W
San José Costa Rica 57 9.59N 84.04W
San José Guatemala 56 13.58N 90.50W
San Jose U.S.A. 52 37.20N121.55W
San Juan Argentina 61 31.33S 68.31W
San Juan r. Costa Rica 57 10.50N 83.40W
San Juan Puerto Rico 57 18.29N 66.08W
San Juan r. U.S.A. 52 37.20N110.05W
San Juan Mts. U.S.A. 52 37.30N107.00W
San Lázaro, C. Mexico 56 24.50N112.18W
San Lucas, C. Mexico 56 22.50N110.00W
San Luis Potosi Mexico 56 22.10N101.00W
San Luis Potosí d. Mexico 56 23.00N100.00W
San Marino Europe 22 43.30N 13.00E
San Matias, G. of Argentina 61 41.30S 64.00W
San Miguel El Salvador 57 13.28N 88.10W
San Miguel de Tucumán Argentina 61 26.47S 65.15W
San Pedro Dom. Rep. 57 18.30N 69.18W
San Pedro Coahuila Mexico 56 25.50N102.59W
San Pedro Sula Honduras 57 15.26N 88.01W
San Salvador i. Bahamas 57 24.00N 74.32W
San Salvador El Salvador 57 13.40N 89.10W
San Sebastián Spain 21 43.19N 1.59W
Santa Ana El Salvador 57 14.00N 89.31W
Santa Barbara U.S.A. 52 34.25N119.41W
Santa Clara Cuba 57 22.25N 79.58W
Santa Cruz Bolivia 60 17.58S 63.14W
Santa Cruz Is. Solomon Is. 47 10.30S166.00E
Santa Fé Argentina 61 31.38S 60.43W
Santa Fe U.S.A. 52 35.41N105.57W
Santa María Brazil 61 29.40S 53.47W
Santander Spain 21 43.28N 3.48W
Santarém Brazil 60 2.26S 54.41W
Santa Rosa Argentina 61 36.00S 64.40W
Santa Rosa Honduras 57 14.47N 88.46W
Santa Rosalía Mexico 56 27.20N112.20W
Santiago Chile 61 33.30S 70.40W
Santiago Dom. Rep. 57 19.30N 70.42W
Santiago Panama 57 8.08N 80.59W
Santiago Spain 21 42.52N 8.33W
Santiago de Cuba Cuba 57 20.00N 75.49W
Santiago del Estero Argentina 61 27.48S 64.15W
Santo Domingo Dom. Rep. 57 18.30N 69.57W
Santos Brazil 61 23.56S 46.22W
San Valentin, Cerro mtn. Chile 61 46.33S 73.20W
San Vicente El Salvador 57 13.38N 88.42W
São Francisco r. Brazil 60 10.10S 36.40W
São Francisco do Sul Brazil 61 26.17S 48.39W
São José do Rio Prêto Brazil 61 20.50S 49.20W
São Luís Brazil 60 2.34S 44.16W
Saona i. Dom. Rep. 57 18.09N 68.42W
Saône r. France 21 45.46N 4.52E
São Paulo Brazil 61 23.33S 46.39W
São Paulo de Olivença Brazil 60 3.34S 68.55W
São Roque, C. Brazil 60 5.00S 35.00W
São Tomé i. São Tomé & Príncipe 38 0.19N 6.43E
São Tomé & Príncipe Africa 38 1.00N 7.00E
Sapporo Japan 35 43.05N141.21E
Sarajevo Yugo. 22 43.52N 18.26E
Saransk U.S.S.R. 28 54.12N 45.10E
Saratov U.S.S.R. 28 51.30N 45.55E
Sarawak d. Malaysia 33 3.00N114.00E
Sardinia i. Italy 21 40.00N 9.00E
Sarek mtn. Sweden 24 67.10N 17.45E
Sarh Chad 38 9.08N 18.22E
Sarmiento Argentina 61 45.38S 69.08W
Särna Sweden 24 61.40N 13.10E
Sasebo Japan 35 33.10N129.42E
Saskatchewan d. Canada 50 55.00N105.00W
Saskatchewan r. Canada 51 53.25N100.15W
Saskatoon Canada 52 52.10N106.40W
Sassandra Ivory Coast 38 4.58N 6.08W
Sassari Italy 21 40.43N 8.33E
Saudi Arabia Asia 30 24.00N 45.00E
Sault Sainte Marie Canada 54 46.32N 84.20W
Sault Sainte Marie U.S.A. 54 46.29N 84.22W
Saurimo Angola 41 9.38S 20.20E
Sava r. Yugo. 22 44.50N 20.26E
Savannah U.S.A. 53 32.10N 81.00W
Savannah Ga. U.S.A. 53 32.09N 81.01W
Save r. Mozambique 41 20.59S 35.02E
Savona Italy 21 44.18N 8.28E
Sayula Mexico 56 19.52N103.36W
Scafell Pike mtn. U.K. 19 54.27N 3.12W
Scammon Bay town U.S.A. 50 61.50N165.35W
Scandinavia f. Europe 9 65.00N 18.00E
Scarborough U.K. 19 54.17N 0.24W
Schefferville Canada 51 54.50N 67.00W

INDEX

Schelde r. Neth. 20 51.14N 4.25E
Schenectady U.S.A. 55 42.28N 73.57W
Schwaner Mts. Indonesia 33 0.45S113.20E
Scilly, Isles of U.K. 19 49.55N 6.20W
Scioto r. U.S.A. 54 38.43N 83.00W
Scotland d. U.K. 19 56.30N 4.00W
Scottsdale Australia 45 41.09S147.31E
Scranton U.S.A. 55 41.25N 75.40W .
Seal r. Canada 51 59.00N 95.00W
Seattle U.S.A. 52 47.35N122.20W
Sebago L. U.S.A. 55 43.37N 71.20W
Sebastian Vizcaino B. Mexico 56 28.20N114.45W
Seberang Perai d. Malaysia 34 5.15N100.28E
Sebha Libya 38 27.04N 14.25E
Segamat Malaysia 34 2.30N102.50E
Segovia Spain 21 40.57N 4.07W
Seine r. France 20 49.28N 0.25E
Seistan f. Iran 30 31.00N 61.15E
Sekondi-Takoradi Ghana 38 4.59N 1.43W
Selangor d. Malaysia 34 3.25N101.30E
Selkirk Mts. Canada 52 50.00N116.30W
Selvas f. Brazil 60 9.00S 68.00W
Selwyn Mts. Canada 50 63.00N130.00W
Semarang Indonesia 33 6.58S110.29E
Seminoe Resr. U.S.A. 52 42.05N106.50W
Semipalatinsk U.S.S.R. 28 50.26N 80.16E
Sendai Japan 35 38.20N140.50E
Seneca L. U.S.A. 55 42.35N 77.07W
Senegal Africa 38 14.15N 14.15W
Senegal r. Senegal/Mauritania 38 16.00N 16.28W
Sennar Sudan 41 13.31N 33.38E
Senneterre Canada 55 48.24N 77.16W
Seoul S. Korea 32 37.30N127.00E
Sepik r. P.N.G. 44 3.54S144.30E
Sept Iles town Canada 51 50.13N 66.22W
Serdang Malaysia 34 3.01N101.44E
Seremban Malaysia 34 2.42N101.57E
Serov U.S.S.R. 28 59.22N 60.32E
Serowe Botswana 41 22.22S 26.42E
Serpukhov U.S.S.R. 25 54.53N 37.25E
Setubal Portugal 21 38.31N 8.54W
Seul, Lac l. Canada 53 50.25N 92.15W
Sevastopol' U.S.S.R. 22 44.36N 33.31E
Severn r. Canada 51 56.00N 87.40W
Severn r. U.K. 19 51.50N 2.21W
Severnaya Zemlya is. U.S.S.R. 29 80.00N 96.00E
Severodvinsk U.S.S.R. 25 64.35N 39.50E
Seville Spain 21 37.24N 5.59W
Seward U.S.A. 50 60.05N149.34W
Seward Pen. U.S.A. 50 65.00N164.10W
Seychelles Indian Oc. 7 5.00S 55.00E
Seydhisfjördhur Iceland 24 65.16N 14.02W
Seymour U.S.A. 54 38.57N 85.55W
Sfax Tunisia 38 34.45N 10.43E
Shah Alam Malaysia 34 3.06N101.35E
Shahjahanpur India 31 27.53N 79.55E
Shakhty U.S.S.R. 28 47.43N 40.16E
Shamva Zimbabwe 41 17.00S 31.38E
Shanghai China 32 31.13N121.25E
Shannon r. Rep. of Ire. 19 52.39N 8.43W
Shantar Is. U.S.S.R. 29 55.00N138.00E
Shantou China 32 23.22N116.39E
Shaoguan China 32 24.53N113.31E
Shasta, Mt. U.S.A. 52 41.35N122.12W
Shawano U.S.A. 54 44.46N 88.38W
Shawinigan Canada 55 46.33N 72.45W
Shebelle r. Somali Rep. 39 0.30N 43.10E
Sheboygan U.S.A. 54 43.46N 87.44W
Sheffield U.K. 19 53.23N 1.28W
Shelikof Str. U.S.A. 50 58.00N153.45W
Shellharbour Australia 45 34.35S150.52E
Shenyang China 32 41.50N123.26E
Shepparton Australia 45 36.25S145.26E
Sherbrooke Canada 55 45.24N 71.54W
Sheridan U.S.A. 52 44.48N107.05W
Shetland Is. U.K. 19 60.20N 1.15W
Shevchenko U.S.S.R. 28 43.40N 51.20E
Shijiazhuang China 32 38.03N114.26E
Shikoku i. Japan 35 33.30N133.00E
Shikoku sanchi mts. Japan 35 34.00N134.00E
Shilka r. U.S.S.R. 29 53.20N121.10E
Shillong India 31 25.34N 91.53E
Shimizu Japan 35 35.08N138.38E
Shimo jima i. Japan 35 32.10N130.30E
Shinano r. Japan 35 37.58N139.02E
Shiono misaki c. Japan 35 33.28N135.47E
Shirane san mtn. Japan 35 35.42N138.12E
Shiraz Iran 30 29.36N 52.33E
Shire r. Mozambique 41 17.46S 35.20E
Shiriya saki c. Japan 35 41.24N141.30E
Shkodër Albania 23 42.03N 19.30E
Sholapur India 31 17.43N 75.56E
Shreveport U.S.A. 53 32.30N 93.46W
Shrewsbury U.K. 19 52.42N 2.45W
Shropshire d. U.K. 18 52.35N 2.40W
Shumagin Is. U.S.A. 50 55.00N160.00W
Sialkot Pakistan 31 32.29N 74.35E
Siauliai U.S.S.R. 24 55.51N 23.20E
Siberia f. U.S.S.R. 9 65.00N120.00E
Sibiu Romania 23 45.47N 24.09E

Sibut C.A.R. 40 5.46N 19.06E
Sicily i. Italy 23 37.30N 14.00E
Sidi bel Abbès Algeria 38 35.15N 0.39W
Siena Italy 21 '43.19N 11.20E
Sierra Blanca mtn. U.S.A. 52 33.23N105.49W
Sierra Leone Africa 38 8.30N 12.00W
Sierra Morena mts. Spain 21 38.10N 5.00W
Sierra Nevada mts. Spain 21 37.04N 3.20W
Sierra Nevada mts. U.S.A. 52 37.30N119.00W
Siglufjördhur Iceland 24 66.09N 18.55W
Sikasso Mali 38 11.18N 5.38W
Sikhote-Alin Range mts. U.S.S.R. 29 45.20N136.50E
Silesian Plateau f. Poland 22 50.30N 20.00E
Siljan l. Sweden 24 60.50N 14.40E
Simard, L. Canada 55 47.37N 78.40W
Simcoe, L. Canada 55 44.25N 79.20W
Simferopol' U.S.S.R. 22 44.57N 34.05E
Simpson Desert Australia 44 25.00S136.50E
Sinai pen. Egypt 39 29.00N 34.00E
Sinaloa d. Mexico 56 25.00N107.30W
Singapore Asia 34 1.20N103.50E
Singapore town Singapore 34 1.16N103.50E
Singapore, Straits of Indonesia/Singapore 34 1.15N104.00E
Sintang Indonesia 33 0.03N111.31E
Sint Eustatius i. Leeward Is. 57 17.33N 63.00W
Sint Maarten i. see St. Martin i. Leeward Is. 57
Sioux City U.S.A. 53 42.30N 96.28W
Sioux Falls town U.S.A. 53 43.34N 96.42W
Sioux Lookout town Canada 53 50.07N 91.54W
Siracusa Italy 23 37.05N 15.17E
Sirte Libya 38 31.10N 16.39E
Sirte, G. of Libya 38 31.45N 17.50E
Sishen R.S.A. 41 27.46S 22.59E
Sittang r. Burma 33 17.30N 96.53E
Sivas Turkey 30 39.44N 37.01E
Skagerrak str. Norway/Denmark 24 57.45N 8.55E
Skagway U.S.A. 50 59.23N135.20W
Skalintyy mtn. U.S.S.R. 29 56.00N130.40E
Skeena r. Canada 50 54.10N129.08W
Skellefteå Sweden 24 64.45N 21.00E
Skopje Yugo. 23 41.58N 21.27E
Skovorodino U.S.S.R. 29 54.00N123.53E
Skye i. U.K. 19 57.20N 6.15W
Slaney r. Rep. of Ire. 19 52.21N 6.30W
Slave r. Canada 50 61.10N113.30W
Slavgorod R.S.F.S.R. U.S.S.R. 28 53.01N 78.37E
Sleetmute U.S.A. 50 61.40N157.11W
Sligo Rep. of Ire. 19 54.17N 8.28W
Sligo d. Rep. of Ire. 18 54.10N 8.35W
Smith's Falls town Canada 55 44.54N 76.01W
Smolensk U.S.S.R. 25 54.49N 32.04E
Snake r. U.S.A. 52 46.15N119.00W
Snowdon mtn. U.K. 19 53.05N 4.05W
Snowy r. Australia 45 37.49S148.30E
Snowy Mts. Australia 45 36.25S148.15E
Sobat r. Sudan/Ethiopia 41 9.30N 31.30E
Sobral Brazil 60 3.45S 40.20W
Sochi U.S.S.R. 28 43.35N 39.46E
Society Is. Pacific Oc. 47 17.00S150.00W
Socorro I. Mexico 56 18.45N110.58W
Socotra i. S. Yemen 30 12.30N 54.00E
Sofia Bulgaria 23 42.41N 23.19E
Sogne Fjord est. Norway 24 61.10N 5.50E
Sokoto Nigeria 38 13.02N 5.15E
Solent str. U.K. 19 50.45N 1.20W
Solihull U.K. 19 52.26N 1.47W
Sollefteå Sweden 24 63.09N 17.15E
Solomon Is. Pacific Oc. 47 10.00S160.00E
Solomon Sea Pacific Oc. 44 7.00S150.00E
Solway Firth est. U.K. 19 54.52N 3.30W
Somali Republic Africa 39 5.30N 47.00E
Somerset d. U.K. 18 51.09N 3.00W
Somerset I. Canada 51 73.00N 93.30W
Songea Tanzania 41 10.42S 35.39E
Songhua Jiang r. China 32 47.46N132.30E
Songkhla Thailand 34 7.12N100.35E
Sonora d. Mexico 56 29.20N110.40W
Sonora r. Mexico 56 28.45N111.55W
Sorel Canada 55 46.03N 73.06W
Sorocaba Brazil 61 23.30S 47.32W
Soroti Uganda 41 1.42N 33.37E
Sosnowiec Poland 22 50.18N 19.08E
Sources, Mt.-aux- Lesotho 41 28.44S 28.52E
Souris r. Canada 52 49.38N 99.35W
Sousse Tunisia 38 35.48N 10.38E
South America 60
Southampton U.K. 19 50.54N 1.23W
Southampton I. Canada 51 64.30N 84.00W
South Atlantic Ocean 61
South Australia d. Australia 44 29.00S135.00E
South Bend Ind. U.S.A. 54 41.40N 86.15W
South Carolina d. U.S.A. 53 34.00N 81.00W
South China Sea Asia 33 12.30N115.00E
South Dakota d. U.S.A. 52 44.30N100.00W
South East C. Australia 45 43.38S146.48E
Southend-on-Sea U.K. 19 51.32N 0.43E
Southern Alps mts. New Zealand 46 43.20S170.45E
Southern Cross Australia 44 31.14S119.16E
Southern Uplands hills U.K. 19 55.30N 3.30W
Southern Yemen Asia 30 16.00N 49.30E

South Georgia i. Atlantic Oc. 61 54.00S 37.00W
South Glamorgan d. U.K. 18 51.27N 3.22W
South I. New Zealand 46 43.00S171.00E
South Korea Asia 32 34.00N128.00E
Southland f. New Zealand 46 45.40S167.15E
South Nahanni r. Canada 50 61.00N123.20W
South Orkney Is. Atlantic Oc. 61 60.50S 45.00W
Southport Australia 45 27.58S153.20E
Southport U.K. 19 53.38N 3.01W
South Sandwich Is. Atlantic Oc. 61 58.00S 27.00W
South Sandwich Trench f. Atlantic Oc. 61 57.00S 25.00W
South Saskatchewan r. Canada 52 50.45N108.30W
South Uist i. U.K. 19 57.15N 7.20W
South West C. Australia 45 43.32S145.59E
Southwest C. New Zealand 46 47.15S167.30E
South Yorkshire d. U.K. 18 53.28N 1.25W
Sovetskaya Gavan U.S.S.R. 29 48.57N140.16E
Spain Europe 21 40.00N 3.30W
Sparta Wisc. U.S.A. 54 43.57N 90.50W
Spence Bay town Canada 51 69.30N 93.20W
Spencer G. Australia 44 34.30S136.10E
Spey r. U.K. 19 57.40N 3.06W
Spitsbergen is. Arctic Oc. 62 78.00N 17.00E
Split Yugo. 22 43.32N 16.27E
Spokane U.S.A. 52 47.40N117.25W
Springfield Ill. U.S.A. 54 39.49N 89.39W
Springfield Mass. U.S.A. 55 42.07N 72.35W
Springfield Miss. U.S.A. 53 37.11N 93.19W
Springfield Ohio U.S.A. 54 39.55N 83.48W
Springs town R.S.A. 41 26.16S 28.27E
Sredne Kolymskaya U.S.S.R. 29 67.27N153.35E
Sri Lanka Asia 31 9.00N 81.00E
Srinagar Jammu & Kashmir 31 34.08N 74.50E
Stafford U.K. 18 52.49N 2.09W
Staffordshire d. U.K. 18 52.50N 2.00W
Stamford Conn. U.S.A. 55 41.03N 73.32W
Stanley Falkland Is. 61 51.45S 57.56W
Stanovoy Range mts. U.S.S.R. 29 56.00N125.40E
Stanthorpe Australia 45 28.37S151.52E
Stara Zagora Bulgaria 23 42.26N 25.37E
Stavanger Norway 24 58.58N 5.45E
Stavropol' U.S.S.R. 28 45.03N 41.59E
Sterlitamak U.S.S.R. 28 53.40N 55.59E
Stewart Island mts. U.S.S.R. 55 55.56N130.01W
Stewart I. New Zealand 46 47.00S168.00E
Stikine r. Canada 50 56.45N132.30W
Stikine Mts. Canada 50 59.00N129.00W
Stirling U.K. 19 56.07N 3.57W
Stockholm Sweden 24 59.20N 18.05E
Stockport U.K. 19 53.25N 2.11W
Stockton Calif. U.S.A. 52 37.59N121.20W
Stoke-on-Trent U.K. 19 53.01N 2.10W
Stony Tunguska r. U.S.S.R. 29 61.40N 90.00E
Storavan l. Sweden 24 65.45N 18.10E
Store Baelt str. Denmark 24 55.30N 11.00E
Stornoway U.K. 19 58.12N 6.23W
Storsjön l. Sweden 24 63.10N 14.20E
Stralsund E. Germany 20 54.18N 13.06E
Stranraer U.K. 19 54.54N 5.02W
Strasbourg France 21 48.35N 7.45E
Stratford New Zealand 46 39.20S174.18E
Strathclyde d. U.K. 18 56.00N 5.00W
Straumnes c. Iceland 24 66.30N 23.05W
Stromboli i. Italy 23 38.48N 15.14E
Sturgeon Falls town Canada 54 46.22N 79.57W
Sturt Desert Australia 45 28.30S141.12E
Stuttgart W. Germany 20 48.47N 9.12E
Suakin Sudan 41 19.04N 37.22E
Sucre Bolivia 61 19.05S 65.15W
Sudan Africa 39 14.00N 30.00E
Sudbury Canada 54 46.30N 81.01W
Sudd f. Sudan 41 7.50N 30.00E
Sudeten Mts. Czech./Poland 22 50.30N 16.30E
Suez Egypt 39 29.59N 32.33E
Suez, G. of Egypt 39 28.48N 33.00E
Suez Canal Egypt 39 30.40N 32.20E
Suffolk d. U.K. 18 52.16N 1.00E
Suir r. Rep. of Ire. 19 52.17N 7.00W
Sukhona r. U.S.S.R. 28 61.30N 46.28E
Sukkur Pakistan 31 27.42N 68.54E
Sulaiman Range mts. Pakistan 31 30.50N 70.20E
Sula Is. Indonesia 33 1.50S125.10E
Sullana Peru 60 4.52S 80.39W
Sulmona Italy 23 42.04N 13.57E
Sumatra i. Indonesia 33 2.00S102.00E
Sumba i. Indonesia 33 9.30S119.55E
Sumbawa i. Indonesia 33 8.45S117.50E
Sumgait U.S.S.R. 28 40.35N 49.38E
Sumy U.S.S.R. 22 50.55N 34.49E
Sunbury Penn. U.S.A. 55 40.52N 76.47W
Sundarbans f. India/Bangla. 31 22.00N 89.00E
Sunderland U.K. 19 54.55N 1.22W
Sundsvall Sweden 24 62.22N 17.20E
Sungai Petani Malaysia 34 5.38N100.29E
Sungai Siput Malaysia 34 4.48N101.05E
Sunyani Ghana 38 7.22N 2.18W
Suo nada str. Japan 35 33.45N131.30E
Superior Wisc. U.S.A. 54 46.42N 92.05W
Superior, L. N. America 54 48.00N 88.00W
Sura r. U.S.S.R. 25 51.52N 46.00E

Surabaya Indonesia 33 7.14S112.45E
Surakarta Indonesia 33 7.32S110.50E
Surat India 31 21.10N 72.54E
Surinam S. America 60 4.30N 56.00W
Surrey d. U.K. 18 51.16N 0.30W
Surtsey i. Iceland 24 63.18N 20.37W
Susquehanna r. U.S.A. 55 39.33N 76.05W
Sutlej r. Pakistan 31 29.26N 71.09E
Suva Fiji 47 18.08S178.25E
Suzhou China 32 31.22N120.45E
Suzu misaki c. Japan 35 37.30N137.21E
Sverdlovsk U.S.S.R. 28 56.52N 60.35E
Svobodnyy U.S.S.R. 29 51.24N127.50E
Swan Hill town Australia 45 35.23S143.37E
Swansea U.K. 19 51.37N 3.57W
Swaziland Africa 41 26.30S 32.00E
Sweden Europe 24 63.00N 16.00E
Swettenham, Gunung mtn. Malaysia 34 4.35N101.28E
Swift Current town Canada 52 50.17N107.49W
Swindon U.K. 19 51.33N 1.47W
Switzerland Europe 21 47.00N 8.00E
Sydney Australia 45 33.55S151.10E
Sydney Canada 51 46.10N 60.10W
Syktyvkar U.S.S.R. 28 61.42N 50.45E
Syracuse N.Y. U.S.A. 55 43.03N 76.10W
Syr Darya r. U.S.S.R. 28 46.00N 61.12E
Syria Asia 30 35.00N 38.00E
Syrian Desert Asia 30 32.00N 39.00E
Syzran U.S.S.R. 28 53.10N 48.29E
Szczecin Poland 22 53.25N 14.32E
Szeged Hungary 22 46.16N 20.08E

T

Tabasco d. Mexico 56 18.30N 93.00W
Tabora Tanzania 40 5.00S 32.50E
Tabriz Iran 30 38.05N 46.18E
Tacoma U.S.A. 52 47.16N122.30W
Tacuarembó Uruguay 61 31.42S 56.00W
Tademait Plateau Algeria 38 28.45N 2.10E
Tadzhikistan S.S.R. d. U.S.S.R. 28 39.00N 71.00E
Taegu S. Korea 32 35.52N128.36E
Taganrog U.S.S.R. 28 47.14N 38.55E
Tagus r. Portugal 21 38.44N 8.57W
Tahan, Gunung mtn. Malaysia 34 4.38N102.14E
Tahat mtn. Algeria 38 23.20N 5.40E
Tahiti i. Pacific Oc. 47 17.00S149.00W
Taihape New Zealand 46 39.40S175.48E
Taipei Taiwan 32 25.05N121.32E
Taiping Malaysia 34 4.51N100.44E
Taivalkoski Finland 25 65.35N 28.20E
Taiwan Asia 32 24.00N121.00E
Taiyuan China 32 37.48N112.33E
Taizhong Taiwan 32 24.11N120.40E
Ta'izz Yemen 30 13.35N 44.02E
Takamatsu Japan 35 34.28N134.05E
Takaoka Japan 35 36.47N137.00E
Talaud Is. Indonesia 33 4.20N126.50E
Talca Chile 61 35.28S 71.40W
Talcahuano Chile 61 36.40S 73.10W
Tallahassee U.S.A. 53 30.28N 84.19W
Tallinn U.S.S.R. 24 59.22N 24.48E
Tamale Ghana 38 9.26N 0.49W
Taman Negara mts. Malaysia 34 4.43N102.30E
Tamanrasset Algeria 38 22.50N 5.31E
Tamar r. U.K. 19 50.28N 4.13W
Tamaulipas d. Mexico 56 24.00N 98.20W
Tambacounda Senegal 38 13.45N 13.40W
Tambov U.S.S.R. 28 52.44N 41.28E
Tampa U.S.A. 53 27.58N 82.38W
Tampere Finland 24 61.32N 23.45E
Tampico Mexico 56 22.18N 97.52W
Tampin Malaysia 34 2.28N102.15E
Tamworth Australia 45 31.07S150.57E
Tana r. Kenya 40 2.32S 40.32E
Tana Norway 24 70.26N 28.14E
Tana r. Norway 24 69.45N 28.15E
Tana, L. Ethiopia 41 12.00N 37.20E
Tanah Merah Malaysia 34 5.48N102.08E
Tanega shima i. Japan 35 30.32N131.00E
Tanga Tanzania 40 5.07S 39.05E
Tanganyika, L. Africa 40 6.00S 29.30E
Tangier Morocco 38 35.48N 5.45W
Tangkak Malaysia 34 2.14N102.33E
Tangshan China 32 39.32N118.08E
Tanimbar Is. Indonesia 33 7.50S131.30E
Tannu Ola Range mts. U.S.S.R. 29 51.00N 93.30E
Tanta Egypt 39 30.48N 31.00E
Tanzania Africa 40 5.00S 35.00E
Tapachula Mexico 56 14.54N 92.15W
Tapajós r. Brazil 60 2.40S 55.30W
Tapis, Gunung mtn. Malaysia 34 4.00N102.53E
Tara r. U.S.S.R. 28 56.30N 74.40E
Taranto Italy 23 40.28N 17.14E
Taranto, G. of Italy 23 40.00N 17.20E
Taree Australia 45 31.54S152.26E
Tarija Bolivia 61 21.33S 64.45W
Tarim He r. China 31 41.00N 83.30E
Tarn r. France 21 44.15N 1.15E
Tarragona Spain 21 41.07N 1.15E

INDEX

Tarrasa Spain 21 41.34N 2.00E
Tartary, G. of U.S.S.R. 29 47.40N141.00E
Tartu U.S.S.R. 24 58.20N 26.44E
Tasek Bera l. Malaysia 34 3.06N102.36E
Tasek Dampar l. Malaysia 34 3.00N102.40E
Tashkent U.S.S.R. 28 41.16N 69.13E
Tasillaq see Ammassalik Greenland 51
Tasman B. New Zealand 46 41.00S173.15E
Tasmania d. Australia 45 42.00S147.00E
Tasman Mts. New Zealand 46 41.00S172.40E
Tasman Sea Australia 47 38.00S163.00E
Tatarsk U.S.S.R. 28 55.14N 76.00E
Tatnam, C. Canada 51 57.00N 91.00W
Taumarunui New Zealand 46 38.53S175.16E
Taunton U.K. 19 51.01N 3.07W
Taupo New Zealand 46 38.42S176.06E
Taupo, L. New Zealand 46 38.45S175.30E
Tauranga New Zealand 46 37.42S176.11E
Taurus Mts. Turkey 30 37.15N 34.15E
Taurus Mts. Turkey 23 37.15N 34.15E
Tawau Malaysia 33 4.16N117.54E
Tay r. U.K. 19 56.21N 3.18W
Taylor, Mt. U.S.A. 52 35.14N107.36W
Taymyr, L. U.S.S.R. 29 74.20N101.00E
Taymyr Pen. U.S.S.R. 29 75.30N 99.00E
Tayshet U.S.S.R. 29 55.56N 98.01E
Tayside d. U.K. 18 56.30N 3.00W
Taz r. U.S.S.R. 28 67.30N 78.50E
Tbilisi U.S.S.R. 28 41.43N 44.48E
Te Anau New Zealand 46 45.25S167.43E
Te Anau, L. New Zealand 46 45.10S167.15E
Te Awamutu New Zealand 46 38.00S175.20E
Tees r. U.K. 19 54.35N 1.11W
Tegucigalpa Honduras 57 14.05N 87.14W
Tehran Iran 30 35.40N 51.26E
Tehuacán Mexico 56 18.30N 97.26W
Tehuantepec, G. of Mexico 56 16.00N 95.00W
Teifi r. U.K. 19 52.05N 4.41W
Tekapo, L. New Zealand 46 43.35S170.30E
Te Kuiti New Zealand 46 38.20S175.10E
Tela Honduras 57 15.56N 87.25W
Tel-Aviv-Yafo Israel 23 32.05N 34.46E
Telukbetung Indonesia 33 5.28S105.16E
Teluk Intan Malaysia 34 4.01N101.03E
Tembeling r. Malaysia 34 4.05N102.19E
Temirtau U.S.S.R. 28 50.05N 72.55E
Temora Australia 45 34.27S147.35E
Temuco Chile 61 38.45S 72.40W
Tenerife i. Canary Is. 38 28.10N 16.30W
Tengiz, L. U.S.S.R. 28 50.30N 69.00E
Tenke Zaïre 41 10.34S 26.07E
Tennant Creek town Australia 44 19.31S134.15E
Tennessee d. U.S.A. 53 36.00N 86.00W
Tennessee r. U.S.A. 53 37.10N 88.25W
Tenterfield Australia 45 29.01S152.04E
Teófilo Otoni Brazil 61 17.52S 41.31W
Tepic Mexico 56 21.30N104.51W
Teplice Czech. 22 50.40N 13.50E
Teresina Brazil 60 4.50S 42.50W
Termez U.S.S.R. 28 37.15N 67.15E
Terminos Lagoon Mexico 56 18.30N 91.30W
Terni Italy 22 42.34N 12.37E
Ternopol U.S.S.R. 22 49.35N 25.39E
Terre Haute U.S.A. 54 39.27N 87.24W
Teruel Spain 21 40.21N 1.06W
Teslin r. Canada 50 62.00N135.00W
Test r. U.K. 19 50.55N 1.29W
Tete Mozambique 41 16.10S 33.30E
Tetuan Morocco 38 35.34N 5.22W
Texarkana Ark. U.S.A. 53 33.28N 94.02W
Texas d. U.S.A. 52 32.00N100.00W
Texoma, L. U.S.A. 53 34.00N 96.40W
Thailand Asia 33 15.00N101.00E
Thailand, G. of Asia 33 10.00N102.00E
Thames r. Canada 54 42.20N 82.25W
Thames New Zealand 46 37.08S175.35E
Thames r. U.K. 19 51.30N 0.05E
Thar Desert India 31 28.00N 72.00E
Thargomindah Australia 45 27.59S143.45E
The Cherokees, L. O' U.S.A. 53 36.45N 94.50W
The Coorong g. Australia 45 36.00S139.30E
The Everglades f. U.S.A. 53 26.00N 80.30W
The Fens f. U.K. 19 52.32N 0.13E
The Gulf Asia 30 27.00N 50.00E
The Hague Neth. 20 52.05N 4.16E
Thelon r. Canada 51 64.23N 96.15W
The Minch str. U.K. 19 58.10N 5.50W
Theodore Roosevelt L. U.S.A. 52 33.30N111.10W
The Pas Canada 51 53.50N101.15W
Thessaloniki Greece 23 40.38N 22.56E
Thetford Mines town Canada 55 46.06N 71.18W
The Wash b. U.K. 19 52.55N 0.15E
The Woods, L. of N. America 53 49.30N 94.30W
Thimbu Bhutan 31 27.29N 89.40E
Thionville France 21 49.22N 6.11E
Thíra i. Greece 23 36.24N 25.27E
Thjórsá r. Iceland 24 63.53N 20.38W
Thorshavn Faroe Is. 20 62.02N 6.47W
Thule Greenland 51 77.30N 69.29W
Thunder Bay town Canada 54 48.25N 89.14W

Thurso U.K. 19 58.35N 3.32W
Tianjin China 32 39.07N117.08E
Tian Shan mts. China 31 42.00N 80.30E
Tianshui China 32 34.25N105.58E
Tibati Cameroon 40 6.25N 12.33E
Tiber r. Italy 21 41.45N 12.16E
Tibesti Mts. Chad 38 21.00N 17.30E
Tibet d. China 31 32.20N 86.00E
Tibetan Plateau f. China 31 34.00N 84.30E
Tiburon I. Mexico 56 29.00N112.25W
Tidjikdja Mauritania 38 18.29N 11.31W
Tierra Blanca Mexico 56 18.28N 96.12W
Tierra del Fuego i. S. America 61 54.00S 68.30W
Tigris r. Asia 30 31.00N 47.27E
Tihama f. Saudi Arabia 30 20.30N 40.30E
Tijuana Mexico 56 32.29N117.10W
Tiksi U.S.S.R. 29 71.40N128.45E
Tilburg Neth. 20 51.34N 5.05E
Timagami L. Canada 54 46.55N 80.03W
Timaru New Zealand 46 44.23S171.41E
Timbuktu Mali 38 16.49N 2.59W
Timişoara Romania 22 45.47N 21.15E
Timmins Canada 54 48.30N 81.20W
Timor i. Indonesia 33 9.30S125.00E
Timor Sea Austa. 44 13.00S122.00E
Tinggi, Pulau i. Malaysia 34 2.19N104.07E
Tínos i. Greece 23 37.36N 25.08E
Tioman, Pulau i. Malaysia 34 2.45N104.10E
Tipperary d. Rep. of Ire. 18 52.37N 7.55W
Tiranë Albania 23 41.20N 19.48E
Tiraspol U.S.S.R. 22 46.50N 29.38E
Tiree i. U.K. 19 56.30N 6.50W
Tîrgu Mureş Romania 22 46.33N 24.34E
Tiruchirapalli India 31 10.50N 78.43E
Tisza r. Yugo. 22 45.09N 20.16E
Titicaca, L. Bolivia/Peru 60 16.00S 69.00W
Titograd Yugo. 23 42.30N 19.16E
Tizimín Mexico 57 21.10N 88.09W
Tlaxcala d. Mexico 56 19.45N 98.20W
Tlemcen Algeria 38 34.53N 1.21W
Toamasina Madagascar 41 18.10S 49.23E
Toba, L. Indonesia 33 2.45N 98.50E
Tobago i. Trinidad 57 11.15N 60.40W
Tobermory U.K. 19 56.37N 6.04W
Tobol r. U.S.S.R. 28 58.15N 68.12E
Tobolsk U.S.S.R. 28 58.15N 68.12E
Tobruk Libya 39 32.06N 23.58E
Tocantins r. Brazil 60 2.40S 49.20W
Tocorpuri mtn. Bolivia 61 22.26S 67.53W
Togo Africa 38 8.30N 1.00E
Tokelau Is. Pacific Oc. 47 9.00S172.00W
Tokoroa New Zealand 46 38.13S175.53E
Tokushima Japan 35 34.03N134.34E
Tokyo Japan 35 35.40N139.45E
Toledo Spain 21 39.52N 4.02W
Toledo U.S.A. 54 41.40N 83.35W
Toliara Madagascar 41 23.21S 43.40E
Toluca Mexico 56 19.20N 99.40W
Tol'yatti U.S.S.R. 28 53.32N 49.24E
Tombigbee r. U.S.A. 53 31.05N 87.55W
Tom Price Australia 44 22.49S117.51E
Tomsk U.S.S.R. 28 56.30N 85.05E
Tona, G. of U.S.S.R. 29 72.00N136.10E
Tonalá Mexico 56 16.08N 93.41W
Tonga Pacific Oc. 47 21.00S175.00W
Tongking, G. of Asia 33 19.50N107.00E
Tonle Sap l. Kampuchea 33 12.50N104.00E
Toowoomba Australia 45 27.35S151.54E
Top, L. U.S.S.R. 25 65.45N 32.00E
Topeka U.S.A. 53 39.03N 95.41W
Topko, Mt. U.S.S.R. 29 57.20N138.10E
Torbay town U.K. 19 50.27N 3.31W
Tornio Finland 24 65.52N 24.10E
Tornio r. Finland 24 65.53N 24.07E
Toronto Canada 55 43.42N 79.25W
Tororo Uganda 40 0.42N 34.13E
Torrens, L. Australia 45 31.00S137.50E
Torreón Mexico 56 25.34N103.25W
Torres Str. Australia 44 9.58S142.30E
Tortosa Spain 21 40.49N 0.31E
Tortue i. Haiti 57 20.05N 72.57W
Toruń Poland 22 53.01N 18.35E
Tottori Japan 35 35.32N134.12E
Touggourt Algeria 38 33.08N 6.04E
Toulon France 21 43.07N 5.53E
Toulouse France 21 43.33N 1.24E
Tours France 21 47.23N 0.42E
Tovada r. U.S.S.R. 28 57.40N 67.00E
Townsville Australia 44 19.13S146.48E
Toyama Japan 35 36.42N137.14E
Trabzon Turkey 30 41.00N 39.43E
Trafalgar, C. Spain 21 36.10N 6.02W
Trail Canada 52 49.04N117.39W
Tralee Rep. of Ire. 19 52.16N 9.42W
Trans Antarctic Mts. Antarctica 62 85.00S150.00E
Transvaal d. R.S.A. 41 24.30S 29.00E
Transylvanian Alps mts. Romania 22 45.35N 24.40E
Traralgon Australia 45 38.12S146.32E
Travers, Mt. New Zealand 46 42.05S172.45E
Traverse City U.S.A. 54 44.46N 85.38W

Trelew Argentina 61 43.13S 65.15W
Trengganu d. Malaysia 34 4.50N103.00E
Trengganu r. Malaysia 34 5.19N103.06E
Trenque Lauquen Argentina 61 35.56S 62.43W
Trent r. U.K. 19 53.41N 0.41W
Trento Italy 21 46.04N 11.08E
Trenton N.J. U.S.A. 55 40.15N 74.43W
Três Marias Dam Brazil 61 18.15S 45.15W
Trier W. Germany 20 49.45N 6.39E
Trieste Italy 22 45.40N 13.46E
Triglav mtn. Yugo. 22 46.21N 13.50E
Trinidad Bolivia 60 15.00S 64.50W
Trinidad Cuba 57 21.48N 80.00W
Trinidad & Tobago S. America 57 10.30N 61.20W
Trinity r. U.S.A. 53 29.55N 94.45W
Tripoli Lebanon 23 34.27N 35.50E
Tripoli Libya 38 32.58N 13.12E
Tripolitania f. Libya 38 29.45N 14.30E
Tristan da Cunha i. Atlantic Oc. 6 38.00S 12.00W
Trois-Rivières town Canada 55 46.21N 72.34W
Troitsko Pechorsk U.S.S.R. 28 62.40N 56.08E
Trollhätten Sweden 24 58.17N 12.20E
Trömso Norway 24 69.42N 19.00E
Trondheim Norway 24 63.36N 10.23E
Trout L. Ont. Canada 53 51.10N 93.20W
Trowbridge U.K. 18 51.18N 2.12W
Troy N.Y. U.S.A. 55 42.43N 73.43W
Troyes France 21 48.18N 4.05E
Trujillo Peru 60 8.06S 79.00W
Truro Canada 51 45.24N 63.18W
Truro U.K. 18 50.17N 5.02W
Tsaratanana, Massif de Madagascar 41 14.00S 48.50E
Tselinograd U.S.S.R. 28 51.10N 71.28E
Tshane Botswana 41 24.02S 21.54E
Tshuapa r. Zaïre 40 0.04S 18.28E
Tsugaru kaikyo str. Japan 35 41.30N140.50E
Tsumeb Namibia 41 19.13S 17.42E
Tsuruga Japan 35 35.40N136.05E
Tsushima i. Japan 35 34.30N129.20E
Tuamotu Archipelago is. Pacific Oc. 47 16.00S145.00W
Tuapse U.S.S.R. 28 44.06N 39.05E
Tucson U.S.A. 52 32.15N110.57W
Tucumcari U.S.A. 52 35.11N103.44W
Tula U.S.S.R. 25 54.11N 37.38E
Tullamore Rep. of Ire. 18 53.17N 7.31W
Tulsa U.S.A. 53 36.07N 95.58W
Tulun U.S.S.R. 29 54.32N100.35E
Tumaco Colombia 60 1.51N 78.46W
Tummo Niger 38 22.45N 14.08E
Tumpat Malaysia 34 6.12N102.10E
Tunis Tunisia 38 36.47N 10.10E
Tunisia Africa 38 34.00N 9.00E
Tunja Colombia 60 5.33N 73.23W
Tura U.S.S.R. 29 64.05N100.00E
Turangi New Zealand 46 38.59S175.48E
Turin Italy 21 45.04N 7.40E
Turkana, L. Kenya 41 4.00N 36.00E
Turkestan U.S.S.R. 28 43.17N 68.16E
Turkey Asia 30 38.00N 34.00E
Turkey r. U.S.A. 54 42.58N 91.03W
Turkmenistan S.S.R. d. U.S.S.R. 28 40.00N 60.00E
Turks Is. Turks & Caicos Is. 57 21.30N 71.10W
Turku Finland 24 60.27N 22.15E
Turneffe Is. Belize 57 17.30N 87.45W
Turpan Pendi f. China 32 43.40N 89.00E
Tuscaloosa U.S.A 53 33.12N 87.33W
Tuscola Ill. U.S.A. 54 39.49N 88.18W
Tuvalu Pacific Oc. 47 8.00S176.00E
Tuxpan Mexico 56 21.00N 97.23W
Tuxtla Gutiérrez Mexico 56 16.45N 93.09W
Tuz, L. Turkey 23 38.45N 33.24E
Tuzla Yugo. 22 44.33N 18.41E
Tweed r. U.K. 19 55.46N 1.59W
Twizel New Zealand 46 44.15S170.06E
Two Harbors town U.S.A. 54 47.02N 91.40W
Tyne r. U.K. 19 55.00N 1.25W
Tyne and Wear d. U.K. 18 54.57N 1.35W
Tyrone d. U.K. 18 54.35N 7.15W
Tyrrell, L. Australia 45 35.22S142.50E
Tyrrhenian Sea Med. Sea 21 41.00N 11.00E
Tyumen U.S.S.R. 28 57.11N 65.29E
Tywi r. U.K. 19 51.46N 4.22W

U

Ubangi r. Congo/Zaïre 40 0.25S 17.50E
Ube Japan 35 34.00N131.16E
Uberaba Brazil 61 19.47S 47.57W
Uberlândia Brazil 61 18.57S 48.17W
Ubon Ratchathani Thailand 33 15.15N104.50E
Ubsa Nur l. Mongolia 32 50.30N 92.30E
Ubundu Zaïre 40 0.24S 25.28E
Ucayali r. Peru 60 4.00S 73.30W
Udaipur India 31 24.36N 73.47E
Udine Italy 22 46.03N 13.14E
Uele r. Zaïre 41 4.08N 22.25E
Ufa U.S.S.R. 28 54.45N 55.58E
Uganda Africa 41 1.00N 32.15E
Uglegorsk U.S.S.R. 29 49.01N142.04E
Uíge Angola 40 7.40S 15.09E
Uinta Mts. U.S.A. 52 40.45N110.30W

Ujung Pandang Indonesia 33 5.09S119.28E
Uka U.S.S.R. 29 57.50N162.02E
Ukhta U.S.S.R. 25 63.33N 53.44E
Ukraine S.S.R. d. U.S.S.R. 22 49.30N 32.04E
Ulan Bator Mongolia 32 47.54N106.52E
Ulan-Ude U.S.S.R. 29 51.55N107.40E
Ullapool U.K. 19 57.54N 5.10W
Ulm W. Germany 21 48.24N 10.00E
Ulúa r. Honduras 57 15.50N 87.38W
Ul'yanovsk U.S.S.R. 28 54.19N 48.22E
Uman U.S.S.R. 22 48.45N 30.10E
Ume r. Sweden 24 63.43N 20.20E
Umeå Sweden 24 63.50N 20.15E
Umtata R.S.A. 41 31.35S 28.47E
Uncompahgre Peak U.S.A. 52 38.04N107.28W
Undur Khan Mongolia 32 47.20N110.40E
Ungava B. Canada 51 59.00N 67.30W
Union of Soviet Socialist Republics Europe/Asia 28 60.00N 80.00E
United Arab Emirates Asia 30 24.00N 54.00E
United Kingdom Europe 19 54.00N 3.00W
United States of America N. America 52 39.00N100.00W
Unst i. U.K. 19 60.45N 0.55W
Upernavik Greenland 51 72.50N 56.00W
Upper Hutt New Zealand 46 41.07S175.04E
Upper Taymyr r. U.S.S.R. 29 74.10N 99.50E
Uppsala Sweden 24 59.55N 17.38E
Ural r. U.S.S.R. 28 47.00N 52.00E
Ural Mts. U.S.S.R. 28 55.00N 59.00E
Ural'sk U.S.S.R. 28 51.19N 51.20E
Uranium City Canada 50 59.32N108.43W
Urmia, L. Iran 30 37.40N 45.28E
Uruapan Mexico 56 19.26N102.04W
Uruguaiana Brazil 61 29.45S 57.05W
Uruguay S. America 61 33.00S 55.00W
Uruguay r. Uruguay 61 34.00S 58.30W
Ürümqi China 32 43.48N131.59E
Ushant i. France 21 48.28N 5.05W
Üsküdar Turkey 23 41.00N 29.03E
Ussuriysk U.S.S.R. 29 43.48N131.59E
Ustinov U.S.S.R. 28 56.49N 53.11E
Ust'kamchatsk U.S.S.R. 29 56.14N162.28E
Ust-Kamenogorsk U.S.S.R. 28 50.00N 82.40E
Ust Kut U.S.S.R. 29 56.40N105.50E
Ust'Maya U.S.S.R. 29 60.25N134.28E
Ust Olenek U.S.S.R. 29 72.59N120.00E
Ust'Tsilma U.S.S.R. 28 65.28N 53.09E
Ust Urt Plateau f. U.S.S.R. 28 43.30N 55.20E
Utah d. U.S.A. 52 39.00N112.00W
Utica N.Y. U.S.A. 55 43.06N 75.15W
Utrecht Neth. 20 52.05N 5.07E
Utsunomiya Japan 35 36.40N139.52E
Uttaradit Thailand 33 17.38N100.05E
Uwajima Japan 35 33.13N132.32E
Uweinat, Jebel mt. Libya/Sudan 39 21.54N 24.58E
Uyuni Bolivia 61 20.28S 66.47W
Uzbekistan S.S.R. d. U.S.S.R. 28 42.00N 63.00E

V

Vaal r. R.S.A. 41 29.00S 23.57E
Vaasa Finland 24 63.06N 21.36E
Vadodara India 31 22.19N 73.14E
Valdai Hills U.S.S.R. 25 57.10N 33.00E
Valdez U.S.A. 50 61.07N146.17W
Valdivia Chile 61 39.46S 73.15W
Val d'Or town Canada 55 48.07N 77.47W
Valence France 21 44.56N 4.54E
Valencia Spain 21 39.29N 0.24W
Valencia Venezuela 60 10.14N 67.59W
Valladolid Spain 21 41.39N 4.45W
Valledupar Colombia 60 10.10N 73.16W
Valenciennes France 20 50.22N 3.32E
Valletta Malta 23 35.53N 14.31E
Valleyfield Canada 55 45.15N 74.08W
Valparaíso Chile 61 33.05S 71.40W
Vals, C. Indonesia 33 8.30S137.30E
Valverde Dom. Rep. 57 19.37N 71.04W
Van, L. Turkey 30 38.35N 42.52E
Vancouver Canada 52 49.13N123.06W
Vancouver I. Canada 50 50.00N126.00W
Vänern l. Sweden 24 59.00N 13.15E
Vännäs Sweden 24 63.56N 19.50E
Vantaa Finland 24 60.13N 25.01E
Vanuatu Pacific Oc. 47 16.00S167.00E
Varanasi India 31 25.20N 83.00E
Varangen Fjord est. Norway 25 70.00N 29.30E
Varna Bulgaria 22 43.13N 27.57E
Västerås Sweden 24 59.36N 16.32E
Vatnajökull mts. Iceland 24 64.20N 17.00W
Vättern l. Sweden 24 58.30N 14.30E
Växjö Sweden 24 56.52N 14.50E
Vaygach i. U.S.S.R. 28 70.00N 59.00E
Vega i. Norway 24 65.40N 11.55E
Velikiye-Luki U.S.S.R. 25 56.19N 30.31E
Vellore India 31 12.56N 79.09E
Venezuela S. America 60 7.00N 66.00W
Venezuela, G. of Venezuela 60 11.30N 71.00W
Veniaminof Mtn. U.S.A. 50 56.05N159.20W
Venice Italy 21 45.26N 12.20E
Venta r. U.S.S.R. 24 57.22N 21.31E